Quick Guid

This guide is org
together, with a few b
the end. The Species
manner:

MW00984369

BIRDS OF SOUTHERN CALIFORNIA

By

Kimball L. Garrett
Jon L. Dunn
Brian E. Small

R.W. Morse Company
Olympia, Washington

KLG and JLD dedicate this book to George Willett, whose popular and scholarly works on the birds of Southern California written in the early 1900s were inspirational.

BES dedicates this book to the two people who've had the greatest positive impact on his life: his father Dr. Arnold Small and his beautiful wife Ana.

Published by the R.W. Morse Company, Olympia, Washington
Copyright ©2012 by the R.W. Morse Company

Library of Congress Control Number: 2011937208
EAN 9780964081086 $19.95 Softcover
First Edition 2012
Second Printing 2013

Printed by
> Imago

Authors
> Kimball L. Garrett, Jon L. Dunn, Brian E. Small

Design
> Nick Hausman

Map
> Shawn K. Morse

Bird Drawings
> Eric Kraig

Cover Photograph of California Quail
> Brian E. Small

Contents

Common Local Birds

Here are some of the most common birds in Southern California. For more information about each bird, go to its Species Account. Images on the next five pages are not to scale.

Mallard
page 40
(male)
(female)

Brown Pelican
page 84

California Quail
page 66

Great Blue Heron
page 88

Cooper's Hawk
page 114

Double-crested
Cormorant
page 80

Red-tailed Hawk
page 120

Willet
page 158

American Coot
page 136

Killdeer
page 144

Sanderling
page 168

California Gull
page 196

Western Gull
page 194

Eurasian Collared-Dove
page 216

Rock Pigeon
page 212

Mourning Dove
page 218

Anna's Hummingbird
page 248

Western Scrub-Jay
page 300

Allen's Hummingbird
page 252

Common Raven
page 306

Black Phoebe
page 280

American Crow
page 304

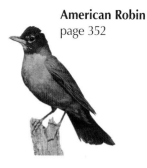

American Robin
page 352

Bushtit
page 322

**European
Starling**
page 358

Northern Mockingbird
page 354

**California
Towhee**
page 390

**Yellow-rumped
Warbler**
page 376

**White-crowned
Sparrow**
page 408

(male)

Red-winged Blackbird
page 422

(female)

Brewer's Blackbird
page 428

(male)

(female)

Hooded Oriole
page 434

Bullock's Oriole
page 436

House Finch
page 440

(male)

(female)

Lesser Goldfinch
page 444

House Sparrow
page 450

x

Introduction

Bird watching, or birding, has become one of America's most popular outdoor activities. It is estimated that one-fifth of all Americans – 46 million people – either watch or feed birds. Birding can be great family entertainment. It is easy to get started, inexpensive, healthy, and allows us to understand and appreciate the natural world.

Birds of Southern California is for beginning bird watchers who wish to identify the birds of the southern half of California. This guide will also appeal to experienced birders who wish to learn more about the behavior, habitats, and seasonal occurrence of our local birds.

Given the popularity of bird watching and the wide array of habitats and birds in Southern California, it is little wonder that the people of this area enjoy seeing and studying our local birds. The local habitats range from ocean waters and coastal estuaries to chaparral, open grasslands, oak woodlands, forested mountains, and desert scrub. Urban plantings and parks, agricultural areas, reservoirs and the inland Salton Sea add more habitat diversity. Since different birds live in each type of habitat, this offers a large assortment of birds throughout the area, with over 570 species found in the region. In this book we include accounts for nearly 350 species; most of these are commonly observed year-round residents or annual visitors, but we also include a few scarcer species that are especially sought-after in Southern California in order to convey the tremendous diversity of bird life in the area. These scarcer species are usually treated in conjunction with the account for a more common or widespread species that is similar.

GEOGRAPHICAL COVERAGE

Birds of Southern California includes the ten southernmost California counties, from San Luis Obispo, Kern and San Bernardino counties south to the Mexican border. We exclude Inyo County, though it is often considered part of southern California. This book encompasses the major metropolitan areas of Los Angeles/Long Beach,

Orange County, San Diego, and the "Inland Empire" (San Bernardino/Riverside and environs) as well as the less urbanized north coastal counties (San Luis Obispo, Santa Barbara and Ventura), and a number of small to mid-sized cities in the Mojave desert and the Coachella Valley and Imperial Valleys.

The map inside the front cover shows the geographical area covered by this book. This area also includes offshore waters from the mainland coast to beyond the Channel Islands, although we focus mainly on those offshore ("pelagic") species which can often be seen from shore or observed on half-day boat outings. The area extends from the Pacific Ocean through the Coast, Transverse, and Peninsular mountain ranges, peaking at 11,500' at the summit of Mt. San Gorgonio in the San Bernardino Mtns. In the rain shadow of the mountains are the "high deserts" (Mojave Desert) and the "low deserts" (Colorado Desert), including the Lower Colorado River Valley and Salton Sink (within which lies the vast but beleaguered Salton Sea, whose surface is currently about 230 feet below Sea Level). Average annual precipitation ranges from about 3 inches (Salton Sink) to over 35 inches in the highest mountains.

CONSERVATION

With over twenty-two million people living in the area covered by this guide, it is clear that environmental change has been dramatic and that most natural habitats have been severely altered. Through agriculture, then urban development and associated flood control efforts, and finally the sprawl of suburbs and new cities, nearly all lowland habitats in the coastal slope and much of the deserts have been completely transformed. Rivers and streams have been channelized, most coastal estuaries have been drained or modified, the high desert areas are rapidly urbanizing, and even our mountains have seen changes. Chronic air pollution has weakened native forests, and pesticides have impacted a host of species. Non-native vegetation now dominates lowland urban and suburban areas, and invasive exotic plants are transforming many natural areas. All of this change has resulted in the loss (or near loss) of some breeding species from the region (such as Fulvous Whistling-Duck, California Condor, Yellow-billed Cuckoo, Willow Flycatcher) and strong population declines in others. Conversely, some native species have adapted well to our current highly modified habitats and a suite of non-native species also now thrives in the region. Extensive protected areas remain within national and state parks, national forests, and a variety of nature reserves, and smaller areas of protected and restored habitat are becoming refreshingly more common.

Protecting native birds and their habitats requires scientific knowledge, financing, education, and political and grassroots activism. Those who enjoy birds and wish to protect them can contribute in some or all of these areas. We urge you to join and become active in one or more of the many conservation organizations such as local Audubon chapters (there are 21 chapters in this area), The Nature Conservancy of California, The Endangered Habitats League, The Center for Biological Diversity, and many local and regional organizations focused on particular habitat preservation issues.

A NOTE ON TAXONOMY

We strictly follow the taxonomy (English names, scientific names, and species sequence) used by the American Ornithologists' Union through its 53rd checklist supplement published in 2012. However, one major new sequence change (moving the falcons and parrots to a place between the woodpeckers and the flycatchers) could not be accommodated so close to press time for this book, so you will find the falcons and parrots in their more "traditional" places in the first edition of this book.

Identifying Birds

It can be confusing when you first start trying to identify birds. They move around, they hide, and many species are distressingly similar to others! A holistic approach to bird identification means paying attention not just to colors and patterns, but to size, structure, shape, behaviors and sounds. First, look at the general shape, size, and color of the bird. Check the Common Local Birds (pages vi - x) and see if it is there. If not, scan through the Species Account pages. Read the description—especially the **boldfaced** text—to see how it matches your bird. Compare range, similar species, voice, and habitat. Keep comparing until you have a match.

The different colors and patterns of a bird's feathering ("plumage") and bare parts (bill, legs, feet, eyes) provide some of the best ways to identify a bird. Beware, however, that plumages may vary within the same species between the sexes, between adults and younger birds, by season, and by geographical location. Learn the parts of a bird; consult the diagram on pages 5 and 6. Most often birds can be identified by head pattern alone.

In some species the male and the female have distinctly different plumages. Good examples are Mallard, Anna's Hummingbird, House Finch, and Red-winged Blackbird. Usually the males have more brilliant colors, as in these examples, while the females have muted colors. Other species such as Rock Pigeon, Western Scrub-Jay, American Crow, and California Towhee show no plumage differences between the sexes.

Most birds seen in Southern California in spring and summer display what is known as their breeding ("summer" or "alternate") plumage. Birds seen here in winter are usually in their non-breeding ("winter" or "basic") plumage. Often, the breeding plumage is more colorful or highly patterned and the non-breeding plumage is more muted; many species, however, look the same year round.

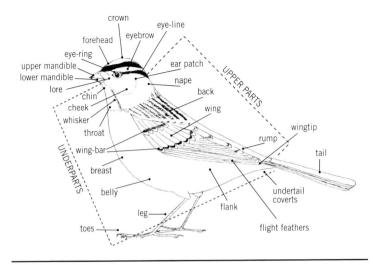

Parts of a Bird. It is helpful to know the names of the different parts of a bird. These sketches of a White-crowned Sparrow and an in-flight Mallard show the terms used to describe bird anatomy in this guide.

Molting is the process of replacing worn feathers with new, fresh ones. Most local birds replace some or all of their feathers in a molt in summer or early fall when they change into their non-breeding plumage. Many birds undergo a partial molt again in late winter or spring to change into a breeding plumage. These molts occur over a period of several weeks or months. In some species, such as the European Starling, the bright "breeding plumage" results from the wearing of dull feather tips (revealing brighter colors underneath) rather than an actual molt. Many songbirds have only a very limited molt of head and body feathers before the breeding season. Molting is generally a longer and more complex process in larger birds than in small songbirds. Most birds have different plumages as they mature. This is particularly true for gulls, which take up to four years and several plumage stages to

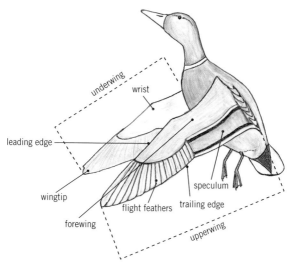

underwing

wrist

leading edge

wingtip

forewing

flight feathers

speculum

trailing edge

upperwing

gain their adult plumage. The term "juvenal plumage" refers to the first true plumage worn by a young bird (a "juvenile") after it loses its initial downy feathers. Some species hold this plumage for only a few weeks after fledging while others may hold it into winter. "First-year plumage" refers to the plumage held during the first 12 months of a bird's life. "Immature" refers to all plumages before the bird gains its adult plumage. For many species in which the plumages of the sexes differ as adults, immature males may closely resemble females.

Colors, patterning, and size may vary considerably among birds of the same species and plumage stage which belong to different geographical populations. For instance, the Fox Sparrows that nest in the high mountains of Southern California differ markedly in color, bill size, tail length, and voice from the dark brown northwestern birds that winter over much of the region. Differences can be great even within the same local population; for example, the majority of our Red-tailed Hawks have light breasts and underwings, yet a certain percentage of birds have dark brown to blackish underparts and underwings with lighter-colored flight feathers. Such consistently different types are called "color morphs" (or just "morphs"); the word "phase" is often incorrectly used in this context.

Don't expect every bird you see to look exactly like the photographs in this guide. Birds, like people, are individuals. To appreciate how variable birds of the same species can be, study the ones that come regularly to your backyard feeder. Male House Finches, for example, can show a wide range of coloration from rich, deep red to golden yellow. You may find that, with practice, you can learn to recognize individual birds by the subtle differences in their markings.

In this book the birds are presented in family groupings, as shown in the Quick Guide to Local Birds on page 23. Learning the characteristics of the different bird families will make bird identification both easier and quicker. Birds in the same family tend to show similarities in appearance and behavior. Hummingbirds, for example, are all very small, with long, thin bills, extremely fast wing beats, and hovering flight. Once you see a bird with these characteristics, you are well on your way to identifying it as a hummingbird. A bird's structure, including head shape, general slimness or roundness of the body, and the shape and length of its wings, tail, legs, and bill, provide important clues to both the family to which it belongs and, often, its species.

Although we have focused above on colors, patterns and shapes, the field identification of birds is greatly simplified by behaviors and, especially, vocalizations that are unique to a species. Experienced birders can recognize virtually all of the area's species by their calls and songs alone. Be sure to use the sections on Voice to arrive at your identifications, and pay close attention in the field to the sounds that birds make.

Observing Local Birds

Many birdwatchers are quite content just to watch the birds in their yards. Some, however, get more involved and begin to look for birds beyond their immediate neighborhood. To get the most out of birding in the field, take time to look, listen, and move slowly. Try to keep conversations to a minimum.

To help locate birds, watch for their movement and listen for their calls. Most often we see birds fly to a nearby branch or flit around in a tree. Their movement catches our attention. But an important part of bird watching is listening and, many times, it is its song or call that draws us to the bird.

Bird songs and calls are a good way to identify birds. Each bird species has unique vocalizations, and, with practice, you can learn to differentiate these sounds. You can purchase tapes, CDs, iPhone applications or visit web sites that allow you to study bird vocalizations at your leisure. With experience, you will be able to identify birds simply by their songs and calls. Be aware, however, that there can be important geographical variations (dialects) in the songs of a given species, and also that confusion may be generated by mimicking species such as Northern Mockingbirds, European Starlings, and Lesser and Lawrence's Goldfinches.

WHEN TO GO BIRDING

Small birds tend to be most active when they are feeding early in the morning (as early as daybreak). Shorebirds tend be most active while they are feeding on incoming and especially outgoing tides; they often rest at high tides. Hawks become active in the morning after rising temperatures create thermals that allow them to soar through the air. Most owls are nocturnal and are most active in the evening or just before dawn. Birders should adapt to these varied schedules shown by different birds.

Birds in Southern California vary in abundance with the season.

Species like Northern Mockingbirds, Western Scrub-Jays and House Sparrows stay throughout the year while others (e.g. Black-chinned Hummingbird, Ash-throated Flycatcher and Hooded Oriole) arrive in the spring and have mostly departed by late summer or fall. Other species (such as American Wigeon, Sharp-shinned Hawk, Cedar Waxwing, and Golden-crowned Sparrow) migrate into our area from the north or the interior of the continent and spend the winter. Yet other species are pure transients, passing through during their migrations; these include Sooty Shearwaters, Rufous Hummingbirds, Baird's Sandpipers and nearly all of our Willow Flycatchers.

Spring is a great time of year for birding. Trees and shrubs have buds and blossoms, insect activity increases, and the birds, many in bright breeding plumages, return from their wintering grounds. The males start singing and the local nesting birds seek mates, build nests, and start to raise young. Wintering birds depart for their breeding grounds, and songbirds, seabirds and shorebirds stream through en route to northerly breeding areas. Spring is prolonged in Southern California; the earliest migrants arrive in January, when some resident species are already nesting, and the latest migrants may still be passing through in the first half of June.

Through the spring and summer, the local young birds hatch, are cared for by their parents for varying periods (depending on the species), and eventually become independent. By July and August, summer visitors are beginning to head south for their wintering grounds. In many of our brighter species (orioles, grosbeaks, hummingbirds) the adult males head south earlier than the females and young. By late summer (even as early as late June) prairie and Arctic-breeding shorebirds are passing through on their way south. Late summer also sees an influx of subtropical waterbirds from Mexico to the Salton Sea area and the coast. Autumn songbird migration is even more prolonged than in spring, with peak passage occurring from late July through October, depending on the species. As fall changes to winter, flocks of waterfowl appear on our lakes and ponds, gull species diversity increases along the coast, and wintering raptors reach peak numbers in the open interior valleys. Our resident birds continue to use neighborhood bird feeders, joined by winter visitors from more northerly or interior regions.

KEEPING RECORDS

Some people keep a checklist of all the birds that appear in their yard ("yard list") or of all the birds seen in their county, state, or lifetime ("life list"). As lists grow, so does a sense of personal accomplishment. Along with the pleasure of finding new and different birds comes an incentive to learn more about them. Many dedicated birdwatchers keep a detailed journal of what they see, when and where, and the birds' behaviors. Careful record keeping by knowledgeable observers can contribute greatly to scientific understanding of birdlife. On-line checklist submission and personal record-keeping through the Cornell Laboratory of Ornithology's "**eBird**" initiative at **http://ebird.org** is especially rewarding and contributes to a vast, real-time, continent-wide database of bird abundance and distribution. Other "citizen science" projects include Audubon's annual mid-winter "Christmas Bird Counts" and various monitoring programs for sensitive bird species.

An index and checklist of the Southern California birds is provided on pages 491 – 495. To obtain access to a full list of the species seen in Southern California, go to **www.rwmorse.com.** Naturalist clubs, Audubon chapters, parks, and nature sanctuaries often produce checklists for local areas. Inquire about these at nature stores and visitor centers. Use checklists and book and journal references to learn the status and distribution of birds in the area – identification mistakes often result from poor knowledge of which species are to be expected when and where.

Bird Habitats of Southern California and Their Birds

The environment that provides the resources for a bird or other living creature to live is termed its "habitat." Birds are quite diverse in the nature and specificity of their habitat requirements. You won't see a Wrentit in arid creosote scrub or a Nuttall's Woodpecker in a salt marsh, nor will you see Killdeer in trees or loons in grasslands. The secret to finding and identifying birds is knowing their habitats and developing an understanding of which birds are likely to be seen where. The more types of habitat you explore, the greater the variety of birds you will see.

We identify below 14 major habitat categories or unique geographical features in Southern California, only hinting at the incredible ecological complexity of the region. These habitats can merge into one another and overlap in complex ways, and each habitat type has many variations. Bird diversity is highest where various habitats adjoin. Some species, like the Mourning Dove or Red-tailed Hawk, are at home in a great variety of habitats, whereas others may seek habitats as specialized as a rocky shorelines (Surfbird, Black Turnstone) or cliffs and boulder-strewn canyon bottoms (Canyon Wren).

OFFSHORE MARINE WATERS

These are open ocean waters in the San Pedro and Santa Barbara Channels and farther off our coasts. Shearwaters, fulmars, and storm-petrels forage here, as do auklets and murres. Sabine's Gulls, jaegers, and Red-necked Phalaropes move through these waters on their annual migrations. Seabirds congregate around productive waters associated with undersea features, such as waters around the northern Channel Islands, Redondo Canyon in Santa Monica Bay, the San Pedro Escarpment off the Palos Verdes Peninsula, Newport Canyon and Lausen Knoll off Newport Beach, and several shallow banks off San Diego.

PROTECTED MARINE WATERS

Few large sheltered bays occur in Southern California (Morro Bay, Los Angeles/Long Beach Harbor, Upper Newport Bay, Mission Bay and San Diego Bay are examples), but these bays and other relatively protected inshore waters in the lee of coastal headlands host scoters, Red-breasted Mergansers, loons, grebes, Brown Pelicans, cormorants, gulls, terns, and skimmers. Impressive flights of migrating Brant, scoters, and loons may be seen passing coastal sea watching points, especially from March – May; such sites include Pt. Piedras Blancas, Goleta Point, Pt. Mugu, Pt. Dume, Pt. Vicente, the Newport Pier, and La Jolla.

ROCKY SHORE, BREAKWATERS AND JETTIES

Natural rocky shore habitat occurs extensively on the San Luis Obispo County coast and the Channel Islands, and more locally southward along the coast. These rocky shores are also mimicked by our larger breakwaters and jetties, as at Santa Barbara, Ventura and Channel Islands Harbors, Marina del Rey, the Los Angeles/Long Beach Harbor breakwater, Dana Point Harbor, Oceanside Harbor, and Mission/San Diego Bays. Tattlers, turnstones, and Surfbirds, cormorants, pelicans, and gulls occur on these rocky shores, and scoters feed on shellfish in adjacent waters.

SANDY SHORE, MUD FLATS, ESTUARIES AND SALT MARSH

Important coastal estuaries with tidal flats and saltmarsh vegetation are found at Morro Bay, Santa Maria River mouth, Goleta Slough, Carpinteria Salt Marsh, Mugu Lagoon, Seal Beach, Bolsa Chica, and Upper Newport Bay, several lagoons on the central San Diego County coast, and south San Diego Bay and the Tijuana River estuary. There are many smaller sites at river mouths along the entire coastline. Vast numbers of shorebirds, waterfowl, terns, and herons congregate at productive estuaries, and our most important tern and skimmer breeding colonies are found in some of these sites. Sandy beaches in the area tend to be crowded with people and heavily groomed, but better protected beaches still attract many shorebirds, gulls, and terns, including Snowy Plovers and Least Terns. Although encased in concrete, the lower Los Angeles River channel from Maywood and Bell Gardens south through Long Beach is a premier site for shorebirds in summer and fall.

Fresh Water Lakes, Reservoirs, and Marshes

Although relatively arid, Southern California receives much runoff from the mountains that border the basins and valleys and once hosted extensive lowland wetlands. Urbanization has eliminated nearly most such wetlands, but a variety of created or restored freshwater wetlands exist. Flood basins or created wetlands in urban areas can be very productive, including the Sepulveda, Hansen, Whittier Narrows, Santa Fe and Prado flood control basins, the Ballona Freshwater Marsh in Playa del Rey, the San Joaquin Marsh (Irvine), portions of the Santa Clara, Los Angeles, San Gabriel, and Santa Ana rivers, and the wetlands of the Tijuana River Valley below San Diego. Many local reservoirs and park lakes teem seasonally with birds. The few desert wetlands are important magnets for birds because of their arid surroundings – these include Piute Ponds on the Edwards Air Force Base (permission required) and water treatment plants near several desert cities (not all are open to birders). Large inland reservoirs providing good habitat include Lake Isabella, Lake Cachuma, Lake Casitas, Castaic Lagoon, Quail Lake, Lake Perris, Lake Henshaw, and Lake Havasu. Inland National Wildlife Refuges (Kern, Salton Sea, Havasu) can host large numbers of marshbirds and waterfowl, as do the state wildlife areas in the San Jacinto Valley and the Imperial Valley.

Herons, cormorants, and Belted Kingfishers feed in these waters, along with coots and a variety of grebes and ducks. Shorebirds can be abundant on exposed mudflats, and rails, gallinules and Least Bitterns skulk in marsh vegetation. Cattails or bulrushes support nesting yellowthroats, Red-winged (and locally Tricolored) Blackbirds, and Marsh Wrens). Northern Harriers, White-tailed Kites, Peregrine Falcons and many other raptors forage in the marshy areas and Ospreys and (locally, in winter) Bald Eagles fish in the lakes.

Riparian Woodlands

Most of the important rivers in urban regions have been channelized or otherwise modified, but portions of these rivers, smaller streams, and flood control basins have important riparian woodlands of willows, cottonwoods and sycamores that attract many breeding and migrating birds. Narrower mountain canyons are dominated by alders and willows. Widespread riparian breeders include Downy Woodpeckers, Common Yellowthroats, Song Sparrows, and Bullock's Orioles. Extensive willows in the major flood control basins attract breeding Bell's Vireos, Yellow Warblers, Yellow-breasted Chats, and Blue Grosbeaks. Shaded canyons host Pacific-slope Flycatchers, Warbling Vireos, Swainson's Thrushes, and Purple Finches. Wet thickets in the high mountains may host breeding MacGillivray's and Wilson's Warblers. Major rivers with good riparian woodlands include: Santa Maria and Santa Ynez Rivers, Santa Clara River, Santa Ana River, San Luis Rey and Santa Margarita Rivers, and, in the interior, portions of the Mojave and lower Colorado Rivers. Deserving of special mention are the extensive and well-protected riparian woodlands of the South Fork of the Kern River.

Coastal Sage Scrub and Chaparral

Much of the coastal slope of the Region was originally cloaked in scrub habitat, from low coastal prairie through coastal sage scrub ("soft chaparral") and true ("hard") chaparral. Chaparral still abounds on foothill and mountain slopes, and extensive areas are protected within our National Forests, state parks, and other reserves. Common species include Bewick's Wren, Wrentit, California Thrasher, and various sparrows. Our scrub habitats are fire-adapted, but unnaturally frequent and/or intense fires have greatly changed their composition and allowed exotic plants to flourish. Coastal sage scrub has been greatly diminished by suburban growth; some of its key species (California Gnatcatcher, coastal populations of Cactus Wrens, Greater Roadrunners and Sage Sparrows) are now highly threatened through this habitat loss.

Oak Woodlands

Coast live oak woodlands are found in foothills over much of the region, with extensive oak habitat in the coastal ranges of San Luis Obispo, Santa Barbara and Ventura counties, in the Santa Monica Mountains (such as Malibu Creek and Topanga State Parks), and in various canyons and slopes on the coastal face of the Transverse and Peninsular mountain ranges south through San Diego. Characteristic birds of these woodlands, as well as savannas of valley oaks and mountain woodlands of canyon and interior live oaks and California black oaks include Western Screech-Owl, Acorn and Nuttall's Woodpeckers, Hutton's Vireo, Oak Titmouse, White-breasted Nuthatch, Western Bluebird, and (in Santa Barbara and San Luis Obispo Counties) Yellow-billed Magpie.

Coniferous Forest

Our mountain forests, protected as National Forests but still exposed to intense recreational pressures, host many birds not found at lower elevations. Lower mountain canyons are cloaked in big-cone Douglas-fir and canyon live oak; a transitional zone of Coulter pine, ponderosa pine, incense cedar and California black oak gives way to extensive areas of white fir and Jeffrey, sugar, and lodgepole pines. Many mountain slopes are cloaked in a chaparral of *Ceanothus*, mountain mahogany and manzanita. Pinyon pines dominate the drier, east and north slopes of our higher mountains. Typical mountain birds include Hairy and White-headed Woodpeckers, Steller's Jay, Mountain Chickadee, nuthatches, Brown Creeper, Cassin's Finch, and summering Western Tanager, Fox Sparrow, and Green-tailed Towhee. Drives to Mount Pinos, along the Angeles Crest Highway through the San Gabriel Mtns., on the many highways through the San Bernardino Mountains, or to the Idyllwild area of the San Jacinto Mtns. will traverse most of the important montane habitats in the region. Conifers also grow in the northernmost coastal areas, such as around Cambria in San Luis Obispo County – "mountain" birds such as Steller's Jays and Pygmy

Nuthatches are found here, along with most of our Chestnut-backed Chickadees. Just to our north, the high mountains flanking the Owens Valley give the birder a taste of the birdlife of the Great Basin (in the White Mountains) and the high Sierra Nevada (west of Bishop and Big Pine). Patches of coniferous forest on the highest peaks on the eastern Mojave Desert are more difficult to reach, but rewarding for the hardy explorer.

DESERT SCRUB AND WOODLANDS

Vast areas of the Southern California deserts are cloaked in creosote scrub, saltbush, sagebrush, or open Joshua tree woodlands. Extensive protected desert habitats are found in Joshua Tree National Park, Anza-Borrego Desert State Park, the East Mojave National Preserve, and in smaller desert parks; large areas of desert habitat, however, are being modified by renewable energy development and urbanization. Important widespread desert species include Ladder-backed Woodpecker, Verdin, Cactus Wren, Black-tailed Gnatcatcher, Le Conte's Thrasher, Phainopepla, Scott's Oriole (spring and early summer), and Sage and Black-throated Sparrows. Desert habitats are by no means uniform, and many additional, more localized desert species occur in our region.

URBAN AND SUBURBAN PARKS AND RESIDENTIAL AREAS

The planting and irrigation of a diverse array of non-native vegetation has transformed urban and suburban habitats and made them attractive to many birds. Our yards and local parks may host Cooper's Hawk, Anna's and Allen's hummingbirds, Nuttall's and Downy Woodpeckers, Black Phoebe, Western Scrub-Jay, American Crow, Bushtit, Northern Mockingbird, Yellow-rumped Warbler (winter), Cedar Waxwing (winter and spring), Brewer's Blackbird, Hooded Oriole (spring and summer), House Finch, and such non-natives as Rock Pigeon, European Starling, House Sparrow, and even parrots. With an abundance of exotic fruiting and nectar-producing trees and shrubs, urban parks can be magnets for migrant birds and a great diversity of wintering species; birders in the region scour well-planted urban parks and residential neighborhoods in winter and migration, turning up an impressive variety of rarities.

FARMLAND, PASTURES, AND GRASSLANDS

Southern California has long been one of the most productive agricultural regions in the nation; Los Angeles, Orange, Ventura, and western Riverside and San Bernardino counties in particular hosted vast acreages of orchards, vineyards, row crops, and pastures, though urbanization has greatly reduced the importance of agriculture in these areas. The southern San Joaquin Valley in Kern County is intensively farmed, and large areas of interior San Luis Obispo and Santa Barbara Counties have been converted to vineyards. Important agricultural valleys include the Oxnard Plain of southeastern Ventura County, portions of the Antelope and other Mojave Desert valleys, the Coachella Valley, the lower Colorado River Valley (especially in the vicinity of Needles, Blythe, Palo Verde and Winterhaven), and the Imperial Valley. The Imperial Valley, lying south and southeast of the Salton Sea, has hundreds of square miles of irrigated croplands; flood irrigation here attracts tens of thousands of ibis, shorebirds, and gulls and the fields also host a large year round population of Burrowing Owls and wintering flocks of Mountain Plovers. The Colorado River is the source of the Imperial Valley's water, but transfers of water from the Imperial Valley to urban areas is diminishing agricultural acreage, changing irrigation practices (to the detriment of foraging birds), and shrinking the Salton Sea (see below).

Natural grasslands are all but gone from Southern California, and grassland species have suffered greater declines than any other group of birds. Native grasslands have been painstakingly restored in just a few areas (such as the Santa Rosa Plateau preserve south of Lake Elsinore) but important and extensive semi-natural grasslands are found on the Carrizo Plain (Kern/San Luis Obispo County border region), the southern flanks of the San Joaquin Valley, and in the western Antelope Valley. Open fields and agricultural areas host such grassland birds such as pipits (winter), Horned Larks, sparrows, and blackbirds. In pasturelands and fields of alfalfa and Bermuda grass Long-billed Curlews, Mountain Plovers, Mountain Bluebirds and a variety of raptors may be found in winter. Once-common open country birds such as Burrowing Owl, Loggerhead Shrike, Grasshopper Sparrow and Western Meadowlark have virtually disappeared as breeders on the coastal slope. Abundant lawns at golf courses, cemeteries, and urban parks are generally too "sterile" to attract a variety of birds.

THE SALTON SEA

California's largest inland lake, the Salton Sea, filled in its present form around 1905 and has supported teeming numbers of waterfowl, wading birds, shorebirds and fish-eating seabirds ever since. This is the only place in the United States to find the Yellow-footed Gull and the best place in Southern California to find such species as Laughing Gull, Wood Stork, Stilt Sandpiper, and the "Large-billed" subspecies of Savannah Sparrow. Many waterbird species that occur regularly at the Salton Sea are rare elsewhere in the interior. Bird watching around the Salton Sea is always fascinating; geese and ducks abound in winter, and lively breeding colonies of herons, ibis, cormorants, terns, and skimmers are found in season. The Salton Sea is intimately tied to the heavily irrigated agricultural areas that border its northwestern, southern and southeastern shores, and many birds move back and forth from these fields to the sea's shores. Always dynamic, the Salton Sea is now at a crossroads, with bird habitats disappearing as the shrinking Sea is starved of freshwater input due to the sale of agricultural water to urban areas.

THE CHANNEL ISLANDS

The eight Channel Islands off the Southern California coast range from tiny and nearly treeless Anacapa and Santa Barbara Islands to the four large and partly wooded islands of Santa Cruz, Santa Rosa, Santa Catalina and San Clemente. The most accessible island, Santa Catalina, is reached by regular public ferries from San Pedro, Long Beach and Orange Co.; Anacapa, Santa Cruz, Santa Barbara and

San Miguel Islands can be reached by regular charters from Santa Barbara or Ventura/Oxnard. San Nicolas and San Clemente (military) and Santa Rosa (largely private) are generally off-limits. The islands are noteworthy, in addition to spectacular scenery, for their breeding seabirds (including Scripps's Murrelets, Pigeon Guillemots, Western Gulls, Ashy Storm-Petrels, Brown Pelicans, and cormorants) and some unique landbirds, including the Island Scrub-Jay whose entire world population lives only on Santa Cruz Island.

Birding In Southern California

One of the best ways to see new birds is to join the local Audubon chapter or other nature club on a field trip. Participants often visit new areas, learn how to identify new birds, and meet people who share a common interest. After studying the birds in your yard, visit local parks and open areas.

It is beyond the scope of this guide to describe specific birding locations in Southern California; there are simply too many excellent areas in every part of the region. Some of the top birding locations have been mentioned above. We highly recommend Brad Schram's "A Birder's Guide to Southern California" for detailed descriptions of birding sites and directions for finding them.

Helpful Resources

REGIONAL PUBLICATIONS:

California Bird Records Committee (Robert A. Hamilton, Michael A. Patten and Richard A. Erickson, eds.). 2007. *Rare Birds of California.* Camarillo: Western Field Ornithologists.

Daniel S. Cooper. 2004. *Important Bird Areas in California.* Audubon California.

Sylvia Gallagher. 1997. *Atlas of Breeding Birds, Orange County, California.* Sea and Sage Audubon Society, Irvine, CA.

Robert A. Hamilton and Douglas R. Willick. 1996. *The Birds of Orange County, California, Status and Distribution.* Sea and Sage Audubon Society, Irvine, CA.

Paul Lehman. 1994. *The Birds of Santa Barbara County, California.* Vertebrate Museum, University of California, Santa Barbara

Joan Easton Lentz. 2006. *Introduction to Birds of the Southern California Coast.* University of California Press.

Michael A. Patten, Guy McCaskie and Phil Unitt. 2003. *Birds of the Salton Sea: Status, Biogeography and Ecology.* University of California Press.

Kenneth V. Rosenberg, Robert D. Ohmart, William C. Hunter and Bertin W. Anderson. 1991. *Birds of the Lower Colorado River Valley.* Tucson: University of Arizona Press.

Brad Schram. 2007. *A Birders' Guide to Southern California.* American Birding Association, Inc.

Phil Unitt. 2004. *San Diego County Bird Atlas.* San Diego Natural History Museum, Ibis Publishing Co.

IDENTIFICATION GUIDES:

Jon L. Dunn and Jonathan Alderfer. 2011. *Field Guide to the Birds of North America, 6th ed.* Washington, D. C.: National Geographic Society.

Kenn Kaufman. 2000. *Birds of North America*. New York: Houghton Mifflin.

Roger Tory Peterson. 2010. *A Field Guide to Birds of Western North America, 4th ed.* Boston: Houghton Mifflin Harcourt.

David Allen Sibley. 2003. *The Sibley Field Guide to Birds of Western North America*. New York: Alfred A. Knopf.

PHOTOGRAPHIC GUIDES:

Edward S. Brinkley. 2007. *National Wildlife Federation Field Guide to Birds of North America*. New York: Sterling Publ. Co.

Ted Floyd. 2008. *Smithsonian Field Guide to the Birds of North America*. New York: Collins.

Paul Sterry and Brian E. Small. 2009. *Birds of Western North America: A Photographic Guide*. Princeton: Princeton University Press.

Donald and Lillian Stokes. 2010. *The Stokes Field Guide to the Birds of North America*. Little, Brown and Co., New York.

JOURNALS

North American Birds (indispensable quarterly reports of bird sightings and related articles and summaries; published by the American Birding Association)

Western Birds (the quarterly journal of the Western Field Ornithologists)

ON-LINE BIRDING RESOURCES

Birds of Santa Barbara County:
   https://sites.google.com/site/bosbc2012

California Bird Records Committee:

http://californiabirds.org

Cornell Laboratory of Ornithology's BirdSource, including eBird, Christmas Bird Counts, Great Backyard Bird Count, Feeder Watch, and other citizen science projects:

http://www.birdsource.org

Joe Morlan's California Birding pages:

http://fog.ccsf.cc.ca.us/~jmorlan

J. Siler's archives of all local birding listserves:

http://birdingonthe.net

Western Field Ornithologists

http://westernfieldornithologists.org

Natural History Museum of Los Angeles County:

Ralph W. Schreiber Hall of Birds; satellite Page Museum of La Brea Discoveries: the Los Angeles Region's birds and other fauna from recent pre-history to 400,000 years ago. **http://www.nhm.org**

Other excellent natural history museums, all with bird displays and collections, include the Santa Barbara Museum of Natural History, San Diego Natural History Museum, and San Bernardino County Museum.

Nature Centers, Nature Stores and Information Centers

There are a number of good nature stores in Southern California. Their staffs are always eager to answer your bird and bird-feeding questions. The yellow pages of the telephone directory or web search engines will locate the closest nature store.

Species Accounts

The following pages present accounts and photographs of the most familiar bird species of Southern California. Information on each species is presented in a standardized format: see the sample page (opposite) for an explanation. Species are grouped by families, color-coded and thumb-indexed. Nineteen species commonest in the higher mountains are presented separately at the end (pages 456–465) as are another 27 found mostly in the deserts including the Imperial Valley and Salton Sea (pages 466–479), and 19 of the most common oceanic species (those best seen from boats at sea, but sometimes from shore) are shown in pages 480-489. The Quick Guide on page 23 will help you locate the birds.

Many species are treated in conjunction with the account for a more common or widespread species that is similar.

The following terms are used to describe the relative abundance of each species and the likelihood of finding it in a particular season. These definitions were developed by the American Birding Association.

- **Common:** Found in moderate to large numbers, and easily found in appropriate habitat at the right time of year.
- **Fairly Common:** Found in small to moderate numbers, and usually easy to find in appropriate habitat at the right time of year.
- **Uncommon:** Found in small numbers, and usually—but not always—found with some effort in appropriate habitat at the right time of year.
- **Rare:** Occurs annually in very small numbers. Not to be expected on any given day, but may be found with extended effort over the course of the appropriate season(s).

Birds shown in the photographs in the Species Accounts are adults unless the captions indicate otherwise.

NAME OF SPECIES
Its Latin name

Description: Length (and wingspan for larger species), followed by a description that includes differences in plumages between sexes and ages. Key field marks—unique markings or structural characters visible in the field that help distinguish one species from another—are shown in **boldfaced** type.

Voice: Describes the main song and calls of the species; these can be very important for species identification. Note that most species have a much greater vocal repertoire than described here.

Behavior: Highlights behaviors characteristic of this species, including feeding behavior, distinctive movements and displays, flight style, and breeding behavior.

Similar Birds: Identifies similar-appearing species and describes how to tell them apart.

Where, When to Find: Describes the general locations and habitats where this bird may be found in Southern California, sometimes suggesting some of the better locations to search for this species. Identifies the times of year that the species is here and its relative abundance (see facing page for definitions of abundance terms).

Did you know? Provides other interesting facts about this species.

Date and Location Seen? A place for you to record the date and location of your sighting of this species.

Immature

Adult

Description: 28", wingspan 53". A **gray-brown** goose with **pinkish bill** and **orange** legs. The **rear underparts are contrastingly white**, and there is a **white band across the base of the tail** and narrow white tail tip. ADULT: **white feathering at base of bill**, irregular **black bars across the belly**. JUVENILE: lacks white on face and black belly bars.

Voice: Common flight call is a rather high yelping *kah-la-luck*.

Behavior: Grazes on lawns, pastures, short marshy vegetation; roosts in shallow water.

Similar Species: Various domestic geese, mostly derived from Greylag and Swan Geese of the Old World, can be common at city park lakes. They resemble White-fronteds, but are larger-billed, pot-bellied, and often tame or even aggressive; they lack White-front's black belly bars and distinct white face patch. Canada Goose (p. 31) has black neck, bill and legs, and broad white chin strap.

Where, When to Find: Uncommon migrant (mainly January to March, and mid-September through October) through lowlands, with a few through winter; individuals or small flocks sometimes stop at coastal lagoons, inland lakes. The largest numbers move through the inland valleys, deserts, and Salton Sea. A few wild birds may tame down and stay for extended periods (even years) at park lakes. Our birds nest mainly in western Alaska and winter in western Mexico. Formerly more common.

Did you know? These geese are called "speckle-bellies" by hunters.

Date & Location Seen: _____

_____

Snow Goose
Immature

Snow Goose
Adult

Ross's Goose
Immature

Ross's Goose
Adult

Description: 28"/23", wingspan 54"/44". Both are medium-large **white** geese with **black wingtips**. In Snow, pink bill shows a black "grinning patch" along the sides where the mandibles meet; **much smaller Ross's has stubbier bill** with blue-gray base, much less black on bill sides. JUVENILE Snow in first fall and early winter is washed with gray on the neck, back, and wings; bill is dull pinkish-gray; juvenile Ross's whiter (gray limited to crown, back, wings). "Blue" plumage morph of Snow, rare in our region, is variably slate-gray on the back, breast, and neck.

Voice: Call is a raucous, fairly high yelping "rowk" or "wow;" call of Ross's higher.

Behavior: Grazes on grasses, grain, marsh vegetation, foraging in shallow water as well as land.

Similar Species: Beware white domestic geese and outsized white domestic Mallards (these all lack the distinct black wingtips), common around park lakes. Hybrid Snow X Ross's Geese are known.

Where, When to Find: Flocks of thousands of Snows and hundreds of Ross's winter, November to March, at refuges at the south end of the Salton Sea; small flocks of Snows winter locally elsewhere and formerly occurred in large flocks in coastal areas. Away from Salton Sea, Ross's usually found singly or in small groups, sometimes taming down and taking up residence with domestic waterfowl at park lakes.

Did you know? Ross's Goose also has a "blue" morph, though very rare; darker than blue Snows, with white face contrasting with dark head and neck.

Date & Location Seen: _____

_____

Canada Goose
Adult

Cackling Goose
minima

Cackling Goose
"Aleutian" *leucoparaeia*

Description: 35-45", wingspan 53-60". A familiar large brown goose with **black neck** and **white "chin strap."** Undertail and band across rump white. Bill and legs black. Size varies with subspecies.

Voice: Call is a low honking *h-lonk*.

Behavior: Grazes in fields, lawns, and on aquatic vegetation in shallow water; roosts on open bodies of water. Nests are in marshy or shrubby lakeshores.

Similar Species: Cackling Goose (*Branta hutchinsii*; 25-27") is like miniature Canada (only slightly larger than a Mallard), but with darker underparts (especially subspecies *minima*), small and stubby bill, and higher, squeakier calls. "Aleutian" subspecies (*leucoparaeia*) of Cackling shows broad white ring at base of black neck and is slightly paler on the breast than *minima*. Both Cackling subspecies are rare winter visitors (November to March) to lakes, ponds, parks.

Where, When to Find: Migratory Canadas are uncommon to common winter visitors (October to March), with flocks found where grasslands or lawns border lakes. Winter flocks declining with loss of open foraging areas, but still found locally in inland valleys such San Jacinto Valley southeast of Riverside and the San Pascual valley and L. Henshaw in San Diego County and more locally near the coast. A rapidly growing non-migratory population now breeds commonly at many park lakes, golf course ponds and other wetlands in the area, and it is now normal to see flocks in spring and summer throughout the coastal slope.

Did you know? Canada and Cackling Geese were only recently "split" as separate species.

Date & Location Seen: _____

Description: 25", wingspan 42". A small, stocky, dark coastal goose with **black head and neck**, irregular white ring on upper neck, **blackish brown breast and belly**, and **extensively white rear end** that nearly hides the black tail. The flanks are marked with white. Bill and legs black. JUVENILE: lacks white neck ring. Our birds are "Black Brant" of the subspecies *nigricans*.

Voice: Flocks make a low, hoarse *cronk* call, but usually silent in our area.

Behavior: Feeds on eelgrass in coastal estuaries and large bays; in our region seen mostly as a migrant offshore, where it flies in disorganized lines (sometimes mixing with scoters).

Similar Species: Canada and Cackling geese always show a conspicuous have white chin strap and are browner overall.

Where, When to Find: Common migrant along the coast from March to mid-May, where best seen from coastal points such as Pt. Vicente, Pt. Dume, Pt. Mugu and Goleta Point. The fall passage (November-December) is farther offshore and largely bypasses our coastline. Flocks winter at large estuaries (Morro Bay, San Diego Bay), and a few individuals or small flocks sometimes winter at smaller estuaries such as Pt. Mugu or Bolsa Chica. Rare spring migrant through the interior; regular in flocks at Salton Sea (a few summer), with some records for the Antelope Valley and elsewhere.

Did you know? Huge flocks of Brant winter both to the north of us and south of us (at many large lagoons in Baja California and the coast of the western Mexican mainland).

Date & Location Seen: _____

Male

Female

Description: 18 ½", wingspan 30". This distinctive duck sports a **drooping crest** and appears **long tailed** in flight. BREEDING MALE: **Colorful** green, black and white head pattern, **red bill base and eye ring**, deep reddish breast bordered behind by vertical black and white bars, glossy black upperparts, tan-yellow sides, and an iridescent blue wing patch. Non-breeding male (summer, fall) much duller but retains basic pattern. FEMALE: Broad **white ring around eye**, pointed in rear. Gray above, gray spotted with white below.

Voice: Calls include various high whistles and squeaks; wings make whistling sound in flight.

Behavior: Often perches low in trees or on fallen branches over the water. Feeds on invertebrates and plants in shallow water; does not dive. Nests in tree cavities (in our area, mostly in nest boxes provided for them).

Similar Species: Unmistakable, but beware escaped Mandarin Ducks (*Aix galericulata*, 18"); male Mandarin is equally colorful but very different; female much like female Wood, but paler with long, thin white extension to eye-ring, large white spots below.

Where, When to Find: Uncommon resident on wooded park lakes, ponds in wooded areas. Local populations have become established with provision of nest boxes. Some favored sites include Oceano, Lake Cachuma, Prado Basin, Laguna Lake (Fullerton), and Descanso Gardens in La Canada Flintridge. In winter (late September to March) a few migrate in from the north to same habitats. Rare migrant on the southern deserts.

Did you know? The downy young jump from the nest cavity when about a day old.

Date & Location Seen: _____

_____

Male

Female

Description: 20", wingspan 33". Ducks of the genus *Anas* are "dabblers", tipping the rear end up to feed just underwater rather than diving below the surface. Gadwall is rather plain but always shows squarish head, orange legs, white belly and a **square white patch on speculum** of wing. MALE: **Plain gray-brown** (actually intricately patterned at close range), with paler gray head, **black rear end**; bill dark gray. FEMALE: Mottled brown and white, with white belly; **orange sides to bill** forms a straight line; white wing patch often visible when at rest.

Voice: Female gives a nasal quack; male's call is a reedy *rep, rep*.

Behavior: Forages on vegetation in shallow water by picking at surface or "tipping up"; also grazes along shore. Usually found in pairs or small groups, often with other dabblers.

Similar Species: Square white speculum patch is unique among our dabblers. Female Mallard (p. 41) is larger, warmer brown, mottled brown on the belly, shows more orange blotches on the bill, and has blue speculum (bordered with white). Female American Wigeon (p. 39) has orange tones to breast, flanks and small gray bill.

Where, When to Find: Fairly common winter visitor (October to March) to estuaries, marshes and freshwater lakes throughout the region; smaller numbers remain through the spring and summer, breeding around marshy lakes and brackish estuaries.

Did you know? Gadwalls are among the few prairie-nesting ducks to have increased in population; some three million birds now breed in North America.

Date & Location Seen: _____

American Wigeon
Male

American Wigeon
Female

Eurasian Wigeon
Male

Eurasian Wigeon
Female

Description: 20″, wingspan 32″. A familiar wintering duck that grazes on lawns. Small **bill is blue-gray with black tip**. MALE: Pinkish brown with **white (or buffy) forehead**, **green patch behind eye**, white flank patch and black undertail. In flight shows white belly and **large white patch on forewing** (in adult). FEMALE: Gray-brown head, **brown breast and flanks, white belly**. In flight forewing is gray bordered behind by white.

Voice: Male's call is an emphatic two- to three-note whistle, *whee whew!* Female gives a low quack.

Behavior: Flocks graze on lawns that border park lakes; also feed by picking vegetation from the surface in shallow water or mudflats.

Similar Species: Eurasian Wigeon (*Anas penelope;* 20″) occurs regularly in small numbers with winter flocks of Americans, especially in coastal areas; hybrids also occur. Male Eurasian has bright orange-rufous head, gray back and sides; female closely resembles American but with browner head not contrasting with breast and gray (not white) underwing linings.

Where, When to Find: Common winter visitor (late September to early April) to freshwater lakes and estuaries throughout the region; very common on golf courses and park lawns with lakes or ponds where it often grazes with coots. They breed mainly in Alaska and Canada, and winter south to southern Mexico.

Did you know? Wigeon are called "Baldpates" by hunters.

Date & Location Seen: _____

_____

Male

Female

Description: 23″, wingspan 35″. Our most familiar duck; large and heavy-bodied, with a blue speculum bordered in front and back by white, white underwings, orange legs. MALE: **Green head**, **white neck ring**, **reddish breast**, pale gray body, curled black feathers at base of tail; bill yellow. FEMALE: Mottled brown, with dark line through eye, orange and dusky bill.

Voice: Female's quacking is the quintessential duck noise; male gives a short, rasping whistle.

Behavior: Feeds in shallow water by tipping up; also grazes on land. Feral birds around park lakes can be tame, even aggressive. Nests in vegetation near water; increasingly Mallards have been nesting in residential areas around swimming pools, small ponds.

Similar Species: Male is unmistakable; female Gadwall (p. 37) has white speculum, female Northern Shoveler (p. 45) has much larger, spatulate bill.

Where, When to Find: Common resident in a variety of wetlands from estuaries to freshwater lakes, urban parks; many of these populations consist at least in part of feral domestic birds. A few breed on lakes in the high mountains. There is also an influx of wintering birds from October to March to wetlands throughout the region.

Did you know? Feral Mallards are abundant at park lakes; these are descended from a variety of domestic breeds and can vary greatly in size and color. These flocks may include "monster" hybrids with Muscovy Ducks and even geese.

Date & Location Seen:

Cinnamon Teal
Male

Cinnamon Teal
Female

Blue-winged Teal
Male

Blue-wingedTeal
Female

Description: 16", wingspan 23". A small dabbling duck with a **light blue forewing patch** and green speculum (both mostly hidden when at rest) orange-yellow legs. MALE: **Deep cinnamon-red** nearly throughout, with a black bill, red eyes, black undertail. FEMALE: Mottled brown with a plain brown head; bluish forewing patch distinctive in flight.

Voice: Females quacks, males give a low chatter.

Behavior: Forages by tipping up in shallow water and by dabbling with the bill in mud. Nests in low, grassy vegetation near water.

Similar Species: Blue-winged Teal (*Anas discors*; 15 ½") is similar in size and shape, but has slightly smaller, less spatulate bill; male has slate-gray head, spotted brown body, **white face crescent and flank patch**. Female much like Cinnamon, but slightly grayer with stronger face patterning, smaller bill. Blue-winged as an uncommon winter visitor and migrant (August to April) throughout; has nested at Bolsa Chica Ecological Reserve. See Green-winged Teal (p. 49).

Where, When to Find: Common spring migrant (late January to April) and fall migrant (mainly August and September) in wetlands throughout the region. Uncommon winter visitor in coastal areas and at Salton Sea. Uncommon to locally fairly common breeder in marshes and ponds in the coastal lowlands, Antelope Valley and Salton Sea; a few even breed in the Los Angeles River channel near Griffith and Elysian Parks.

Did you know? As with most of our ducks, adult males wear a dull, female-like plumage for a brief period in late summer and early fall.

Date & Location Seen: _____

Male

Female

Description: 19". A medium-sized dabbler with an **oversized, spatulate bill**. The large bill gives a front-heavy appearance in flight. MALE: Green head with yellow eye, white breast, cinnamon sides. In flight shows light blue-gray forewing with broad white rear border. FEMALE: Mottled brown with broad buffy-white edges to side and flank feathers; gray forewing with narrow white rear border. Female's large spoon-shaped bill with orange sides distinctive.

Voice: Females quack; males give a soft *thup-tup*.

Behavior: Feeds in flocks in shallow water by tipping up, and by sifting through the water and mud with their outsized bills with sweeping motions. Flocks fly in bunches or loose lines.

Similar Species: Many other female ducks are similar in general plumage, but none shows the large, expanded bill of the shoveler.

Where, When to Find: Common winter visitor (late August to April) to lakes, marshes, estuaries throughout the region; can be especially abundant on sewage treatment ponds. Up to 25,000 winter in the Salton Sea area. A few may remain rarely through the summer, and on a handful of occasions shovelers have nested in the region. Flocks of migrants are sometimes seen over the open ocean.

Did you know? Northern Shovelers have fringes along the sides of the bill that help them filter food items from water and mud.

Date & Location Seen: _____

Male

Female

Description: 21", wingspan 33". A slender, long-necked dabbling duck with a **gray bill** and long **pointed tail**. MALE: **Brown head**, white breast, **white stripe up side of neck**. Gray body with elongated black and white feathers on the sides of the back; black undertail, **long pointed central tail feathers**. The speculum is green, bordered in front by buff, behind by white. FEMALE: Plain pale brown head and neck, mottled gray-brown body; central tail feathers pointed; in flight shows white trailing edge to inner half of wing; bill plain gray.

Voice: Female gives hoarse quacks; males give a thin, wheezy whistle and a musical *droop* call (often doubled).

Behavior: Typically feeds by tipping up, with long tail pointed skyward and head and neck underwater. Flies in lines or "V"s, appearing slim and long-necked.

Similar Species: Other dabbling ducks have shorter, stockier necks and lack the pointed tail. Female Redhead (p. 51) is stockier, more solidly gray-brown on the body, and has pale gray flight feathers.

Where, When to Find: Common winter visitor (mainly August to March) to larger estuaries (such as Upper Newport Bay, Mugu Lagoon), lakes, and river bottoms (large numbers are found in the San Gabriel River channel in El Monte and Pico Rivera). Very common at the Salton Sea. Has nested in the north coastal counties, at Bolsa Chica, and on the desert at Piute Ponds on the Edwards Air Force Base. Fall migrants often found well at sea.

Did you know? North American populations now number well above the all-time low of about two million, but below the peak count of nearly ten million.

Date & Location Seen:

Male

Female

Description: 14″, wingspan 23″. The smallest dabbling duck; all show a **bright green speculum** with a buffy-white border in front. Bill is small and dark. MALE: **Bright green ear patch** borders **chestnut crown and face**; body gray with **white vertical stripe behind the breast**; undertail is pale yellow and black. FEMALE: Mottled brown; dark line through eye bordered indistinctly by buffy-brown lines; buffy or whitish patch on sides of the undertail.

Voice: Males give a high, peeping *dreep*. Female gives short, rough quacks.

Behavior: Feeds by dabbling at the surface of shallow water, but also routinely feeds shorebird-style on mudflats. Flocks spring vertically from the water when disturbed.

Similar Species: Female Cinnamon and Blue-winged Teal (p. 43) are larger with larger bills, blue-gray forewing patch; they lack buff or whitish patch below tail.

Where, When to Find: Common winter visitor (mainly late September to early April) to marshes, estuaries, ponds and river bottoms throughout the lowlands (including desert wetlands).

Did you know? "Eurasian" Green-winged Teal, males of which show a white horizontal stripe above the wing instead of the vertical breast stripe, occurs very rarely in winter with flocks of American Green-wings.

Date & Location Seen: _____

Redhead Male

Canvasback Male

Redhead Female

Canvasback Female

Description: 21/19", wingspan 29/29". Gray diving ducks with chestnut heads and black chests and rear ends (females are plainer but retain distinctive shapes of males). CANVASBACK: Male has nearly **whitish body**, deep chestnut head, red eyes, **long sloping forehead** and **long black bill**; female is pale gray with light brown head and chest, pale gray wings. REDHEAD: Male is medium gray with bright rufous-red head, **rounded forehead**, and shorter **blue-gray bill** with black tip preceded by a white line; female is plain gray-brown; pale gray flight feathers contrast with darker forewing.

Voice: Canvasbacks generally silent in our area; male Redheads on breeding grounds give a loud cat-like *ooaaoh*.

Behavior: Both species dive underwater for aquatic vegetation, some invertebrates. Canvasbacks can occur in large rafts; Redheads in our area are usually in smaller groups. Redheads breed in marshes; their pale yellow downy young are often seen at Piute Ponds near Lancaster and the Salton Sea.

Similar Species: Canvasback is told from Redhead by head and bill shape and much paler body color. Female Redhead could be confused with female Ring-necked Duck (p. 53) or scaup (p. 55).

Where, When to Find: Canvasback is an uncommon to fairly common winter visitor (mainly November to March) to deepwater lakes and reservoir as well as brackish coastal lagoons. Redheads are found in similar areas, October to March, and breed locally in marshes.

Did you know? Female Redheads sometimes lay their eggs in other Redhead nests, or in nests of other duck species.

Date & Location Seen:

Male

Female

Description: 17", wingspan 25". A small diving duck that would better be called "**ring-billed** duck" – the gray bill has white rings at the base and near the tip; bill tip is black; **head is peaked at rear of crown**. In flight gray flight feathers contrast with darker forewing. MALE: Appears all black with **white crescent behind black breast**, pale gray sides; head is glossed purplish, chestnut neck ring is hard to see. FEMALE: Dark slaty-brown above, brown below; white eye ring and diffuse white feathering at base of bill contrast with gray face.

Voice: Generally silent in our area.

Behavior: Dives for aquatic plants, invertebrates. Usually found in small flocks; can be quite tame at some park ponds.

Similar Species: Differs from scaup (p. 55) in having white rings on bill and more peaked head and lacking white wing stripe. Male scaup have gray (not black back), whitish (not gray) sides; female scaup have distinct white patch at bill base, lack eye ring. Female Redhead (p. 51) larger, paler brown, with more rounded head.

Where, When to Find: Fairly common winter visitor (mid-October to early April) to freshwater lakes and ponds throughout the lowlands and foothills. Usually scarce in coastal lagoons and estuaries. Ring-neckeds are more likely to be found on small, wooded ponds and small park lakes than the other diving ducks of the genus *Aythya*.

Did you know? As with most members of its genus, Ring-necked Duck males have bright yellow eyes; the eyes of females are duller, browner.

Date & Location Seen: _____

Lesser Scaup
Female

Lesser Scaup
Male

Greater Scaup
Female

Greater Scaup
Male

Description: 16 ½", wingspan 25". A common diving duck; in all plumages shows a white stripe on inner half of wing in flight, gray bill with small black "nail" on tip. MALE: **Iridescent purple (sometimes greenish) head** with slight bump at rear of crown (less evident on actively diving birds); chest, rump and undertail black; remaining **upperparts pale gray**, underparts white. FEMALE: Brown throughout with white belly, **white patch at the base of the bill**.

Voice: Grating calls of females and rough whistles of males are rarely heard in our area.

Behavior: Dives for aquatic invertebrates, some plant food. Often found in large flocks, sometimes mixed with other species of diving ducks.

Similar Species: Greater Scaup (*Aythya marila*, 18"), is an uncommon to locally fairly common winter visitor (mainly November to March) to deeper reservoirs (such as Quail Lake), Colorado River dam outflows, and coastal lagoons (especially San Diego Bay); it is very similar to Lesser, but is larger with larger bill, rounder head (not peaked at rear), longer white wing stripe.

Where, When to Find: Common winter visitor (October to early April) to freshwater lakes and reservoirs, coastal lagoons.

Did you know? Though the iridescence of the male's head is usually purple in male Lesser Scaup and green in Greater Scaup, such color is highly variable and dependent on the lighting and should not be used for species identification.

Date & Location Seen:

Surf Scoter
Adult Male

Surf Scoter
Female

White-winged Scoter
Adult Male

White-winged Scoter
Immature

Black Scoter
Adult Male

Black Scoter
Immature Female

Description: 20", wingspan 30". A heavy-set, dark diving duck of salt water. MALE: Entirely black except for **white patches on hindneck, forehead. Swollen bill has orange tip, white base with large black spot**; eyes white. FEMALE: Dark brown with blackish crown, **whitish patches on cheek** and at base of bill. Immatures of both sexes browner, with pale belly.

Voice: Generally silent when in our region.

Behavior: Dives for mussels and other mollusks in marine waters, especially around pier pilings, rocky shorelines, and bays with rocky bottoms. Often found in large flocks. Flips forward when launching into a dive. Large flocks fly in loose lines past coastal points in spring.

Similar Species: White-winged Scoter (*Melanitta fusca*; 21") and **Black Scoter** (*Melanitta nigra*, 19") are rare winter visitors (mainly November to March), usually with flocks of Surf Scoters. White-winged's large white speculum may be hidden when at rest; look for sloping forehead and feathering extending well out the bill (whitish in females and immature males). Male Black Scoter has yellow-orange swelling at base of thin, upturned black bill; female has plain whitish sides of more rounded head contrasting with blackish cap, small concave bill.

Where, When to Find: Common winter visitor and migrant along the coast, November to April; found both in protected bays and harbors and on exposed coastlines. Rare migrant on lakes and reservoirs inland, though small flocks occur annually at Salton Sea (other scoter species are casual inland).

Did you know? All three scoters nest on ponds and lakes in tundra and taiga regions which include Canada and Alaska; White-winged has declined markedly in our region in recent decades.

Date & Location Seen: _____

Bufflehead
Male

Bufflehead
Female

Common Goldeneye
Adult Male

Common Goldeneye
Female

Description: 13 ½″, wingspan 21″. Our **smallest duck**, with small gray bill. MALE: White below, mostly black above with **large white area on back of head**, large white wing patch. In good light, shows purple and green gloss to black of head. FEMALE: Dark gray throughout with **oval white patch on side of head**, small white speculum.

Voice: Generally silent in our area.

Behavior: Found in small, loose flocks; dives for aquatic invertebrates, small fish; surfacing only briefly when actively feeding. Flight is rapid, whirring.

Similar Species: Common Goldeneye (*Bucephala clangula*; 18 ½″) is an uncommon winter visitor (November to March) to deepwater reservoirs such as Quail Lake, the Salton Sea, Colorado River and sometimes coastal estuaries such as Bolsa Chica. Larger than Bufflehead; male has green-glossed black head, large white spot at bill base; female is gray with dark brown head, often some yellow at tip of bill. Barrow's Goldeneye (*B. islandica*; 18″), not shown here, is regular (with Commons) only below dams on Colorado River; it differs from Common in more extensive black in plumage and white crescent (not spot) at bill base of male, steep puffy forehead, smaller stubbier bill (orange-yellow in most females).

Where, When to Find: Fairly common winter visitor (November to April) to lakes, ponds, estuaries and rivers throughout the region. Seen less commonly on salt water, but a few winter in protected harbors.

Did you know? This cavity-nesting species generally breeds well north of our region, but one exceptional nesting record occurred at Piute Ponds north of Lancaster.

Date & Location Seen: _____

Male

Female

Description: 18". A small, thin-billed, long-tailed diving duck with a unique puffy crest. MALE: **Puffy white crest outlined in black**; when folded back, white of crest is reduced to a long thick stripe. Black above, tawny on sides, with **two vertical black bars on side of white breast**, long white. FEMALE: Dusky above, gray-brown on breast, sides; belly white; **puffy light tawny-brown crest**; bill has much yellow on sides. Immature male like female but with black bill, hint of adult's head pattern.

Voice: Generally silent in our area, though wings make whistling sound in flight.

Behavior: Dives for small fish and aquatic invertebrates. In our area found singly or in small groups. Very slender and bullet-like in flight, with rapid wing beats.

Similar Species: Male can suggest male Bufflehead (p. 59); latter has pure white sides, stubby gray bill. Female not likely to be confused with much larger, orange-billed Red-breasted and Common Mergansers (p. 63)

Where, When to Find: Uncommon winter visitor (late October to March) to small lakes and ponds, especially those with wooded margins. Consistent sites include Lake Cachuma, Whittier Narrows, Hansen Dam, Los Encinos Historical Monument (Encino), Big Canyon Pond at Upper Newport Bay. One nesting record (in a Wood Duck nest box) at the Prado Basin.

Did you know? Formerly considered rare in the region, the Hooded Merganser has increased its local wintering numbers since the 1970s.

Date & Location Seen: _____

Common Merganser
Adult Male

Common Merganser
Female

Red-Breasted Merganser
Adult Male

Red-breasted Merganser
Female

Description: 23/25", wingspan 30/34". Low-slung diving ducks with slender bills. RED-BREASTED: **Bill reddish-orange**. Adult male has **dark green head with shaggy thin crest**, white neck ring, mottled reddish-brown breast bordered behind by black and white patch; mostly blackish above, gray and white below, with white wing patch. Female and young male show **tawny brown head with thin shaggy crest**, gray body. COMMON: **Bill thin but deep-based, bright red**. Adult male has **green head** with short, smooth crest; **body mostly white** with black down center of back. Female and young male have **deep rusty head sharply separated from white chin and pale chest**, gray breast and flanks.

Voice: Low croaking calls; rarely heard in our area.

Behavior: Both species dive for fish; flocks sometimes move together, herding fish. Red-breasteds may chase fish in shallow water around foraging herons.

Similar Species: Only likely to be confused with each other. Larger Common has deeper-based, brighter red bill; female Common shows sharp demarcation between chestnut neck and gray and white breast.

Where, When to Find: Red-breasted is a fairly common November to early April in coastal lagoons, bays, and harbors; rare inland where occasionally seen in migration and rarely winter on deep water lakes and reservoirs. Common local but fairly common November to March on deepwater inland lakes; favored sites include Lake Isabella, Quail Lake, Lake Casitas, Bonelli Regional Park, and Lake Perris. Common is rare in salt water; it has bred on Upper Santa Ynez River (Santa Barbara County) and Piru Creek (Ventura County).

Did you know? Merganser "teeth" – good for holding and helping grasp fish – are projections on the horny covering of the bill, not true teeth.

Date & Location Seen: _____

Breeding Male

Female

Description: 15". A small compact duck with a long **stiff tail, often pointed upward**. MALE: Blackish crown, **large white cheek patch**. Mainly gray-brown (darker above), except March to August, when **body is entirely deep chestnut** color and **bill is sky blue**. FEMALE: Resembles non-breeding male, but with **dark line across the whitish cheek**.

Voice: Mostly silent except when male displays with an accelerating series of low popping notes ending in a low croak: *fup fup fup fup fuf-fuf-fuf-frrrrrp.*

Behavior: Dives for aquatic plants as well as small fish and invertebrates. More likely to dive than fly when approached; when they do take to the air they patter vigorously along the surface before becoming airborne. Displaying male points tail straight upward, bobs head in time with vocalizations.

Similar Species: Female Bufflehead (p. 59) is grayer with smaller white cheek patch than winter male Ruddy; Bufflehead has shorter tail, white wing patch.

Where, When to Find: Common winter visitor (October to April) to lakes, ponds, marshes and estuaries throughout the region; uncommon on ocean, but common on the Salton Sea. Fairly common spring and summer breeder in freshwater marshes and lakes with vegetated borders.

Did you know? Adult male Ruddies are in the bright breeding plumage for only about five months, a much shorter period than for most other ducks.

Date & Location Seen: _____

Male

Female

CALIFORNIA QUAIL
Callipepla californica

Description: 10". A plump gray game bird with short, rounded wings, medium-length tail, small black bill, and **curved black topknot. Belly is scaled with white**, brown flanks have white streaks. MALE: **Black throat outlined in white**; dark brown crown; conspicuous forward-curved topknot, dark chestnut belly patch. FEMALE: Gray-brown head; small, nearly straight topknot.

Voice: Call includes a cawing *waaaw* and a three-noted *chi-ca-go*. Flocks give sharp *pit, pit* calls.

Behavior: Feeds in flocks on the ground, scratching with the feet for seeds and insects. One or more males stand watch as "sentinels." When flushed quail explode into flight with whirring wing beats. Clutches are large – groups of a dozen or more young are seen in late spring.

Similar Species: Gambel's Quail (p. 467) of s. and e. deserts similar, male has reddish cap, unscaled buff-white belly with black patch; female is paler on belly; these species sometimes hybridize, as at Anza-Borrego State Park. Mountain Quail (p. 459) has long straight topknot, vertical white bars on chestnut flanks, rusty undertail; usually found at higher elevations.

Where, When to Find: Common resident in chaparral and oak and riparian woodland understory in lowlands and foothills throughout the coastal slope; also in Joshua-tree woodlands, desert scrub on parts of the western Mojave Desert, and at fringes of Coachella and Borrego Valleys. Found on Santa Catalina I. (and introduced to Santa Cruz and Santa Rosa Is.). A few small populations persist within the heavily urbanized coastal regions, such as the Baldwin Hills, Palos Verdes Peninsula, and Point Loma.

Did you know? This species, sometimes called the "Valley Quail", is the State Bird of California.

Date & Location Seen: _____

67

Juvenile

Breeding Adult

Description: 25", wingspan 36". Loons are heavy-bodied, dagger-billed swimming and diving birds; not normally seen on land in our area. Red-throated is the smallest loon, with **thin, slightly upturned bill held tilted upwards**. NON-BREEDING: **Gray above with small white spots**. Adult has gray cap, white face and throat; neck of juveniles is washed with gray. BREEDING: Head and neck gray, brick **red patch on throat**. In flight looks plain gray on neck, upperparts; feet appear relatively small.

Voice: Generally silent in our area.

Behavior: Pursues fish underwater; often forages close inshore, even among the breakers. In flight the neck usually droops below horizontal.

Similar Species: Pacific (p. 71) and Common (p. 73) loons larger, show larger feet in flight. Pacific darker above, with dark neck sides contrasting with white throat, straighter bill; breeding birds have white patches on sides of back, black throat. Western and Clark's Grebes (p.79) have much longer and thinner necks, yellow bills. Compare also with Red-breasted Merganser (p. 63) and immature Double-crested Cormorant (p. 81).

Where, When to Find: Fairly common winter visitor (November to March) in inshore ocean waters, harbors, bays. Migrants pass by in small loose groups off coastal points in March and April. Occurs very rarely on inland deep water lakes, mainly in late fall.

Did you know? The legs of loons are set far back on the body, so they cannot walk efficiently on land.

Date & Location Seen: _____

Non-breeding Adult

Breeding Adult

Description: 25", wingspan 36". Medium-sized loon with straight bill. NON-BREEDING: Dark brown upperparts, crown (to the eyes) and **neck sides, contrasting sharply with white throat** and underparts. Juveniles are barred with whitish gray above and have paler gray hindneck. Most non-breeders show a thin dark "chinstrap," sometimes lacking in juveniles. BREEDING: **Hindneck pale gray**, contrasting with **black throat**. Checkered **white patches on either side of the back (the scapulars)**. At close range, thin vertical white streaks on sides of neck.

Voice: Generally silent in our region.

Behavior: Pursues fish underwater. Migrants fly low over the water, usually in loose flocks.

Similar Species: Common Loon (p. 73) is larger with a heavier bill. Non-breeding Commons have more irregular separation of dark and white on neck, white markings around eyes; in breeding plumage Common has completely black head, white collar, white checkers over entire back.

Where, When to Find: Fairly common to common winter visitor along the coast, November to April. Large numbers of migrants pass by coastal points in April and May, and flocks are often found over the open ocean at this season. Very rare but regular on inland lakes, mainly in late fall and winter.

Did you know? Pacific Loons undertake a long migration from as far south as Baja California to Arctic Alaska and northern Canada. As many as 11,000 have been counted in a single day passing by the Santa Barbara County coast in late April.

Date & Location Seen:

Juvenile

Breeding Adult

Description: 32", wingspan 46". Our **largest loon**, with a **heavy bill**. In flight shows very large feet, broad wings with relatively slow wing beats. NON-BREEDING: Gray-brown above (juvenile has pale gray cross-barring and duskier face), white below. **White partial collar on neck**, with broad dark collar extending forward below this; white arcs around the eyes. BREEDING: Green-glossed **black head and bill**; collar of white vertical bars on neck, with black collar under that; **back checkered black and white**.

Voice: Maniacal yodeling calls are sometimes heard from migrants, but generally silent in our area.

Behavior: Pursues fish underwater with long dives. Sometimes swims along surface with face underwater, looking for prey. Migrants move singly or in small, loose flocks past coastal points, often closer to shore than other loons (even over land); migrating Commons fly higher over water than other loons.

Similar Species: See other loons, especially Pacific (p. 71).

Where, When to Find: Fairly common winter visitor (mid-October to mid-May) along coast, in protected harbors and bays. More likely to be found inland than other loons, with small numbers found in winter and migration on larger inland reservoirs.

Did you know? A few immatures of all three of our loon species occur through the summer as non-breeders along our coast.

Date & Location Seen: _____

Non-breeding

Breeding Adult

Description: 13″. A small diving bird with a **short, thick chicken-like bill**. **Plain tawny brown** throughout. Breeding adult has black throat patch, **whitish bill with black ring near tip**. Bill of non-breeders and immatures is plain pale brownish. Young juveniles and downy young have black and white stripes on the face.

Voice: Often quite vocal. Male's "song" is a loud *kuh kuh kuh kow kow kow kow-ah kow-ah*, etc. Interacting birds give an electric chatter, *huzza-huzza-huzza…*

Behavior: Dives for fish, aquatic invertebrates. When disturbed may slowly sink into water rather than diving. Rarely seen flying. Found in pairs or family groups, rarely in flocks. Nest is a floating platform anchored to emergent vegetation.

Similar Species: Eared Grebe (p. 77) has longer, slimmer neck, thin bill, and more contrasting gray and white plumage.

Where, When to Find: Widespread and fairly common in freshwater lakes, river channels and small ponds throughout the region. Also found (mainly non-breeding) in coastal estuaries and protected bays and harbors, but infrequent on the open ocean.

Did you know? This is one of our most adaptable waterbirds, frequently seen on urban park lakes and even nesting in the river channels near downtown Los Angeles and San Diego.

Date & Location Seen: _____

Horned Grebe
Non-breeding

Eared Grebe
Non-breeding

Horned Grebe
Breeding Adult

Eared Grebe
Breeding Adult

Description: 13″. Small **slim-necked** grebe with **thin, slightly upturned bill**, bright red eyes. Feathering at rear usually fluffed out when resting on water. NON-BREEDING: Gray above, whitish with gray mottling below. **Peaked crown** is dark down to cheek; neck variably washed with gray. BREEDING: Head and **neck black** with patch of yellow plumes on side of head. Breast and flanks chestnut.

Voice: Rising whistles heard mainly at breeding colonies.

Behavior: Dives for small fish, aquatic invertebrates. Often found in large flocks, sometimes tightly concentrated. Nests in colonies on shallow vegetated ponds and lake margins. Like most of our grebes, rarely seen in flight.

Similar Species: Horned Grebe (*Podiceps auritus*; 14″) is an uncommon visitor (November to March) to coastal waters; small numbers also occur regularly on deep water reservoirs inland on the coastal slope, more rarely on the deserts. Non-breeders resemble winter Eared, but have flat black crown, shorter and stockier neck with clean white foreneck, pale spot in front of eye; bill has pale tip.

Where, When to Find: Common winter visitor (late September to April) to freshwater lakes and reservoirs, sewage ponds, and coastal bays and estuaries. Also found on inshore ocean waters and occasionally even well at sea. Abundant at Salton Sea in winter and early spring (at times, well over a million birds here). A few nesting colonies are found on marsh-bordered lakes and reservoirs in the region, such as Piute Ponds in the Antelope Valley, and Baldwin Lake in the San Bernardino Mountains.

Did you know? Grebes are propelled underwater by their feet which have lobes or flaps on the toes rather than webbing.

Date & Location Seen: _____

_____

Clark's Grebe
Non-breeding

Western Grebe
Breeding Adult

Description: 25". Largest grebes, with long slender necks and bright red eyes. **Gray above**, **white foreneck and underparts**, with **black crown**. WESTERN: **Dull yellow to greenish-yellow bill**; black crown extends to eyes. CLARK'S: Best told by **bright orange yellow bill**; eye largely surrounded by white, dark on hindneck more restricted, more extensive white in wings.

Voice: WESTERN: loud grating *kree-kreeeek*; CLARK'S: single, drawn-out *kreeeeek*.

Behavior: Dives for fish. Displaying birds rush along water surface with gracefully curved necks. Floating nests are anchored to vegetation in marshy pond borders. As in all grebes, the small downy chicks may ride on the backs of the parents.

Similar Species: Western and Clark's best distinguished by bill color (dull yellow to yellow olive in Western, orange-yellow in Clark's). Breeding Clark's show white surrounding eye, but face pattern difference is less clear in winter. Horned Grebe (p. 77) much smaller and shorter-necked.

Where, When to Find: WESTERN: Common winter visitor to inshore waters, bays, and harbors along the coast; non-breeders uncommon through summer. Also common on some deep water inland lakes (e.g. hundreds on Castaic Lake). CLARK'S: makes up a small percentage (usually <10%) of birds in the above areas. Small breeding colonies of both species occur on inland lakes, e.g. Lake Palmdale, gravel pit lakes in Irwindale, Piute Ponds, Oso Reservoir near Mission Viejo, and Lake Hodges (and other reservoirs) in San Diego County.

Did you know? These two species were formerly considered different plumage morphs of a single species; breeding colonies in southern California often include mixed pairs, and intermediate-looking birds, likely hybrids, are frequently seen.

Date & Location Seen:

Breeding Adult

Immature

DOUBLE-CRESTED CORMORANT
Phalacrocorax auritus

Description: 33", wingspan 52". Large, with conspicuous **bare yellow or orange skin on the face and chin**, thick neck and relatively long wings. ADULT: Black head, neck and underparts; scaled above with gray and black. Bright orange-yellow skin in front of eyes and on throat. Breeding birds have white, black, or mixed double crest plumes. IMMATURE: Varies from brown to almost whitish on the neck and breast; belly darker; bare face skin yellow. Our only cormorant normally seen inland.

Voice: Generally silent, but breeding and roosting birds make low guttural croaking sounds.

Behavior: Pursues fish underwater; at the surface rides low in the water, with bill angled upwards. Often seen perched on shore, rocks or in trees with wings spread. More likely to fly high above the water than other cormorants. Stick nests are built in tall trees near water, often among nesting herons; nests on rocky slopes on the Channel Islands.

Similar Species: See Brandt's Cormorant (p. 83). Very pale immatures on the water can be confused with loons.

Where, When to Find: Common year-round visitor to inshore marine waters and estuaries along the coast and in lakes and river channels throughout the lowlands. Small breeding colonies are found at some coastal slope lakes and river bottoms, such as Anaheim Lake and ponds near the San Gabriel R. and Rio Hondo in El Monte and Pico Rivera, and coastally at Morro Bay, south San Diego Bay, and some Channel Islands. Large numbers nest at the Salton Sea when abundant tilapia prey is available.

Did you know? Populations of this cormorant have greatly increased; they now commonly feed on fish stocked into park lakes.

Date & Location Seen: _____

_____

**Brandt's Cormorant
Adult**

**Brandt's Cormorant
Immature**

**Pelagic Cormorant
Breeding Adult**

**Pelagic Cormorant
Immature**

BRANDT'S CORMORANT/PELAGIC CORMORANT
Phalacrocorax penicillatus/pelagicus

Description: 34/28", wingspan 48/39". Restricted to marine waters and coastlines. BRANDT'S: Large, with relatively short wings, **short tail**, black bill. Adult **entirely black** with **buff chin patch**; breeding birds have blue-green gloss, thin white head plumes, bright blue bare pouch at bill base. Immature duller, with light brown breast. PELAGIC: **"Pencil-necked" and tiny-headed**, with the **very thin bill** that appears "pushed" into the facial feathering; **tail long**. Chin and throat feathering always dark. Adult black throughout, glossier than our other cormorants; breeding birds (February to May) show a **white patch on the flanks**, thin white plumes on the neck, and small red facial patch. Immature blackish-brown throughout.

Voice: Generally silent.

Behavior: Pursue fish underwater, Brandt's sometimes feeding in large flocks. Resting birds sit on rocky outcrops, jetties and breakwaters, Pelagic favoring more vertical substrates. Fly with neck held nearly straight. Nests are placed on the ground on rocky slopes (Pelagic on more vertical cliffs).

Similar Species: Double-crested Cormorant (p. 81) has yellow bare throat pouch and partly yellow bill, thicker neck shows strong kink in flight, wings longer, more pointed.

Where, When to Find: BRANDT'S: Found year-round along the coast, especially along rocky shorelines and around breakwaters; can be very common far at sea. Breeds on the Channel Islands, and locally on the coast of San Luis Obispo County and at La Jolla. PELAGIC: Uncommon to fairly common along the immediate coast, especially rocky coastlines and jetties; numbers greatest in winter, but non-breeders remain on the mainland coast through year. Breeds on the Channel Islands, Morro Bay.

Did you know? Despite its name, the Pelagic Cormorant is the least "pelagic" of our three cormorants.

Date & Location Seen: _____

American White Pelican
Non-breeding Adult

Brown Pelican
Breeding Adult

Brown Pelican
Juvenile

Description: 50″, wingspan 79″. An unmistakable **huge** seabird, generally gray-brown with **long hooked bill and pouch**. ADULT: **Dark brown underparts**, frosted gray upperparts, **whitish head and neck**; courting and breeding adults have brown hindnecks and bright red markings on bill and pouch. IMMATURE: Juveniles have **dark brown necks and upperparts**, **white bellies**; adult plumage develops over 3-4 years.

Voice: Silent away from breeding colonies.

Behavior Plunges from 10-30′ in the air to catch fish under the surface, using pouch as a scoop. Fly in lines or Vs, with necks folded. Flocks rest on breakwaters, rocky islets, pier pilings, sand flats.

Similar Species: Larger **American White Pelican** (*Pelecanus erythrorhynchos*; 62″) is all white, with black flight feathers and huge yellow to orange bill (beware adult Browns that can appear very pale above in some lighting). White Pelicans migrate, sometimes in large flocks, through the foothills and deserts in March-April and October; small numbers winter on some inland lakes and coastal lagoons and they are abundant in winter and migration at the Salton Sea.

Where, When to Find: Common through the year along the coast; largest numbers are usually found June to September after the breeding on Channel Islands and Baja California. Mainly inshore, but also found far at sea. Flocks visit the Salton Sea from summer through early winter; otherwise casual on inland lakes, mainly in summer, fall. Numbers have recovered from steep declines caused by organochlorine pesticides, though breeding success varies from year to year.

Did you know? Dr. Ralph Schreiber, curator at the Natural History Museum of Los Angeles County from 1976 to 1988, was a leading expert on the biology of this species.

Date & Location Seen: _____

Least Bittern
Breeding Adult Male

Least Bittern
Female

American Bittern

Description: 13″, wingspan 17″. A tiny, secretive heron found very locally in our region. Large buff patch on shoulders is conspicuous in flight. Bill and legs yellowish. ADULT: Cinnamon-buff throughout, with buff patch on shoulders, dark back (blackish in males), and buff stripes on white breast. JUVENILE: More strongly striped below than adult; back dusky with buff fringes.

Voice: Best detected by voice, a harsh *kek-kek-kek-kek* that slows at the end. Soft cooing heard on breeding territory.

Behavior: Feeds within bulrushes (tules) and cattails, clambering about low over the water's surface. Often suns early in the morning at edge of reeds; otherwise hard to see except when flying between patches of reeds.

Similar Species: American Bittern (*Botaurus lentiginosus*; 28″) is a rare and declining winter visitor (mainly October to April) to freshwater and brackish marshes such as San Joaquin Marsh and Upper Newport Bay, San Jacinto Wildlife Area, Salton Sea. It is much larger, intricately marbled brown buff and gray; note long black stripe below cheek, dark flight feathers contrasting with paler shoulder area. Compare Least with immature Green Heron (p. 97), American with immature Black-crowned Night-Heron (p. 99).

Where, When to Find: Uncommon and local resident in freshwater ponds and lakes with extensive margins of reeds (bulrushes, cattails)**.** Seen most consistently at refuges at Salton Sea and Colorado River; also at Whittier Narrows, Harbor Lake (Ken Malloy Harbor Regional Park), El Dorado Park; also often at San Joaquin Marsh, Ballona Freshwater Marsh. Absent from marshes in the Antelope Valley.

Did you know? The common contact call described above is undescribed in most literature; once learned, it's the best way to detect this species.

Date & Location Seen:

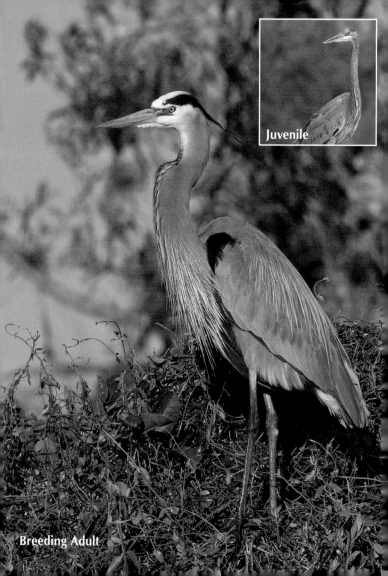

Juvenile

Breeding Adult

Description: 46", wingspan 72". Our **largest and most widespread heron**. Largely **gray**, with darker flight feathers; **cinnamon or chestnut "thigh" feathering**, strong, dagger-like bill shows much yellow; legs grayish. ADULT: **Whitish face, pale crown, long black head plumes**, plain pale lavender-gray neck. JUVENILE: Dark crown, much gray streaking on foreneck and breast.

Voice: Calls are loud, deep and harsh, e.g. *grake* or *kronk*.

Behavior: Patiently hunts for fish, crayfish, frogs and other prey, standing on shore or in shallow water. Sometimes hunts mice in open fields. Often perches high in trees; stick nests are built in tall trees. Flies with ponderous wingbeats, neck folded and retracted.

Similar Species: Often mistakenly called "crane" by non-birders. Our true crane (Sandhill Crane, p. 467) flies with shallow wingbeats and outstretched neck and has shorter legs, solid gray plumage with red cap.

Where, When to Find: Common year-round resident; more numerous and widespread in winter (September to March). Found in all wetlands, including rivers, ponds, reservoirs, estuaries and even rocky coastlines. Small breeding colonies are found in tree groves near wetlands throughout the lowlands; increasingly these herons are nesting in residential areas, park lakes.

Did you know? This is the most widespread breeding heron in North America.

Date & Location Seen:

Description: 39", wingspan 51". A **large**, **all white** heron with very long, slender neck, a **yellow bill**, and **black legs and feet**. All plumages are similar, but breeding adults have long white plumes on the breast, lower back and rump.

Voice: Very low, harsh grating calls.

Behavior: Hunts very patiently, standing still for long periods or wading very slowly through shallow water. Feeds on a great variety of vertebrates, including fish, frogs, and rodents; also takes crayfish. Often feeds in open fields, and (along with the Great Blue Heron) sometimes seen foraging from rafts of kelp just offshore.

Similar Species: Snowy Egret (p. 93) is much smaller, with slender black bill, yellow feet. Cattle Egret (p. 95) also has dark legs and yellow bill, but is much smaller with a short neck and bill. These smaller egrets fly with faster wingbeats.

Where, When to Find: Year-round visitor to coastal estuaries and to freshwater wetlands throughout the lowlands; generally uncommon in summer, but fairly common to common from September through March. Small breeding colonies are found in lakes along the Santa Ana and San Gabriel Rivers and very locally elsewhere on the coastal slope; larger nesting colonies are found at Salton Sea/Imperial Valley, and at Topock Marsh near Needles.

Did you know? Although white like Snowy and most other egrets, it is more closely related to the Great Blue Heron and recently has been placed in the same genus.

Date & Location Seen: _____

Snowy Egret
Breeding Adult

Snowy Egret
Non-breeding

Little Blue Heron
Juvenile

Description: 24". A **small pure white egret** with a **slender black bill**, dark legs with **yellow feet**. ADULT: Bare **skin between eye and bill deep yellow**; mostly black legs contrast with yellow feet. Breeding birds get a white crest and long white plumes on the breast and rump. JUVENILE: Lacks plumes, facial skin dull yellow-green, legs greenish.

Voice: Rasping, grating notes, higher in pitch than calls of Great Egret.

Behavior: Uses a variety of feeding behaviors, from slow stalking to active running; often dabbles the surface with the bill to lure fish, or stamps feet to flush prey. Forages almost exclusively in shallow water or at water's edge (not in dry fields).

Similar Species: Compare with Great Egret, Cattle Egret. Immature **Little Blue Heron** (*Egretta caerulea*; 24") has thicker, gray bill, gray-green legs, and dull yellow facial skin, and most show hint of dusky in wingtips (adult is dark blue-gray and maroon); regular on San Diego area coast, very rare elsewhere.

Where, When to Find: Fairly common and widespread winter visitor (mainly September to early April) to coastal wetlands; extends uncommon to inland wetlands on the coastal slope. Breeds very locally on coastal slope. Mainly a migrant through deserts in April-May and August-September, but breeding colonies found at Salton Sea and Imperial Valley.

Did you know? Population reductions of Great Egrets and this species by plume hunters in the late 1800s motivated preservationists and led to the establishment of what is now the National Audubon Society.

Date & Location Seen: _____

Breeding Adult

Non-breeding

Description: 20". Small and short-necked egret, white with **short yellow bill** and **blackish legs**; BREEDING ADULTS have orange bill and legs, orange-buff patches on back, chest, crown.

Voice: Constant murmuring and *ruk-ruk* calls heard at breeding colonies, but generally silent otherwise.

Behavior: Feed mainly in fields, often around livestock or tractors, taking advantage of disturbance to insects; huge flocks may gather as fields are flood-irrigated in the Imperial Valley.

Similar Species: Bare part colors suggest Great Egret (p. 91), but much smaller, stockier. Shorter-legged and shorter-billed than a Snowy (p. 93), which has black bill. In flight, wingbeats more rapid than those of other egrets.

Where, When to Find: Very common in agricultural areas of the Imperial Valley and found less commonly in many other agricultural areas (pastures, dairies, hay crops). Migrants occasionally visit coastal estuaries. A large breeding colony (mixed with other herons, Double-crested Cormorants) is found at Ramer Lake, part of a state refuge near Calipatria in the Imperial Valley.

Did you know? Cattle Egrets were unknown in the New World until the late 1800s and did not become well-established until the 1950s, having colonized from Africa; they reached California in the early 1960s. Populations have declined somewhat in recent years.

Date & Location Seen:

Adult

Juvenile

Description: 18", wingspan 26". A small thick-necked, short-legged heron of wooded ponds, marshes and riparian areas. ADULT: **Slaty above** with only a hint of a green sheen; feathers of the wings have neat, narrow pale fringes. **Chestnut neck** with white stripe down the front, gray belly, **yellow to orange legs** and feet. IMMATURE: Streaked with rufous on neck, breast; legs dull yellow; juvenile has feathers of wings boldly edged with buff.

Voice: Call is a loud *keeeow*, usually given when flushed; also a low *kuk, kuk*.

Behavior: Solitary or in pairs; hunts patiently from shore or from branches low over water. Flicks tail when nervous. May perch well within willows or other riparian trees. Solitary nester, building a stick nest in low to middle heights of trees, usually close to water.

Similar Species: Juvenile can suggest smaller Least Bittern (p. 87) but is darker (less buffy overall) and lacks buff wing patch.

Where, When to Find: Fairly common migrant and winter visitor to wetlands, small ponds, and riparian areas, mid-August to April. A few occur in coastal estuaries and even rocky ocean shores. Uncommon but widespread breeder in riparian areas, vegetated borders of small ponds and lakes; some have nested in residential areas. Mainly a migrant on deserts away from Salton Sea, Colorado River.

Did you know? Despite its name, this species displays only a hint of a green sheen to the plumage of adults.

Date & Location Seen: _____

Adult

Juvenile

Description: 25". A medium-sized, **stocky** heron with a **short, thick neck**, red eyes. ADULT: **Black crown and back**, white forehead, gray wings, **pale gray underparts**. Bill black, legs yellow. Adults usually show one or two long white head plumes. IMMATURE: Juveniles are streaked gray-brown below and have white spots on the wings and small white streaks on the back. Legs greenish to yellow, bill with much yellow at the base. Older immatures are plainer gray-brown above and pale gray-buff below.

Voice: Call is an emphatic *kwok!* or *quark!*

Behavior: Sluggish, perching motionlessly at the water's edge for long periods before striking a fish, frog, or other prey. Most active at dusk and in the evening, but hunts through the day as well. During the day they are most often encountered as they roost in trees or reeds. Nests in small to large colonies in groves of trees (often planted eucalyptus groves) or in bulrush marshes, especially near coastal estuaries and harbors.

Similar Species: Immature differs from scarce American Bittern (p. 87) in grayer plumage tones, more uniform colored wings, absence of black stripe below cheek. Yellow-crowned Night-Heron (*Nyctanassa violacea*; 24") is a rare visitor and breeder in the San Diego area and at Pt. Mugu, but is only found casually elsewhere.

Where, When to Find: Common year-round resident in coastal estuaries, harbors, lakes, and marshes throughout the region where nearby trees are available for roosting. Often encountered at urban park lakes. Nesting colonies are found locally in coast and valley areas and at the Salton Sea and Colorado River.

Did you know? This species and the Great and Cattle Egrets are the world's most widespread herons.

Date & Location Seen:

Breeding Adult

Non-breeding Adult

Juvenile

Description: 23", wingspan 36". A dark wading bird with a **long, decurved bill**. Appears black in poor light or at a distance. ADULT: Eyes red, bill gray. Breeding birds have **glossy green back and wings** with pink highlights; head, **neck and underparts deep chestnut**. Bare pink skin on face surrounded by thin white line of feathering. Non-breeders are duller slaty (less chestnut) on the body with small white streaks on the neck, only a hint of white lines around limited pink on face. IMMATURE: Resembles non-breeding adult, but less glossy, pink facial skin lacking.

Voice: When flushed gives a low, quacking *waarr, waarr.*

Behavior: Feeds mainly on insects and other invertebrates. Gregarious, flies in tight groups or lines where large numbers occur; in our area, often found singly or in small groups. Feeds in flooded fields, marshes, and along small channels. Nests in extensive freshwater marshes.

Similar Species: Curlews (p. 161) share the long, decurved bill but are mottled gray-brown to cinnamon-brown and have shorter legs.

Where, When to Find: Uncommon and local migrant (mainly August to October) and rare winter visitor to marshy ponds in the lowlands and sometimes coastal salt marshes. Small numbers breed in bulrush marshes at Piute Ponds north of Lancaster and flocks are found very locally in flooded alfalfa fields on the deserts from April to October. Abundant in the Imperial Valley, where small numbers also nest; flocks are also often seen in the San Joaquin Valley portion of Kern County.

Did you know? Range and numbers have expanded; very few were found in the Los Angeles region prior to the 1980s.

Date & Location Seen: _____

_____

Description: 26", wingspan 66". A large, raptor-like bird, distantly related to the hawks and eagles. **Blackish-brown** throughout, with a **bare reddish head** and whitish bill. The **flight feathers of the wing appear pale silvery from below**, contrasting with the darker body and wing linings. Appears small-headed in flight. Juveniles have pale edges to the wing feathers, a dull brownish head, and darker bill.

Voice: Silent.

Behavior: Feeds on carrion, including road kills. Travels long distances searching for food, soaring on slightly uptilted wings. Often rocks back and forth in flight. Can be gregarious; gathers in the late afternoon at roost sites in stands of tall trees. Flocks of migrants ride thermal updrafts.

Similar Species: Distant flying adult Golden Eagle (p. 123) is similar but has more uniform wing color from below larger feathered head, pale brown hindneck and undertail.

Where, When to Find: Fairly common migrant in spring (late January through April) and fall (mainly September and October) through the interior and deserts. Locally common in winter in the coastal lowlands and foothills, especially in the remaining open grasslands and hillsides with sparse scrub. Smaller numbers occur through the summer in all areas, but nesting is mostly limited to remote, mountainous areas.

Did you know? Kenneth E. Stager, bird curator at the Natural History Museum of Los Angeles County from 1946 to 1976, earned his doctorate studying the keen sense of smell in this species, which is used to locate decaying carcasses.

Date & Location Seen:

Description: 46", wingspan 109". A **huge** vulture that soars with very long, broad wings that show finger-like projections at the tips. ADULT: Blackish throughout, with **white underwing linings**, thin white line on upperwings, **bare orange head.** JUVENILE: Dull slaty throughout, with bare gray head. All released birds have lettered/numbers tags on the wings, and most sport antennas for remote tracking.

Voice: Generally silent.

Behavior: Soars in very wide circles, only occasionally giving a couple of deep flaps. Perches on cliff faces, tall bare trees; released birds have shown some tendency to perch on man-made structures. Individuals can travel dozens of miles in day.

Similar Species: Turkey Vulture (p. 103) is much smaller, flies with uptilted wings, has dark wing linings and silvery flight feathers. Golden and Bald eagles (p. 123) are smaller, have feathered heads; first-year Bald shows wing pattern reminiscent of young condor's.

Where, When to Find: Most occur in mountain and foothill country from northern Ventura County to Monterey County, but a few birds sometimes visit hills north of the San Fernando Valley (e.g. along Bear Divide Road).

Did you know? Condors persisted in the wild in the mountains flanking the southern San Joaquin Valley until the mid-1980s; the last wild individuals were taken into captivity on 19 April 1987. Breeding programs at Los Angeles Zoo, San Diego Wild Animal Park and elsewhere have produced hundreds of young, many of which have been released in the wild. Mortality of released birds has been high, but some successful breeding has occurred recently.

Date & Location Seen:

Description: 23", wingspan 63". A large fish-eating hawk with a small, slightly crested head. Mostly **white on head and underparts**; **dark mask through eye**; blackish-brown above. Juvenile is scaled with buffy on back and wings, has buffy wash on breast. Appears **gull-like in flight**, with wings angled and drooped slightly downward.

Voice: Shrill, downslurred whistles are especially heard when birds interact.

Behavior: Often perches conspicuously on poles, bare trees, mudflats. Courses or briefly hovers over water, plunging to surface to grab fish with their large feet; sometimes even submerges and swims for short distances. Nest is a large stick structure on a conspicuous tall pole or tree.

Similar Species: Distant birds can suggest large gulls.

Where, When to Find: Uncommon migrant and winter visitor (late August to April) to estuaries, harbors, lakes and reservoirs and around Salton Sea. Especially widespread late March-April and September-October, when migrants occur widely. Formerly nested at a few coastal sites, and now increasing in the breeding season; young were hatched, fledged at Newport Bay in coastal Orange County in spring 2006. They have also nested recently in coastal San Diego County.

Did you know? Ospreys carry fish their fish prey, often surprisingly large, head first in their talons; their toes and footpads are covered with spike-like projections that help them hang on to prey.

Date & Location Seen:

Immature

Description: 15", wingspan 39". An attractive small raptor with long, narrow wings and a long tail. **White head, underparts and tail**; pale gray upperparts with **black patch on shoulders**. In flight the underwing shows dark gray outer fight feathers and black patches at the "wrists." Juvenile has a wash of cinnamon on the breast, crown and upperparts.

Voice: Short whistled notes; a longer rising whistle.

Behavior: Feeds mainly on rodents. Flies buoyantly and habitually hovers ("kites") while searching for prey; often feeds at dusk. Perches on thin twigs atop trees, shrubs. Large roost gatherings of two dozen or more birds are sometimes noted in fall and winter.

Similar Species: General coloration suggests a gull or large tern, but note black markings midway out the wings and distinctive hovering flight.

Where, When to Find: Uncommon resident In open grasslands, valley oak savannas, marshes, and agricultural areas throughout the lowlands. Numbers are somewhat higher in winter, but occurrence then can be highly localized. Populations have cycled over the decades, with notable increases in the mid-1900s, but since the early 1990s this species has seen a strong decline with the loss of open habitats. Rare in the Imperial Valley and Colorado River.

Did you know? Population cycles in this species are likely related to the abundance of small rodents known as voles, their preferred prey items.

Date & Location Seen:

Juvenile Female

Adult Female

Adult Male

Description: 18″, wingspan 43″. A long-winged, low-flying hawk with a banded tail; always shows a **conspicuous white rump** patch. The small head has an owl-like facial disk. ADULT MALE: **Medium gray** head and upperparts; **whitish below** with some rusty spotting. **Black wing tips**. FEMALE: Brown, with streaked underparts. JUVENILE: **Brown; pale rusty underparts** contrast with dark head.

Voice: Generally silent away from breeding territories, where they give high whistles and lower, barking notes.

Behavior: Feeds by coursing low over marshes, grasslands, and low open scrub, wheeling around to pounce on rodents and other prey. The wings are held slightly above horizontal in flight. Infrequently seen up high in soaring flight compared with other raptors. Nests on the ground in marshes.

Similar Species: Red-tailed Hawks (p. 121) and other *Buteo* have broader wings, lack white rump patch. Cooper's Hawk (p. 115) flies with quick flaps and glides, has shorter wings, and lacks white rump.

Where, When to Find: Uncommon to fairly common migrant and winter visitor (mid-September to early April) to extensive open freshwater and saltwater marshes, grasslands and agricultural fields (common in Imperial Valley agricultural lands). Breeding populations have been virtually extirpated from the urbanized coastal lowlands, but remain in north coastal areas, Camp Pendleton, and the Tijuana River Valley; also breeds in remaining open grasslands and marshes in the interior valleys such as the San Jacinto Valley and Piute Ponds on the Edwards Air Force Base.

Did you know? Formerly called "Marsh Hawk," this is the only harrier normally found in North America. The Eurasian subspecies (sometimes considered a separate species) is called "Hen Harrier".

Date & Location Seen: _____

Adult

Adult

Juvenile

Description: 11-13", wingspan 22-26". A small **short-winged, long-tailed** bird-eating hawk. **The tail is squared at the tip.** ADULT: **Slate-gray above, barred with reddish below**. Tail has gray and blackish bands. JUVENILE: Brown above, with some white spots; underparts have rows of **teardrop-shaped reddish-brown spots**. Females are larger than males.

Voice: Generally silent in our area; gives a series of *kew* notes on the nesting territory.

Behavior: Feeds on birds, which they ambush and chase – often around yards with feeders. Often seen flying between roost sites and feeding areas early in the morning and late in the afternoon. Usually perches within trees, only very rarely more openly and virtually never on utility poles.

Similar Species: Closely resembles the larger Cooper's Hawk (p. 115). Cooper's appears to have relatively longer wings and tail, and larger head projects farther in front of wings in flight. Tail-tip of Cooper's is rounded. Spotting on the underparts of juveniles larger, more teardrop shaped, more reddish in Sharp-shinned; Cooper's has longer, sharper dark brown streaks and more rufous tones to nape.

Where, When to Find: Fairly common migrant and winter visitor, from late September through March. Widespread in woodlands, chaparral, suburban areas and lower mountain areas; generally found in more wooded areas than Cooper's. Generally absent from our region in summer (a few seen in mountains), most nesting farther north (including the Sierra Nevada and northern Coast Ranges).

Did you know? Although very difficult to distinguish from Cooper's in the field, the measurements of smallest male Cooper's and largest female Sharp-shinned do not overlap.

Date & Location Seen: _____

_____

Adult

Juvenile

Juvenile

Description: 15-18", wingspan 30-35". The larger of our two bird-eating hawks. **Tail is somewhat rounded in shape** and usually shows an obvious white band at the tip. ADULT: Blackish cap, **dark gray upperparts**, **reddish barring below**; eyes red. JUVENILE: Brown above with some lighter markings above; thin **dark brown streaks** on the white underparts. Eyes yellow.

Voice: An insistent, clucking *kek-kek-kek-kek-kek* is heard mainly on the breeding territory; juveniles give squealing whistle.

Behavior: Ambushes birds in brushy or wooded areas, often hunting around bird feeders. Perches more openly than Sharp-shinned, often on bare tree tops, utility poles, fence tops. Normally flies with quick wing beats, glides and soars on flat wings. Displaying birds on territory fly high with deep, slow wing beats and white undertail coverts flared. Stick nest is usually high in a tree.

Similar Species: See very similar but smaller Sharp-shinned Hawk (p. 113). Red-shouldered Hawk (p. 117) has relatively longer wings and shorter tail and shows strongly checkered upperparts and upperwings. Larger Northern Goshawk (*Accipiter gentilis*; 22-25") is a rare nester in Mt. Pinos area, Greenhorn Mtns., and interior Santa Barbara County, accidental elsewhere.

Where, When to Find: Fairly common year-round resident throughout the region; found in riparian, oak and conifer woodlands, suburban areas, urban parks, and tree groves in the desert. There is some influx of wintering birds from late September to March and a peak of fall migrants in late September and October.

Did you know? Population declines in much of North American in mid-1900s have reversed; this species has greatly increased in urban and suburban areas in the past 20 years and is now a common sight in many urban areas.

Date & Location Seen:

Adult *elegans*

Juvenile *elegans*

Description: 17", wingspan 40". A striking, attractive hawk of riparian and oak woodlands. Boldly **banded black and white tail**, **checkered pattern on wings**, and translucent **pale patches toward the wingtips**. ADULT: **Rich rufous-orange** on the breast and barred belly, and the shoulder area. Wings boldly patterned in black and white. JUVENILE: Reddish color below more limited to bars, spots; breast streaked with dusky, wing and tail pattern duller.

Voice: Can be quite vocal, giving loud, repeated down-slurred *kee-oo, kee-oo…* calls.

Behavior: Hunts in woodlands and streamsides, feeding on reptiles, frogs, crayfish, rodents and birds. Our birds fly with stiff, rapid wing beats (recalling a Cooper's Hawk). The stick nest is built in a tall tree.

Similar Species: Immature Red-tailed Hawk (p. 121) is larger, with broader wings and tail; it lacks reddish markings on underparts and shoulders and has finely barred brown tail. See Cooper's Hawk (p. 115).

Where, When to Find: Fairly common resident in riparian (especially sycamore) and oak woodlands, and even mature tree plantings in residential areas, in valleys, foothills, and locally in the coastal lowlands. Wanders rarely to ranch yards and agricultural areas on the deserts and up to about 7,000' in the mountains.

Did you know? Our California subspecies (*elegans*) is distinctive in its rich red coloration and quick wing beats; other subspecies occur in the eastern U. S.

Date & Location Seen: _____

**Adult
Light Morph**

Juvenile

**Adult
Dark Morph**

Description: 19", wingspan 51". A buteo with relatively slender, **pointed wings** and a fairly long tail. Variable, but always shows, **dark chest**, **light undertail**. Often shows small whitish band on rump. Typical ADULT has **white wing linings** contrasting with dark flight feathers from below, white chin, brown chest, and solidly brown upperparts. Some adults are extensively rufous or dark brown below and have rufous or even dark wing linings. JUVENILE: mottled dusky and white; usually shows dark whisker mark and chest, pale chin; whitish or buffy wing linings are variably mottled with dusky.

Voice: On breeding territory gives a long, drawn-out *keeeeeah* scream.

Behavior: A buoyant flyer, sometimes catching large insects and consuming them on the wing; also feeds on rodents. Migrants may occur in flocks of up to a hundred or more birds. Nests are built in isolated tall trees in open areas.

Similar Species: Red-tailed Hawk (p. 121) has broader, blunter wing, shorter and wider fan-shaped tail, and dark markings along the leading edge of the inner underwing.

Where, When to Find: Migrates, sometimes in large groups, through the Borrego Valley in eastern San Diego County, then along the coastal flank of the San Bernardino and San Gabriel Mountains from mid-February through April. Migrants are also noted in spring (April-May) and fall (September-October) through the northern deserts and more rarely along the coast. A few summer in the Antelope Valley and eastern Mojave Desert, with breeding pairs sometimes found at isolated stands of tall trees in agricultural areas; formerly bred more widely in the region.

Did you know? Most populations of this threatened species winter in Argentina.

Date & Location Seen: _____

Adult

**Adult
Dark Morph**

Juvenile

Description: 19″, wingspan 49″. By far the most common and widespread large hawk in the region; found in all habitats. Bulky and broad winged, with **broad tail**. Nearly always shows **pale mottling on sides of back**. ADULT: Variable, but our birds always have **reddish-orange tails** (color best seen from above). Underparts vary from largely buffy (with streaks across the belly) to reddish brown or blackish. All but blackest birds show a **distinct dark patch along the leading edge of the inner portion of the underwing**. JUVENILE: Most show some white on breast, dark mottling on belly. Tail finely barred blackish and gray-brown.

Voice: Typical call is a harsh, drawn-out scream; also gives shorter, clipped notes.

Behavior: Hunts ground squirrels, gophers and other rodents, as well as snakes and birds. Courting birds fly in tandem with legs dangled; sometimes make long, aerobatic dives and rolls. Nest is a large stick structure in tall tree or cliff ledge.

Similar Species: Red-shouldered (p. 117), Swainson's (p. 119), and Ferruginous (p. 471) hawks differ in shape as well as plumage.

Where, When to Find: Our "default" large hawk, common year-round in nearly all habitats including heavily urbanized areas; also resident on the larger Channel Islands. A winter influx (mainly October to March) brings birds of various color morphs; some dark morph birds also breed locally. Very common in winter in the Imperial Valley, but does not nest there.

Did you know? This species was first described to science from the island of Jamaica, hence the scientific name *jamaicensis*.

Date & Location Seen: _____

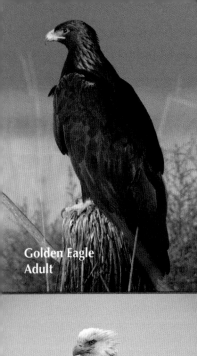

**Golden Eagle
Adult**

**Golden Eagle
Juvenile**

**Bald Eagle
Adult**

**Bald Eagle
Juvenile**

Description: 30", wingspan 79". A very large **dark brown** raptor, now rather scarce in the region. **Very long wings**, sometimes angled slightly upward when soaring. Legs are feathered; toes are bright yellow. ADULT: Dark plumage relieved by pale golden-brown hindneck, light brown undertail, and grayish tail base. JUVENILE: **Large white patches** at base of tail and at base of flight feathers on wing.

Voice: Generally silent in our area; weak chippering calls heard on breeding territory.

Behavior: Feeds on rabbits, ground squirrel, and other medium-sized, diurnal mammals. Also scavenges carrion.

Similar Species: Bald Eagle (*Haliaeetus leucocephalus*; 31") is an uncommon winter visitor (November to March) to large reservoirs, lakes and estuaries where it feeds mainly on fish, waterbirds, and carrion; a few have been reintroduced to Santa Catalina and Santa Cruz Islands. Broader wings, longer neck and bill than Golden; white head and tail of adult unmistakable; juvenile has dark head and white mottling on wing linings; older immatures have much white mottling on head, body.

Where, When to Find: A bird of remote mountain and desert areas, now found only rarely near urban centers and along the immediate coast. Best found in the inner coast ranges of San Luis Obispo, Santa Barbara and San Diego Counties, the mountains ringing the southern San Joaquin Valley, the desert slopes of the Transverse Ranges, and areas of relief on the deserts. A few move into agricultural valleys (such as the Antelope and San Jacinto Valleys, Carrizo Plain) in winter.

Did you know? The Golden Eagle is the most commonly represented bird species entrapped in the Rancho La Brea asphalt pits.

Date & Location Seen:

Adult Male

Adult Male

Female

Description: 10", wingspan 21". A small **dainty** falcon with slender, pointed wings, a long tail and buoyant flight. Note distinctive **black stripes on sides of head**. MALE: Blue-gray wings, **rusty back, rusty tail** with black tip; buff below with black spotting (immature has brown streaks). FEMALE: Larger, with barred rusty back, wings and tail; underparts with reddish streaking.

Voice: High *killy killy killy killy.* series.

Behavior: Perches openly on wires, antennas, treetops. Flight is buoyant, with rapid, shallow wing beats. Often hovers to spot prey, including large insects, lizards, small rodents and birds. Nest is in tree cavity or hollow within palm fronds.

Similar Species: Merlin (p. 127) is a stockier falcon with more powerful flight; usually shows white eyebrow, heavily streaked underparts, solid gray or brown upperparts. Sharp-shinned Hawk (p. 113) has short, rounded wings, solid gray or brown back, very different hunting behavior.

Where, When to Find: Fairly common to common year-round resident, with an influx of additional birds in winter (September to March). Found in most open and lightly wooded lowland habitats, including urban areas (though declining in the most urbanized regions). Also resident on many of the Channel Islands.

Did you know? Various subspecies of kestrels live from Alaska all the way to the southern tip of South America.

Date & Location Seen: _____

"Black" *suckleyi*

Adult Male
richardsoni

Juvenile
columbarius

Description: 11″, wingspan 23″. A **small** but **powerfully built** falcon. Variable. **Tail usually banded black on gray**. All dark wings range from gray to sooty brown. Head shows **white eye-stripe** (lacking in darkest birds) but no strong markings. Adult males are grayer above than females and immatures; all are **streaked below** (heavily in darkest birds). *COLUMBARIUS*: Our more common subspecies ranges from dark gray to sooty above. *RICHARDSONII*: Paler, with wide gray to whitish bands on tail; male is blue-gray above, streaked with reddish below; female, immatures are pale gray-brown above. *SUCKLEYI:* very dark, tail bands very narrow.

Voice: Not very vocal in our area; gives a series like a kestrel, but huskier.

Behavior: Primarily hunts flocking birds in open areas with fast, powerful flight. Perches almost exclusively in trees, often on a conspicuous bare tip.

Similar Species: American Kestrel (p. 125) is more slender and dainty, strongly marked with rufous on the back. Merlin shows a shorter tail and more pointed wingtip than kestrel. Peregrine Falcon (p. 129) has similar powerful flight, but is much larger (can be hard to judge) with relatively broader wings and shorter tail.

Where, When to Find: Birds of the subspecies *columbarius* are uncommon winter visitors, mainly late September to March; found in open agricultural areas with scattered trees, wooded parks and residential areas in the coastal lowlands, and around lakeshores and large estuaries. Subspecies *richardsonii*, which breeds on the northern prairies, is a rare winter visitor, found mostly on the deserts and interior valleys. Subspecies *suckleyi* rare winter visitor from coastal British Columbia.

Did you know? Populations of Merlins are increasing in many areas, in part due to adaptability to urbanization.

Date & Location Seen:

Adult

Juvenile

Description: 16", wingspan 42". A heavy, fairly **short-tailed** falcon with amazingly fast and powerful flight. At rest wingtips reach or nearly reach tail tip. Always shows a **thick black "whisker mark"** on the side of the face. ADULT: **Slate-gray above**; white to creamy buff underparts with **black barring on lower breast and belly**. Tail gray with narrow black bars; underwing barred with black. JUVENILE: Sooty-brown above; heavily streaked below.

Voice: A harsh *ray ray ray* series and softer *ee-chup* calls.

Behavior: Hunts for birds ranging from swallow to duck size by stooping upon them in a rapid dive and hitting them with the large, powerful feet. Perches on bare limbs, cliff faces, utility poles and building ledges. The nest is usually on a ledge on a cliff face, but ledges on tall buildings and bridges are used in urban areas.

Similar Species: Compare with smaller Merlin (p. 127). Prairie Falcon (p. 471) is a paler brown falcon of open deserts, rocky hills and grasslands. Underparts white with brown streaks or spots; flanks and "wingpits" blackish.

Where, When to Find: Uncommon but widespread year-round resident, with some influx of birds in migration. Hunts over estuaries, wetlands, open fields; well-known urban nest sites occur in downtown Los Angeles, Long Beach, Newport Beach, the San Diego waterfront, and elsewhere.

Did you know? Through intensive management (including captive breeding) and bans on certain pesticides Peregrines have recovered from severe declines in the middle decades of the 20th century.

Date & Location Seen:

Virgina Rail

Clapper Rail
yumanensis

Clapper Rail
levipes

Description: 9 ½". A small, dark, short-tailed marsh bird that usually stays well hidden. **Long, thin, slightly decurved bill** is mostly red-orange. ADULT: Gray face, **bright rusty underparts** with **black and white vertical bars on flanks**. Feathers of upperparts are edged rusty. JUVENILE: Upperparts and breast blotched with sooty; little rusty coloration.

Voice: Common calls include a grunting, accelerating *wek, wek, wek, wek…*; a sharp *gi-dik, gi-dik*; and various other high, sharp notes.

Behavior: Feeds mainly on invertebrates, small fish and amphibians. Walks through marsh vegetation, flicking the short, raised tail. Sometimes feeds more openly on mudflats, pond shores, but usually shy and hidden. Flight appears weak and labored.

Similar Species: The **Clapper Rail** (*Rallus longirostris*; 14 ½"), endangered in California, is like a much larger, thicker-billed version of Virginia's; the upperparts are duller and the flanks are barred with gray, not black. Subspecies *levipes* is restricted to extensive tidal salt marshes, mainly at Seal Beach, Bolsa Chica, and Upper Newport Bay; extremely high tides often bring many birds into view. A slightly duller subspecies *yumanensis*, the "Yuma" Clapper Rail, is found in marshes around the Salton Sea (especially southern end) and the lower Colorado River.

Where, When to Find: Uncommon to fairly common migrant and winter visitor (mainly mid-September through March) to freshwater marshes and estuaries in the coastal lowlands; migrants occur widely and sometimes turn up in very small wetlands. Small numbers breed in some freshwater marshes in the coastal lowlands and in the brackish inland portions of some coastal wetlands. Inland, fairly common resident at the Salton Sea and in marshes scattered through the deserts and interior valleys.

Did you know? Rails are indeed "thin as a rail", being laterally compressed for maneuvering through reeds.

Date & Location Seen: _____

Adult

Juvenile

Description: 8 ¾". This small rail has a **short yellowish bill**. Flicks tail upward, showing creamy-white undertail. ADULT: **Black face mask** (including throat in breeding season), gray neck and breast, barred flanks, scaly black, brown and white upperparts. JUVENILE: Browner than adult, with duller bill, buffy yellow breast; this plumage held into winter.

Voice: Commonest call is a rapid, descending whinny, *wee-ee-ee-ee-ee-ee*…. Also various high, sharp *keek* and *kee-oo* notes.

Behavior: Feeds mostly on invertebrates. Skulks in marshes, but sometimes feeds openly on mudflats close to vegetation – our most frequently seen rail. Flight appears weak and labored, with legs often dangling.

Similar Species: Virginia Rail (p. 131) has longer and thinner red-orange bill, rusty (not gray or buff breast).

Where, When to Find: Fairly common migrant and winter visitor, mainly August to April. Found in freshwater marshes and coastal estuaries, with migrants occurring more widely at small ponds, wet fields, creeks. This species has nested rarely in freshwater marshes in Orange County; and formerly nested more widely on the coast south to San Diego; it has also nested at small marshy ponds in the San Bernardino Mtns. Fairly common late July to May at Piute Ponds north of Lancaster, but even at that location nesting is not documented.

Did you know? This most widespread of North American rails is highly migratory, even though its flight appears weak and uncoordinated.

Date & Location Seen: _____

Adult

Juvenile

Description: 14". A dark, chicken-like marsh bird. **Bill and forehead shield bright red** (brightest in breeding season). **Slaty** head and underparts with a **brown-tinged back**, white horizontal **"racing-stripe" along flanks**, white patches on sides of undertail. Legs and long toes yellow. Juvenile is duller and paler gray below; bill is mostly dusky.

Voice: Various high laughing, cackling notes, a loud *keeek*, and other miscellaneous "marsh sounds."

Behavior: Swims in well-vegetated ponds and marshes while bobbing head back and forth. Also walks nimbly along pond shores and even over floating vegetation. Feeds mainly on aquatic invertebrates and vegetable matter.

Similar Species: American Coot (p. 137) is stockier with a white bill, lobed toes; lacks the white stripe along the flanks.

Where, When to Find: An uncommon fall and winter visitor, mainly from mid-September to early April, to marshes and estuaries in the coastal lowlands. A few remain through the summer, breeding in freshwater marshes; easily found at San Joaquin Wildlife Sanctuary, Irvine. Mainly an uncommon migrant through the deserts, but a fairly common breeding resident at the Salton Sea.

Did you know? This species was recently split from the Old World species known as the Common Moorhen (and the name Common Moorhen is thus found in much of the American literature in recent decades).

Date & Location Seen:

Description: 15″. An abundant and familiar **slaty** bird with a **black head**, suggesting a plump chicken on land and a **white-billed** duck on the water. Small white streaks on sides of undertail (can be flared out when birds are interacting); wing shows a white trailing edge in flight. Small dark red shield on forehead; thin dark band near bill tip. Legs are greenish-yellow; **toes have lobes** which aid in paddling. Juvenile is pale gray below; downy young have bright red markings on the head.

Voice: Coots make a variety of creaking, grating and trumpeting notes.

Behavior: Food consists of aquatic vegetation and invertebrates, obtained by diving and dabbling, and while walking on mudflats. Also grazes on land, especially on lawns. Flies somewhat reluctantly, pattering along the water surface to get airborne; flight is rapid and a bit unsteady.

Similar Species: Duck-like, but note lobed (not webbed) toes and sharply pointed white bill. See Common Gallinule (p. 135).

Where, When to Find: Common on lakes, ponds, marshes and estuaries throughout the region; many occur on urban park lakes. Also found in protected saltwater harbors, but only a few migrants are found on the open ocean.

Did you know? Coots can become so abundant on golf courses and other extensive lawns adjacent to ponds that permitted control measures are sometimes practiced.

Date & Location Seen: _____

**Black-bellied Plover
Breeding Adult Male**

**Black-bellied Plover
Juvenile**

**Pacific Golden-Plover
Adult Non-breeding**

**American Golden-Plover
Juvenile**

Description: 11 ½". A large plover with a stubby black bill. In flight always shows a **prominent white wing stripe**, white rump, and **black patch in the "armpits."** Usually seen here in NON-BREEDING plumage, when gray overall, spotted with whitish above. BREEDING plumage (April to September): face and most of underparts black, more extensive in male; undertail and sides of neck white. JUVENILE resembles winter adult but is slightly browner and more neatly spotted with white above.

Voice: Loud, plaintive whistle, dropping in pitch in the middle, then rising; e.g. *kleee-ooo-weee.*

Behavior: Feeds mainly on beaches and mudflats, with typical plover gait of running and abruptly stopping; picks prey from the surface. Large flocks may roost on salt pans and pickleweed flats.

Similar Species: **Pacific Golden-Plover** (*Pluvialis fulva*; 10") is a rare fall migrant and winter visitor (mid-September to March) along the coast (more regular on the Channel Islands); very rare in the interior. It differs from Black-bellied in having a dark rump, gray "wingpits", faint wing-stripe, and extensive yellowish spotting above; call is a two-noted *chu-weet.* Similar **American Golden-Plover** (*P. dominica*; 10 ½") is a rare migrant (mainly juveniles September-October); like Pacific but smaller-billed, less golden, with longer wing tip projection.

Where, When to Find: Common migrant and winter visitor (July to May) along the coast and at the Salton Sea; a few non-breeders present through summer. Forages on beaches, mudflats, and intertidal rocks; in some areas also in flooded fields and extensive lawns adjacent to wetlands. Uncommon migrant through the remaining interior (mainly April-May, August-October).

Did you know? Black-bellied Plovers are found throughout the world, but breed only in Arctic tundra regions.

Date & Location Seen: _____

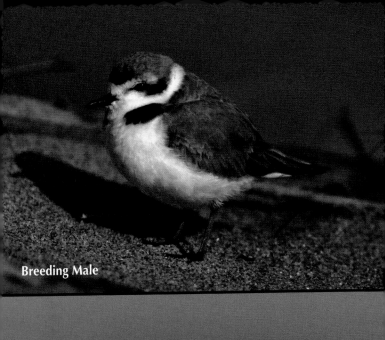

Breeding Male

Non-breeding

Description: 6 ½". A **small, pale** plover of beaches and extensive flats. **Slender black bill**, dark gray to tan legs. The upperparts are sandy-brown; the white underparts show only a **partial band on the sides of the breast**. White wing stripe and tail edges show in flight. Breeding males have black band on forecrown and black patches on sides of breast; all other plumages lack black markings.

Voice: Not very vocal except on breeding territories; calls include a short, hard *krip* and a rising *ch'loooy*.

Behavior: Moves in halting runs, picking at the surface for flies and other invertebrates. Resting birds sit in footprints, tire tracks, other depressions in the beach sand. More active when feeding than Semipalmated, often actively chasing prey. Eggs are laid in a bare scrape in an upper beach, estuary margin, or interior alkali flat.

Similar Species: See Semipalmated Plover (p. 143); also see Sanderling (p. 169), the other small pale shorebird of beaches.

Where, When to Find: Uncommon to fairly common but localized winter visitor to beaches, especially near estuaries, outfalls. Breeds very locally on sandy beach margins on the Channel Islands and on the mainland from San Luis Obispo to Ventura counties and from Bolsa Chica in Orange County south to the Tijuana River mouth south of San Diego. Eliminated as a breeder from the Los Angeles coast. Also breeds around the Salton Sea and on some lake beds on the Mojave Desert (including Rosamond Lake, Piute Ponds). A few migrants occur elsewhere in the interior.

Did you know? Beach development has led to the listing of coastal Snowy Plovers as Threatened by the United States Fish and Wildlife Service.

Date & Location Seen: _____

Breeding Adult Male

Juvenile

Description: 7 ¼". A small plover with a **dark brown back** and **complete dark breast band**. The **bill is stubby** and the **legs are yellow or orange**. In flight shows white wing stripe, black patch at tail tip. Breeding birds have the face and breast band black (males) or mottled black and brown (females); bill has bright orange base. Non-breeding birds lack black areas; juveniles are subtly fringed with whitish on the back feathers.

Voice: Call is a distinctive rich, rising *chu-weep*.

Behavior: Forages with typical plover run-and-stop behavior. Usually feeds on wet flats (Snowies are often on drier flats or sand).

Similar Species: Snowy Plover (p. 141) is paler above, lacks a complete breast band, has dark gray legs and a slim black bill. The much larger Killdeer (p. 145) has two black breast bands and an orange rump.

Where, When to Find. Fairly common migrant throughout region on mudflats of coastal estuaries, lake margins; peak numbers are found from April to mid-May and from late July to early October. In winter mainly restricted to the larger estuaries, with the greatest numbers in coastal Orange and San Diego Counties. Very few winter in Los Angeles County's small remaining estuaries. Breeds in taiga and Arctic regions.

Did you know? "Semipalmated" refers to the partial webbing between the toes, a feature shared by certain other shorebirds.

Date & Location Seen:

143

Description: 10 ½". A familiar, noisy plover of upland as well as wetland habitats. Dark brown above with **orange rump and tail base**. White underparts show **two black breast bands**. In flight appears long-tailed, and the long wings show a white stripe. Juvenile shows pale rusty fringes on the feathers of the back and wings.

Voice: Quite vocal, both day and night. Call is a piercing *kill-deee* frequently repeated. When disturbed also gives a strident *teeeee-deer-deer* and a rapid trill.

Behavior: Forages on a variety of open substrates, from mudflats and gravel washes to lawns, plowed fields and short crops. Often quite active and vocal at night. Found in pairs or family groups in the breeding season, but in fall and winter flocks of dozens or even hundreds of birds are sometimes found.

Similar Species: Our other plovers all have one breast band or lack a band altogether. Compare with Ruddy Turnstone (p. 165), very different in shape and behavior.

Where, When to Find: Our most widespread "shorebird", found throughout the lowlands where mudflats, irrigated lawns, agricultural fields or pond and lake margins provide foraging habitat. The eggs are laid on the ground in a gravelly substrate such as a river or creek bottom, vacant lot, or railroad right-of-way.

Did you know? Along with the poorwill and a few other species, this species is named for its call.

Date & Location Seen:

Adult

Juvenile

Description: 17". A **large blackish bird of rocky shores** with a **bright orange-red, knife-like bill**. Black head and underparts, blackish-brown back. Legs pinkish; eyes yellow, surrounded by a bare red ring. The juvenile has a duller orange bill with a dark tip, slightly duller plumage.

Voice: Loud piping whistles are readily heard over the crashing surf. Calls are often given in a long series, *wheeep, wheeep, wheeep, whee-whee-whee-whee*.

Behavior: Forages on mollusks, barnacles and other intertidal invertebrates on rocky shorelines; the bill can be used to sever the adductor muscles of bivalves. Can be very vocal, with small groups often chasing about. Eggs are laid on a rocky ledge above the high tide line.

Similar Species: Unmistakable. The American Oystercatcher (*Haematopus palliatus*, 17"), found as close as the upper Gulf of California and the west coast of Baja California, has white belly and white on wings, upper tail; it is found casually in our region, but hybrids with Black Oystercatcher occur regularly.

Where, When to Find: Almost exclusively found on rocky shorelines of the Channel Islands, the San Luis Obispo County coast, but also on larger breakwaters and jetties farther south; easily found on the Marina del Rey breakwater and common on the less accessible Los Angeles/Long Beach Harbor breakwater. Scarcest in Orange and San Diego Counties, but often seen on rocky coast from Corona del Mar to Laguna Beach and at Point Loma. Exclusively coastal, but still with an extensive distribution that stretches north much of the way out the Aleutian chain.

Did you know? This species was given its scientific name by J. J. Audubon for his friend, Rev. John Bachman (pronounced "back-min").

Date & Location Seen:

Male

Female

Description: 14". A large, slender **black and white** shorebird with **extremely long pink to red legs**. The **bill is slender and straight**. Crown and hindneck black, rump and underparts white. MALE: Back is glossy black; breeding birds have buffy wash on breast. FEMALE: Back is washed with brown. JUVENILES have paler heads and buffy fringes to the upperpart feathering.

Voice: Call is a high *keek* note, suggesting a Long-billed Dowitcher. On breeding grounds and in large foraging groups throughout the year stilts give an incessant series of yapping notes, *yike! yike! yike!*

Behavior: Forages by walking on mudflats and, especially, in shallow water, picking for invertebrate prey. Often found in large groups. Like many ground-nesting birds, adults will feign injury to lead potential predators away from the nest site.

Similar Species: Unmistakable. American Avocet (p. 151) has upturned bill, white areas on wing, blue-gray legs, and lacks black on neck.

Where, When to Find: Winters widely in the coastal lowlands from July to April. Migrants (late March to early May, July to September) are seen throughout. Abundant at the Salton Sea, and large numbers may also be found year round in the major coastal estuaries, the San Diego Bay saltworks, and the length of the Los Angeles River Channel. Breeds locally in ponds and marshes farther inland, including the Antelope Valley and wetlands in the southern San Joaquin Valley.

Did you know? Stilts may nest on open ground at very hot desert wetland areas; incubating birds wet their belly feathers to cool their eggs.

Date & Location Seen:

Breeding Female

Non-breeding Male

Description: 18". A large black and white shorebird with **long blue-gray legs and long, thin upturned bill**. White back and **pied black and white wings**. BREEDING: Head and neck are a rich tawny color. NON-BREEDING: head and neck grayish. JUVENILES have buffy necks. The male's bill is longer, less strongly upturned than female's.

Voice: High *kleep, kleep*; especially vocal on breeding grounds

Behavior: When actively feeding in shallow water avocets lean forward and sweep the slightly flattened bill from side to side to stir up and grab invertebrate prey. Avocets can swim well for a shorebird. Gregarious, often occurring in flocks of dozens or hundreds. Breeding birds may aggressively dive-bomb predators and human intruders.

Similar Species: Unmistakable; compare with Black-necked Stilt (p. 149).

Where, When to Find: Widespread winter visitor (mostly July through April) to coastal estuaries, larger marshes and river channels; even more widespread in migration. Breeds locally in marshes and saline ponds in the Antelope Valley, and in the coastal lowlands including the lower Los Angeles River in Long Beach, various Orange County estuaries, and coastal San Diego County (such as Batiquitos Lagoon and south San Diego Bay). Abundant year round at the Salton Sea, breeding fairly commonly.

Did you know? At least three cases of hybridization with the Black-necked Stilt (yielding "avostilts") have been reported in the wild.

Date & Location Seen: _____

Spotted Sandpiper
Juvenile

Spotted Sandpiper
Breeding

Solitary Sandpiper
Juvenile

Description: 7 ½". Distinctive in its **constant bobbing, teetering motion**. NON-BREEDING; Brown above with white eyebrow. White below, with brownish patches on the sides of the breast. Bill dark, legs dull greenish-yellow or flesh. BREEDING: Thin dark bars above, heavy black spotting below; bill is extensively pink at the base, legs pinkish orange.

Voice: High staccato whistled notes, *peet-weet*; also a series of *whee-whee-whee-whee* notes.

Behavior: Found singly or in pairs; in migration may occur in small, loose groups. Bobbing, teetering behavior distinctive. Distinctive flight consists of intermittent bursts of rapid, shallow wing beats. Walks along pond and river margins, estuary shores, rocky intertidal areas, often lunging forward to grab insects. Nests are among grasses in cobble creek bottoms or lake shores.

Similar Species: Solitary Sandpiper (*Tringa solitaria*; 8 ½") is a rare migrant, from mid-April to early May and especially mid-August to mid-September. Solitary is darker above than Spotted, with longer greenish legs, brownish breast, white eye-ring; in flight shows dark underwings, black and white barred tail.

Where, When to Find: Fairly common winter visitor (July through May) to wetlands, small ponds, reservoirs, and estuaries. More numerous and widespread as a migrant, especially from late April to early June and July through September. Small numbers breed along gravelly creeks, even very locally on the upper Santa Ana River and the channelized Los Angeles River near Elysian Park. Also nests around lake margins in the San Bernardino Mtns.

Did you know? Spotted Sandpipers are often polyandrous nesters; a female may mate with up to four different males, leaving them to care for the eggs and chicks.

Date & Location Seen:

Breeding

Non-breeding

Description: 11". A **long-winged short-legged shorebird** nearly always associated with rocky coastlines (including man-made jetties). NON-BREEDING: **Overall dark gray**, paler on belly; dark line from eye to bill contrasts with a thin, broken eye ring. BREEDING: Strongly barred with dark gray on the underparts, paler in vent region. **Legs greenish-yellow**. In flight note the uniformly dark, long wings.

Voice: A series of rapid, mellow whistles on one pitch.

Behavior: Walks methodically over rocks, bobbing its tail in a manner reminiscent of a Spotted Sandpiper. Usually solitary, but often loosely with other rocky shorebirds such as turnstones and Surfbirds.

Similar Species: The smaller Spotted Sandpiper (p. 153) has similar behavior, but flies with shallow, rapid wingbeats; Spotteds have mostly white underparts, white wing stripe. Larger Willet (p. 159) has gray legs, striking flight pattern.

Where, When to Find: Uncommon winter visitor to rugged rocky coasts of the mainland and Channel Islands as well as jetties and breakwaters from late July through mid-May; more numerous and widespread in migration, when sometimes also found on sandy beaches and in estuaries. A few non-breeders can remain through the summer. Casual migrant inland.

Did you know? This species breeds mainly in Alaska and the Yukon Territory and winters widely on the Pacific coast from British Columbia to Peru as well as on many islands through the tropical Pacific.

Date & Location Seen:

Greater Yellowlegs

Breeding

Juvenile

Lesser Yellowlegs

Breeding

Juvenile

Description: 14″/10 ½″. Both species have **long, bright yellow legs,** plain wings, and mostly white rump and tail in flight. GREATER is a rather large shorebird with a **long, slightly upturned bill that is gray at the base** (except in breeding plumage). It is grayish with white spots above, pale below. In breeding plumage heavily spotted and barred with blackish above and below. The scarcer LESSER is smaller, with a **shorter and straighter bill that is always uniformly dark**. Plumage like Greater's, but darker gray, especially on the breast; Lesser is less heavily marked in all plumages. Juvenile Greater shows distinct streaks on breast; neck and breast of Lesser is plainer gray.

Voice: GREATER gives loud, shrill three-noted descending whistled, *tew-tew-tew*. LESSER utters softer two-note *tu-tu*, often strung together into a series.

Behavior: Both, but especially Greater, are active feeders, running about in shallow water to pursue small fish and aquatic invertebrates.

Similar Species: Solitary Sandpiper (p. 153) is darker overall, with shorter greenish legs. Larger Willet (p. 159) has grayish legs, stouter bill, and striking wing pattern.

Where, When to Find: GREATER: Widespread in migration and winter (July to May) in small wetlands and channels as well as large estuaries and marshes. LESSER: Rare winter visitor and spring migrant (mainly April), and uncommon fall migrant (July through September; juveniles may be fairly common in August and September). Lessers are less likely than Greater to be seen in small wetlands and creeks.

Did you know? The Greater Yellowlegs is one of the hardiest shorebirds, wintering even in semi-frozen interior regions; "fall" migrants can arrive as early as late June.

Date & Location Seen:

Breeding

Non-breeding

Description: 15". A stocky **gray** shorebird with a **striking black and white pattern in flight**. The **legs are gray**, and the gray, **medium-length bill is straight and fairly stout**. The plumage is mostly gray, becoming whitish on the forehead and belly; in breeding plumage there is some barring and spotting on the underparts, back and wings. Juveniles are neatly marked with small buff-white spots on the back and wings. In flight the rump and tail are mostly white, and the wings show a broad white stripe bordered by black.

Voice: Call is a reeling *kree-ree-reel*; also gives a nasal *yaah-yah* and a low *kip…kip*.

Behavior: Forages for invertebrates (more rarely small fish) on sandy beaches, rocky shores, and estuarine mudflats. Migrants may be found on pond and lake margins, freshwater marshes. Like many related long legged shorebirds, Willets quickly nod their heads up and down when alert.

Similar Species: Greater Yellowlegs (p. 157) is slimmer, with bright yellow legs.

Where, When to Find: Common migrant and winter visitor (late June to early May) along the entire coast, from sandy beaches and estuaries to rocky shorelines and jetties; non-breeders remain uncommonly through the rest of the early summer. Common at the Salton Sea, but otherwise a rare migrant in most areas well away from the coast; can be more numerous in the Antelope Valley (from mid-June through August, and again March-April).

Did you know? Our "Western Willet" (*inornata*) differs in breeding plumage and size from the "Eastern" subspecies (*semipalmata*) that breeds on Atlantic and Gulf coasts and winters in eastern South America.

Date & Location Seen: _____

Whimbrel

Long-billed Curlew

Description: 17 ½". A large mottled grayish brown shorebird with a **bill** that is **strongly decurved**, especially near tip. **Bold dusky and buff head stripes** are diagnostic. In flight the underwings are barred with dusky. All plumages are somewhat similar.

Voice: Rapid series of high-pitched whistles on one pitch, *kee-kee-kee-kee-kee....*

Behavior: Gregarious in migration. Probes in soft mud, but also picks for invertebrates on rocky shorelines.

Similar Species: Long-billed Curlew (*Numenius americanus*; 23") is larger and more cinnamon in color; its bill is thinner and much longer (especially in females), lacks head stripes. In flight shows bright cinnamon in wing linings and flight feathers. Call an upslurred whistle, *cur-leee*. Long-billed is a local winter visitor (July to mid-April) on large estuaries and salt marshes (such as Mugu Lagoon, Bolsa Chica, Upper Newport Bay, San Diego Bay); individuals may occur elsewhere. Also occurs (mainly September to mid-April) in alfalfa fields and other agricultural lands in the Antelope Valley, and is abundant in agricultural fields in the Imperial Valley.

Where, When to Find: Common migrant (March to May, July to September) along the coast. Small numbers winter along coast, especially on rocky coastlines. A push of spring migrants occurs through the interior of the region (where often found on large open lawns, fields); thousands pass through the Imperial and Antelope Valleys in spring as a stopover between wintering areas south of the United States and the Central Valley, which is the next major stopover on their northward migration. Absent from the interior in winter.

Did you know? North American birds (*hudsonicus*) differ from Old World Whimbrels in being more uniformly colored, lacking a pale rump and underwings.

Date & Location Seen: _____

Description: 18". A large **buffy brown** long-legged shorebird with a **long, slightly upturned bill with pink-orange base, dark tip**. In flight note **cinnamon-rufous wing lining and flight feathers**. Breeding birds have dark barring on the underparts.

Voice: Calls have a laughing quality; gives a nasal *kwa-ha* and a *goweeta-goweeta-goweeta* series.

Behavior: Probes into wet sand and soft mud with the long bill. Often found in large flocks in coastal bays (and frequently mixed with Willets and other shorebirds), roosting on islands or patches of pickleweed at high tide.

Similar Species: Whimbrel and Long-billed Curlew (p. 161) are easily told by their decurved bills. Sleeping Long-billed Curlew looks much like a godwit; larger curlew's legs are paler gray.

Where, When to Find: Common winter visitor (July to April) along coast; the largest numbers are found in the major estuaries, but smaller numbers are found on all beaches. Small numbers of non-breeders remain in summer. Uncommon migrant (April-May, July-October) through the Antelope Valley. Like many "coastal" shorebirds, common at the Salton Sea but scarce in most other interior areas.

Did you know? In our godwits and curlews, the females are noticeably larger and longer-billed than the males.

Date & Location Seen: _____

_____

Ruddy Turnstone

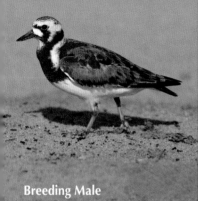

Breeding Male

Non-breeding

Black Turnstone

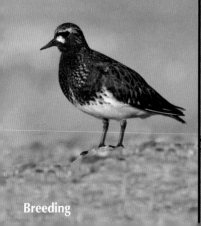

Breeding

Non-breeding

Description: 9 ½". **Stocky, short-legged shorebirds** with stout, **slightly upturned bills** and a **striking pattern of dark and white in flight**. RUDDY: Dark harlequin pattern on head and chest. Legs bright orange. Breeders are extensively rufous above, with much white on the head; males are especially highly patterned. BLACK: Overall blackish with white belly; breeding birds have white spot in front of eye and white spotting on sides of chest. Legs dull orange to dusky red.

Voice: Rapid trilled notes, lower-pitched and more guttural in Ruddy.

Behavior: Forage on rocky shorelines by picking at mussels, barnacles, algae. Ruddies also forage on mudflats and beaches where they dig holes for prey and flip over small stones, small mats of kelp, etc.

Similar Species: Larger Surfbird (p. 167) has thicker, bicolored bill and yellowish legs; it is more uniform gray in overall color and shows simple flight pattern with white tail base and wing stripe.

Where, When to Find: Found mostly on rocky shores. Black is a fairly common winter resident in rocky areas along coast and Channel Islands, mainly mid-July through April. Ruddy is scarcer than Black on rocky coasts but more frequent at larger coastal lagoons and sandy beaches, mainly July-May. Inland, Ruddy is a scarce migrant; the largest numbers are found at the Salton Sea mainly in April and May, but a few are also seen from July through winter; Black has been found casually in the interior, mostly at the Salton Sea.

Did you know? Black Turnstone is endemic to the west coast of North America, breeding in western Alaska. Ruddy is a circumpolar breeder, declining in much of its North American range.

Date & Location Seen: _____

Surfbird

Breeding

Non-breeding

**Red Knot
Juvenile**

**Surfbird
Non-breeding**

Description: 10″. A large, chunky "rock-piper" with short greenish-yellow legs. Overall lead gray with white belly and spots on sides and flanks. Bold white wing stripe and white tail base in flight. Stubby bill has a yellow base. BREEDING: Extensive spotting on head and chest and sides, rufous mottling on sides of the back.

Voice: Largely silent in our area, unlike turnstones (with which they often associate).

Behavior: Probes intertidal rocks, algae for invertebrate prey.

Similar Species: See Black Turnstone (p. 165). **Red Knot** (*Calidris canutus*, 10 ½″) is a stocky pale gray sandpiper with pale eyebrow and medium-length straight bill; whitish underparts have faint spotting. Breeding knots are pale rufous on face, underparts; back and wing feathers of juveniles have dark subterminal markings and pale fringes. Fairly common (late July through April) at large coastal estuaries of Orange County, especially Bolsa Chica, and south San Diego Bay. Rare migrant (April to May, late July through September) elsewhere along the coast and very rare inland, though seen annually at wetlands in the Lancaster area and regular in small flocks at the Salton Sea.

Where, When to Find: Local winter visitor on rocky shores of the mainland and Channel Islands, including constructed jetties and breakwaters. Easily found along the jetties at Playa del Rey; more numerous late March through April when sometimes also found on sandy beaches. Casual inland in spring.

Did you know? Breeds on windswept ridges on Alaskan mountains; its winter range has a greater latitudinal extent than that of nearly any other bird species (southern Alaska to Tierra del Fuego).

Date & Location Seen: _____

Non-breeding

Breeding

Juvenile

Description: 8″. The familiar **small pale gray and white sandpiper** of our sandy beaches. Shows **darker area at "wrist" of wing**, and a prominent white wing stripe in flight. Black bill is fairly short, straight and blunt-tipped; legs and feet dark (hind toe lacking). In breeding plumage there is an extensive but variable rusty wash on the head, upperparts and chest.

Voice: Call is a hard *kip*; similar to call of Red-necked Phalarope but lower.

Behavior: Runs rapidly back and forth on sandy beaches with advance and retreat of waves' picks and probes for invertebrates, eggs. Usually found in small flocks.

Similar Species: Western (p. 171) and Least Sandpipers (p. 173) are smaller, thinner-billed, darker above, and have hind toes; they tend to occur in estuaries, mudflats rather than open, sandy beaches.

Where, When to Find: Common winter visitor to beaches throughout from mid-July through May; a few non-breeders remain through summer. Also occurs on rocky beaches, jetties. Rare inland migrant, mainly in May and late July to early October; can be fairly common at the Salton Sea, mainly in spring (March to May).

Did you know? Sanderlings breed farther north than virtually any other shorebird (mainly on islands in the high Canadian Arctic); the extensive winter range extends south to Chile.

Date & Location Seen: _____

Breeding

Non-breeding

Juvenile

Description: 6 ½". The small *Calidris* sandpipers are collectively known as "peeps". Western has **blackish legs**; a **relatively long bill** (especially in females) **with slight droop toward fine tip**. NON-BREEDING: Gray-brown above, whitish underneath. BREEDING: Variably rufous on crown, cheeks, and on upperparts; breast, sides and flanks marked with dark arrow-shaped spots. JUVENILE: Cleanly marked gray and chestnut above, clean white below (buffy across chest when fresh in August).

Voice: Call is a high, scratchy *djeeet*.

Behavior: Forages on mudflats and in shallow water, picking and probing for small invertebrates. Often found in large flocks (up to many thousand).

Similar Species: Smaller Least Sandpiper (p. 173) is darker in all plumages, with brown wash across the chest; with shorter and thinner bill; greenish-yellow legs diagnostic but beware of discoloration from mud, algae, etc.

Where, When to Find: Locally common winter visitor to larger coastal estuaries throughout, July through April; smaller numbers winter at small coastal lagoons, mouths of river channels, and inland wetlands. The abundant "peep" in migration, from late March through April and again from July through September; large numbers pass through the interior, especially the Salton Sea and Antelope Valley. Counts of over 10,000 in a day have been made in the lower Los Angeles River channel in Long Beach. A few can winter in the Antelope Valley and inland wetlands on the coastal slope; up to a few thousand winter at the Salton Sea.

Did you know? Although a North American species, its breeding range extends west into the Russian Far East.

Date & Location Seen: _____

Breeding

Non-breeding

Juvenile

Description: 6″. The world's smallest sandpiper, but one of the hardiest. Appears **short-winged** in flight; at rest the tips of the wings (primaries) are not visible on the folded wing. **Bill is short and very thin**, slightly arched. NON-BREEDING: **Gray-brown above**, with **brown wash across the breast**. **Legs yellowish to dull greenish**. BREEDING: Breast is strongly streaked; the back feathers have black centers and some rufous fringes. JUVENILE: Rufous fringes to back and wing feathers, variable buffy wash across lightly streaked breast.

Voice: Call is a high trill *treep* or *tree-treep*.

Behavior: Forages on wet mud, lakeshores; usually does not wade into shallow water. Often in flocks, but not the massive numbers seen in Western.

Similar Species: Western Sandpiper (p. 171) has blackish legs, longer bill; in non-breeding plumage has a whiter breast. Pectoral Sandpiper (p. 175) is much larger and longer winged.

Where, When to Find: Common winter visitor (July through April), both in coastal estuaries and creek mouths and at wetlands, lakes, creek channels and marshes inland. Least usually greatly outnumbers Western in winter in the interior; can be common in winter in the Antelope Valley and Salton Sea.

Did you know? Least Sandpipers have the most southerly breeding range of all our "peeps"; they nest extensively through the taiga regions rather than being restricted to high Arctic tundra.

Date & Location Seen: _____

Baird's Sandpiper
Juvenile

Pectoral Sandpiper
Juvenile

BAIRD'S SANDPIPER
Calidris bairdii

Description: 7 ½". A medium-sized, **buffy** sandpiper with **very long wings**; stands with a horizontal posture; legs dark. JUVENILE: Gray-brown back and wings have buff-white fringes to all feathers, yielding a **scaly appearance above**. The **breast is strongly washed with buff**, with short dark streaks on the sides of the breast. Adults seen only very rarely in the region; in breeding plumage they are less scaly than juveniles and have black spotting above.

Voice: Call is a harsh, dry *kreeeel*.

Behavior: Feeds slowly and deliberately on flats and shallow water, but more apt to feed well away from water than most small sandpipers.

Similar Species: Pectoral Sandpiper (*Calidris melanotos*; 8 ¾") is similar in structure but larger, more patterned above, with strong band of streaks across the chest; legs yellowish. Call note is a low, rich *churrk*. Pectoral is an uncommon fall migrant, mainly late August through October; casual in spring. Least Sandpiper (p. 173) vaguely like Pectoral but much smaller, darker, with much shorter wings.

Where, When to Find: Juveniles pass through our region as uncommon migrants in fall (mainly August through September); most numerous at wetlands in the interior, including the Antelope Valley (Piute Ponds, Lancaster Wastewater Treatment Plant) and wetlands elsewhere on the Mojave Desert. Casual transient in spring.

Did you know? In spring most Baird's migrate north through the Great Plains. Pectorals mostly migrate north through the Mississippi and Ohio Valleys; it is among the world's longest-distance migrants.

Date & Location Seen:

Breeding

Non-breeding

Description: 8 ½". A medium sized sandpiper with a **long, drooping bill** and **blackish legs**. NON-BREEDING: Fairly dark and plain **gray-brown above** with a pale brown head, faint whitish eyebrow, and **brown wash across the breast**. BREEDING: Distinctive, with **reddish back**, large **black belly patch**, streaked whitish breast and pale head. JUVENILE: not usually seen in our area.

Voice: Call is a rough *jeeeev*, lower and harsher than Western's call.

Behavior: Often mixed with other shorebirds such as Western Sandpipers and dowitchers; typically wades belly deep into shallow water but also feeds on mudflats.

Similar Species: Winter Western Sandpiper (p. 171) is smaller, shorter-billed and cleaner white on the breast. Dowitchers (p. 179) have much longer, straighter bills, show white lower back in flight.

Where, When to Find: Common winter visitor to coastal estuaries and lagoons. Does not arrive until late September, and remains into early May. A few also winter with Least Sandpipers and Long-billed Dowitchers at inland wetlands (more numerous at the Salton Sea). Fairly common spring migrant in the interior in April and early May, with some passing through again in October.

Did you know? North American Dunlins (including our birds of the subspecies *pacifica*) are among the few shorebirds that molt in the Arctic region after breeding. They arrive in our area relatively late in fall, already in their drab non-breeding plumage.

Date & Location Seen: _____

Short-billed Dowitcher

Non-breeding

Juvenile

Breeding

Long-billed Dowitcher

Non-breeding

Juvenile

Breeding

LONG-BILLED DOWITCHER/SHORT-BILLED DOWITCHER
Limnodromus scolopaceus/Limnodromus griseus

Description: 11″. Rather long-legged medium sized shorebirds with **long straight bills** and a **triangular patch from the rump up the back**. The **tail is barred black and white**. Short-billed is shorter billed, shorter-legged, and usually appears paler tailed. NON-BREEDING: Overall grayish above and across chest, whitish belly; Short-billeds slightly paler, with more evident spotting on breast and relatively broader white bars on tail. BREEDING: Upperparts mottled black, buff and rufous; underparts chestnut-buff. Long-billeds darker rufous above with white feather tips; Short-billeds spotted on sides of neck, Long-billeds barred. Rufous of underparts more extensive in Long-billed. JUVENILE: Buffy across chest (brighter, more spotted in Short-billed); longest feathers on folded wing boldly marked with orange-buff markings in Short-billed, plainer on Long-billed.

Voice: LONG BILLED: high, sharp *keek*, often in an excited series; SHORT-BILLED: Mellow *tu-tu-tu*. Both give aggressive *ju-ju-ju-jweeee-da*.

Behavior: Feed in mud with "sewing-machine" motions. Gregarious, sometimes in mixed species flocks. Short-billeds tend to feed in shallower water.

Similar Species: See Red Knot (p. 167).

Where, When to Find: LONG-BILLED: Widespread migrant and winter visitor from late July through May; all dowitchers in the interior in winter are Long-billeds. SHORT-BILLED: Winters locally on large coastal estuaries; common migrant along the entire coast and uncommon migrant inland (late March through April and July to late September); common migrant at the Salton Sea. Juvenile Short-billeds arrive in early August, but juvenile Long-billeds do not arrive until September.

Did you know? The two dowitchers were considered a single species until intensive studies in the late 1940s by the late Frank Pitelka of the University of California at Berkeley.

Date & Location Seen:

Description: 10 ½". A dumpy brown short-legged shorebird with a **long, straight bill**. The crown and face are striped, and the **back has long creamy white stripes**. The breast and sides are barred with dusky, contrasting with the white belly. The **orange tail** can be conspicuous when the bird is flying away.

Voice: When flushed gives a raspy *scaaip*. Territorial winnowing sounds are rarely heard in our area.

Behavior: Secretive, usually hiding motionlessly within short marshy vegetation; flushes with zig-zag flight, towering into the air then dropping suddenly. Sometimes feeds more openly on mudflats, but rarely far from vegetation. Usually found singly, but in good habitat small loose groups may sometimes be found.

Similar Species: Dowitchers (p. 179) have a white rump, longer legs, and lack the snipe's long pale back stripes; the rapid bill-jabbing feeding movements of dowitchers are very different from the snipe's probing.

Where, When to Find: Uncommon to fairly common migrant and winter visitor, mainly from September to mid-April. Found in the grassy or marshy margins or ponds, lakes, ditches and streams; also found in coastal saltmarshes and wet meadows. Breeds just north of us in the Owens Valley, and there are a few old breeding records for several southern California counties.

Did you know? Formerly known as the Common Snipe, but the lumping of New World and Old World groups in the mid-1940s has recently been "reversed;" Old World birds are still called Common Snipe; *Gallinago gallinago*); one was recently found for the first time in California in the San Jacinto Valley east of Riverside.

Date & Location Seen: _____

Breeding Female

Juvenile

Molting Juvenile

Description: 9 ¼". Phalaropes are unique swimming sandpipers with lobed toes; females are larger than males and brighter in breeding plumage. Wilson's is plump with a **needle-like bill**. In flight shows **plain wings** and **white rump**. NON-BREEDING: Pale grayish above, whitish below. Short legs are greenish yellow. BREEDING: Females have a broad dark brown stripe through the eye and down the sides of the neck; the hindneck is white and the foreneck is apricot; males are similar but duller. JUVENILE: Dark feathering above has buffy edges; buff wash across front of neck in fresh plumage.

Voice: Call is a low, grunting *wump*, often given in a short series.

Behavior: Swims, spinning rapidly to bring food items to the surface. More likely to be seen feeding on mudflats that other phalaropes, walking with forward-lunging gait, picking for brine flies and other prey.

Similar Species: Lesser Yellowlegs (p. 157) has much longer legs, feeds by wading in shallow water. Other two phalaropes (p. 185) are smaller and shorter-billed, show dark eye patches in non-breeding plumages, and have white wing stripes and dark centered tail.

Where, When to Find: Common spring (late April through May) and fall (mid-June through September) migrant in the interior, with large numbers found at the Salton Sea and wetlands of the Antelope Valley. Less common coastally, where it can be fairly common in estuaries and freshwater marshes from mid-April to early May and again from late June to mid-September. This is a prairie and Great Basin breeder which winters mainly in South America.

Did you know? Perhaps our earliest fall migrant shorebird – southbound migrants in mid-June actually cross paths with northbound Willow Flycatchers!

Date & Location Seen: _____

Red-necked Phalarope
Breeding Female

Red-necked Phalarope
Juvenile

Red Phalarope
Breeding Female

Red Phalarope
Fall Adult in Transition

Description: 7 ¾". The smallest phalarope, with a **short, thin bill**. **White wing stripe**, dark central tail feathers. NON-BREEDING: **Dark patch through eye**; **back striped** dark gray and white. BREEDING: Slaty crown and face, white patch on sides of throat, red neck sides; sides of breast dark gray, upperparts gray with gold stripes. Females darker and brighter than males. JUVENILE: Like non-breeding adult, but with dark cap, black and buff upperparts.

Voice: Sharp *kip* recalls Sanderling's call, but a bit sharper.

Behavior: Feeds by spinning rapidly on the water, bringing bits of food to the surface.

Similar Species: Red Phalarope (*Phalaropus fulicaria*; 8 ½"), larger with shorter, thicker bill (yellow at base). Non-breeders have plain gray back; breeders solidly red below (molting birds show red spots, patches). Higher pitched *keet* call. Found offshore; generally uncommon, but occasionally common in late fall; rarely seen onshore except after some late fall and early winter storms; casual inland. Mainly found in May and from August to (especially) October through November. Irregular in small numbers through the winter offshore.

Where, When to Find: Most frequently seen in coastal waters and in estuaries. Irregular in spring; sometimes seen in large flocks (thousands can pass by offshore), mainly in late April and early May. More widespread in fall, July through mid-October, in coastal estuaries. Inland, a common spring (April-May) and very common fall (July-October) migrant at the Salton Sea; large numbers also pass through the Antelope Valley and some other interior wetlands. Most winter off Central and South America.

Did you know? Food items within water drops are drawn up into the mouth from the bill tip by surface tension.

Date & Location Seen: _____

_____

Breeding
Adult

Non-breeding Adult

First-year

Description: 13 ½", wingspan 32". A **small** tern-like gull with a **slender black bill**, pink legs. NON-BREEDING: Pale gray above, white head and underparts with **black spot behind eye**. **White triangle on outer wing, bordered behind by black**. BREEDING: In April adults acquire **complete slaty-black hood**. IMMATURE: Differs from adult in black tail band, dusky bar across upperwing, dark border along entire trailing edge of wing.

Voice: Buzzy, raspy calls.

Behavior: Feeds on small fish, invertebrates, while swimming or dipping to surface in flight; also walks along mudflats, picking at surface. Flies with shallow wingbeats. Can occur in large flocks.

Similar Species: Tern-like (compare with Forster's Tern, p. 207). Several other small to medium-small gulls with dark hoods (in breeding plumage) can occur rarely in the region (see Sabine's Gull, p. 485; Laughing and Franklin's Gulls, p. 469), so always consult field guides.

Where, When to Find: Common spring migrant (April to early May) along the coast and even well offshore. Locally common in winter (late October to early May); favored areas often shift, but flocks often occur around sewage outfalls, wastewater treatment plants, productive ocean waters just offshore. Uncommon migrant inland at sewage ponds, reservoirs; more numerous at some inland lakes (Prado Regional Park, Lake Perris) and Salton Sea where flocks often seen in winter, migration. A few, mostly immatures, may summer on coastal lagoons and at Salton Sea.

Did you know? This species English name honors Charles Lucien Bonaparte, an ornithologist and nephew of Napoleon.

Date & Location Seen:

Breeding Adult

First-year

Description: 19″, wingspan 49″. A distinctive dark-bodied medium-sized gull. ADULT: **Gray overall** (darker above) with a **black tail**, **bright red bill**, black legs. In breeding plumage (late December to July) the head is white. IMMATURE: Juvenile is solidly dark brown; pale fringes to feathers of back and wings have mostly worn away by fall. Bill dull pink at base, dark at tip; legs blackish. Older immatures are progressively grayer; bill is extensively orange-red by second winter.

Voice: Vocal when squabbling for food in groups; calls have a nasal, barking quality.

Behavior: Flocks occur around piers, on beaches, and where food is concentrated offshore. Often associates with feeding Brown Pelicans, seeking fish spilled from pouch. Also forage along the beach tideline like sandpipers, mainly for mole crabs.

Similar Species: Distinctive, but beware dark juvenile gulls such as California and Western. Rarely, adults may show bold white patches on upperwing; these can be mistaken for jaegers, a similarity compounded by Heermann's habit of chasing terns in jaeger-like fashion.

Where, When to Find: Common along the immediate coast and offshore waters. Moves north into region late May from Mexican breeding colonies; common by mid-June. Most stay to January; non-breeders (mainly immatures) may stay through the spring. Casual inland (mainly April and late fall); a few seen in spring, summer and fall at the Salton Sea, and has even attempted to nest there.

Did you know? This species breeds mainly in the Gulf of California, with large numbers moving northward after the breeding season.

Date & Location Seen: _____

_____

Non-breeding Adult

First-year

Description: 16", wingspan 43". A medium-small gull with a rounded head, large dark eye, and **short slender bill**. ADULT: **Small bill is yellowish**, faintly smudged with dusky near the tip in winter; legs yellowish. **Mantle color medium gray** (like California, darker than Ring-billed). **Black wingtips have large white spots** ("mirrors"). In winter head and neck washed with brown. IMMATURE: First-winter birds are washed pale brown with a soft gray back, brownish underwing, almost entirely brown tail; legs pinkish, dull pink bill has dark tip. In second winter much like adult but less white in wingtips, some black near tail tip, black-tipped bill, greenish legs.

Voice: High squealing, mewing notes.

Behavior: Feeds on beaches, but often forages by flying over inshore waters, bays, sewage ponds, dipping to surface for food items.

Similar Species: Ring-billed Gull's (p. 193) thicker bill always dark at or near tip; adult's eye yellow, mantle paler gray. Larger California Gull (p. 197) has longer, thicker bill with red and black spot, adults show less white in wingtips.

Where, When to Find: Uncommon winter visitor (late October to mid-March) along the coast; locally fairly common around sewage outfalls, harbors (Morro Bay, Ventura Harbor, Hyperion, Los Angeles Harbor); scarcer farther south. Regularly moves inland a few miles up the major rivers (especially Santa Ana River), but rare (Salton Sea, Inland Empire) to casual well inland.

Did you know? Our birds are of the subspecies *brachyrhynchus* which is restricted to western North America. Slightly larger birds in the Old World are often called the "Common Gull."

Date & Location Seen:

Breeding Adult

Non-breeding Adult

Description: 17 ½", wingspan 46". A medium sized gull with a fairly short bill. ADULT: **Pale gray above**; black wingtips (with white spots) are sharply set off from pale gray wing. Winter birds get limited brown flecking on the head and neck. **Bill yellow with black ring near tip**; **eye yellowish-white**, **legs yellow**. IMMATURE: First-winter is pale gray on mantle, wings mottled brown above, whitish below; the head and breast are spotted with brown, tail white with darker mottling and blackish band at tip. Bill pink with a black tip, legs pinkish, eyes dark. In second winter similar to adult, but wingtip solidly black, variable small black band on tail tip (often broken); legs greenish-yellow.

Voice: High squealing notes, often with a slightly raspy quality.

Behavior: Feeds on fish, marine invertebrates; also scavenges along beaches and for refuse in parks, parking lots.

Similar Species: California Gull (p. 197) is larger and longer-billed; adult has darker mantle, red spot on bill, dark eye. Sub-adults of many gull species show blackish ring on the bill; in particular second-winter California can suggest first-winter Ring-billed (but note darker mantle, size and shape differences). See Mew Gull (p. 191)

Where, When to Find: Fairly common to common winter visitor (late September through April) to the coast, frequenting beaches, parks, parking lots. Also occurs inland around park lakes and flooded fields throughout the lowlands; abundant in winter at the Salton Sea. Does not venture offshore, being seen only very rarely at sea and around the Channel Islands. Non-breeders remain uncommonly through the summer.

Did you know? Populations of this species have skyrocketed around the Great Lakes; the North American (and world) population now probably exceeds four million birds.

Date & Location Seen: _____

Breeding Adult
wymani

Fourth-year

Juvenile

Juvenile

Description: 25" wingspan 58". An abundant **large coastal gull**, usually the most common species in summer. **Robust bill is thick near the tip**. **Pink legs and feet**. ADULT: White with **dark slaty gray back and upperwings** blending into black wingtips; in flight from below note extensive dark trailing edge to wing. Bill yellow with red spot. Winter adults remain mostly white-headed. IMMATURE: First-winter is overall sooty with white mottling on belly and rump. Underwings dark. Bill black. Progressively whiter on head and underparts and more slaty above through second and third winters.

Voice: Typical gull calls, deeper than our other species; "long call" is a series of *aah aah aah aah* notes.

Behavior: Scavenges on beaches, around harbors, estuaries; also forages for fish, squid and other prey offshore. Increasingly these gulls also move inland to scavenge for garbage.

Similar Species: All other regularly occurring large gulls have paler upperparts. Hybrids with Glaucous-winged Gull not uncommon; these are paler above than pure Westerns. First winter birds resemble Herring Gull (p. 199) but upperparts and wings less scaly, white rump contrasts with dark tail; Herring has a more slender bill, paler underwings. At Salton Sea, see Yellow-footed Gull (p. 469).

Where, When to Find: Common resident along coast, breeding mainly on the Channel Islands. Since 1980s also numerous well inland on the coastal slope, visiting landfills, urban areas, and other sites where garbage, scraps abound; a few appear annually at the Salton Sea, but otherwise almost unknown on the deserts.

Did you know? Our darker, more southerly subspecies *wymani* was named for Luther Wyman, the first Curator of Birds at the Natural History Museum of Los Angeles County.

Date & Location Seen: _____

Breeding Adult

Non-breeding Adult

First-year

Description: 21", wingspan 53". A common medium-large gull with a fairly long, slender bill. ADULT: **Medium gray mantle** and upperwings; extensive black at wingtips shows large white spots. Otherwise white; head and chest are heavily streaked with brown in winter. **Eyes dark**, **legs greenish** (deep yellow in breeding birds), **bill yellow with red and dusky spots near the tip**. IMMATURE: Mottled gray-brown; tail mostly dark, bill pale pink with black tip, legs pink; second-winter birds have gray mantle, pale gray bill with black ring near tip, pale gray-green legs.

Voice: Typical gull cries, some high-pitched, some guttural.

Behavior: Large numbers commute between nighttime roosts on the coast and feeding areas at landfills, parks, schoolyards and other areas with garbage; the most common gull over the urban lowlands in winter.

Similar Species: Ring-billed Gull adult (p. 193) is paler gray above, shorter bill has black ring; immature Ring-billeds mainly white below. Herring Gull adult (p. 199) also paler gray above, has pale eye, pink legs; immatures have all black bill in early winter, pale inner flight feathers on outer wing.

Where, When to Find: Very common winter visitor and migrant, mainly September to early May. Widespread along coast (including well offshore), also moving inland to forage in coastal lowlands. Common migrant (late February to early May, mid-August to mid-October) through the interior, with some wintering. Common in winter at the Salton Sea and 100+ pairs have nested at the Salton Sea National Wildlife Refuge in recent years.

Did you know? The diversion of water for Los Angeles from streams feeding Mono Lake threatened a major breeding colony of this gull until agreements were reached to maintain the lake's level.

Date & Location Seen:

Herring Gull
Non-breeding Adult

Herring Gull
Juvenile

Thayer's Gull
Juvenile

Thayer's Gull
Juvenile

Description: 25", wingspan 58". A large pink-legged gull with long fairly thin bill. ADULT: **Upperparts pale gray**; **limited black in the wingtips**. **Eyes pale yellowish**, **legs bright pink**. In winter adults are streaked and mottled with brown on the head and neck. IMMATURE: Variable. First year birds mottled brown, with the head often noticeably paler. Increasing gray on mantle and white on underparts through second and third years. In flying immatures note that the flight feathers are paler toward mid-wing than at the tip.

Voice: Typical gull squeals and cackles.

Behavior: Associates with other gulls around harbors, estuaries, and landfills.

Similar Species: Thayer's Gull (*Larus thayeri*; 23"), uncommon along the coast and rare inland from late October to March, is similar to Herring but smaller and more delicately built, with a smaller bill. First-winter birds (which predominate here) are frostier, with browner outer wings with conspicuous pale feather tips; wingtips look uniformly pale from underneath. Western X Glaucous-winged hybrids can be similar, but larger with a thick bill.

Where, When to Find: Uncommon winter visitor (October through April) along the coast; fairly common migrant past coastal points in late March and April. Fewer occur inland except in San Joaquin Valley where fairly common and at the Salton Sea, where common. Occurs in numbers well out to sea, even well beyond the Channel Islands.

Did you know? North American Herring Gulls (*smithsonianus*, named for the Smithsonian Institution in Washington, D.C.) may represent a species distinct from populations in Europe; other closely related species are found through much of the rest of Eurasia.

Date & Location Seen: _____

Glaucous-winged Gull
Non-breeding Adult

Glaucous Gull
First- winter

Glaucous-winged Gull
First-year

Description: 26", wingspan 58". Pacific Northwest gull that winters in our region. Structurally very similar to Western Gull, with long heavy bill. Deep pink legs. ADULT: Light gray above; grayish wingtips (same shade as mantle) with white spots. Extensive gray-brown mottling on the head in winter. IMMATURE: First-winter is mottled pale gray-brown throughout, with pale wingtips; heavy all black bill. Worn immatures late in winter can be very pale.

Voice: Much like Western's.

Behavior: A marine gull, usually found along the immediate coast (especially around estuaries, shorelines, and harbors) and offshore waters. Often feeds in rocky intertidal areas.

Similar Species: Western Gull (p. 195) similar but much darker on mantle with black wingtips. Unlike Glaucous-winged, adult Westerns remain mostly white headed in winter. First-winter Thayer's Gull (p. 199) can be nearly as pale as Glaucous-winged, but is more distinctly patterned on back and wings, has darker wing tips and much smaller bill. **Glaucous Gull** (*Larus hyperboreus*; 27") a rare winter visitor to coast, Salton Sea; most are first-winter, overall chalky white with white wing tips, black tip to evenly-proportioned pink-based bill.

Where, When to Find: Uncommon winter visitor along the coast from late October to early April though can be common on San Luis Obispo County coast and common farther south some winters. Generally rare inland on the coastal slope, but a few join Westerns at such localities. A very few remain rarely on the coast through the summer. Rare but regular at the Salton Sea.

Did you know? Glaucous-wingeds hybridize extensively with Western Gulls in the Pacific Northwest and with Herring Gulls in parts of southern Alaska; hybrids are intermediate in mantle and wing tip color.

Date & Location Seen: _____

Breeding Adult

Juvenile

Description: 9", wingspan 20". A **tiny tern** with short yellowish legs and a short, slightly forked tail. BREEDING ADULT: **Bill yellow**. Distinct **white forehead** patch contrasts with black crown and line through eye. Outermost flight feathers of wing blackish, contrasting with pale gray wing. IMMATURE: Juvenile has long dark patch behind eye, streaked crown, brownish barring on back. Older immatures and winter adults, rarely seen in our region, have black bills.

Voice: A high *ki-deek* or *k-seek*, often in a series.

Behavior: Hovers over the water surface, plunging in for tiny fish. Aggressive around nesting colonies, chasing after intruding gulls, crows, and other birds. Nests in loose colonies on sandy islands or (where fenced or otherwise protected from predators) in upper beach areas.

Similar Species: Other terns much larger but compare with Forster's (p. 207).

Where, When to Find: Locally fairly common summer resident along immediate coast, mostly from mid-April through August. Breeding colonies found near Oceano, Oxnard, Marina del Rey, Los Angeles Harbor, Seal Beach, Bolsa Chica, Santa Ana River mouth, Upper Newport Bay, Camp Pendleton, and several sites around San Diego Bay. In mid-summer family groups disperse along entire coast and may feed in wetlands up to several miles inland. Casual inland, but regular in summer at Salton Sea (where it has nested).

Did you know? Our "California" subspecies, *browni*, is classified as endangered and receives intensive management.

Date & Location Seen: _____

Breeding Adult

Description: 21", wingspan 48". The **largest tern**, with a **deep red to red-orange bill**. Tail slightly forked. Always shows **blackish underneath the wingtips**. BREEDING: Black crown, square at rear (not crested); pale gray above, otherwise white. NON-BREEDING: **Crown is peppered black and white**. Immatures show some brown mottling on wings, more dark on upper side of wingtips.

Voice: Call is a deep, raucous *kraa-aay-ow*. Young birds give a high, insistent whistle through the first fall and winter.

Behavior: Like most terns feeds by plunging into the water to catch fish; also dips to surface to catch prey. Stands on beaches, mudflats in loose groups when not feeding, habitually facing into the wind. Nests in mixed tern and skimmer colonies on islets at Bolsa Chica, San Diego Bay, Salton Sea.

Similar Species: Royal Tern (p. 209) is 15% smaller, slightly smaller and thinner bill is more orange, underwing tips mostly whitish; our Royals show an extensive white forehead most of the year (black or streaked with black in Caspian).

Where, When to Find: Fairly common and widespread migrant at lakes, marshes, reservoirs, from late March through early May, August through September. Uncommon winter visitor at coastal estuaries and beaches. Fairly common breeder in tern colony at Bolsa Chica; also breeds at south San Diego Bay and sometimes elsewhere on coast; large colonies have nested in recent years at the south end of the Salton Sea, where a few winter.

Did you know? Caspian Terns began nesting at the Salton Sea in 1927, south San Diego Bay in 1941, and coastal Orange County in 1986; they are also more numerous now in winter than they were decades ago.

Date & Location Seen:

**Forster's Tern
Breeding Adult**

**Forster's Tern
First Winter**

**Common Tern
Breeding Adult**

**Common Tern
First-year**

Description: 13", wingspan 31". Our common medium-small tern; long, **deeply forked tail**. ADULT: Pale gray above; **wings frosted silvery-white**. Breeders (March to August) have all black crown, **orange bill with black tip**; in winter shows white crown, black bill; a **black patch extends back from the eye,** hindneck grayish. IMMATURE: Like winter adult, but wingtips darker; juveniles have pale rusty mottling on back.

Voice: Calls include a prolonged buzzy *keeeurrr* and sharp *kit* notes.

Behavior: Hovers briefly, then plunges into water for small fish. Roosts on beaches, tidal flats in estuaries. Often sits on low pilings, posts surrounded by water. Nests are in more vegetated areas of salt marshes than those of our other terns.

Similar Species: Migrant **Common Terns** (*Sterna hirundo*; 12") occur mainly in May and late July to October, especially on the coast and offshore; they have declined greatly in the region. Common breeding adult has gray underparts, dark wedge near outer wing, red-based bill, short dark red legs; winter adults and immature show black rear hood, dark bar at bend of wing. Most winter south of the United States.

Where, When to Find: Fairly common year-round resident on the coast. Nests mainly at Bolsa Chica and south San Diego Bay, small colonies are sometimes found at other Orange and San Diego County estuaries. Fairly common year round at the Salton Sea, with a few nesting. More widespread and in winter and migration when small numbers occur at inland lakes on the coastal slope, and a few migrants are found in the interior away from the Salton Sea.

Did you know? Unlike Common Tern, Forster's rarely occurs well out over the ocean.

Date & Location Seen:

Royal Tern
Non-breeding Adult

Elegant Tern
Breeding Adult

Elegant Tern
First-year

Description: 20″ / 17″, wingspan 41″ / 34″. Similar terns with orange bills, whitish bodies. ROYAL: Larger than Elegant, with thicker orange bill. Head white most of the year, with black patch from behind eyes back around the nape; breeding birds (February to early June) have all black crown. ELEGANT: Bill is slender, becoming yellow-orange near tip. Breeding birds have black crowns, shaggy black crests, often show pink wash below; from August to February rear crown and crest are black, forehead white. Tail is rather deeply forked. Immatures of both species have some dusky markings on the wings, paler yellow-orange bills.

Voice: Both give a grating *keer-rick* (lower and more mellow in Royal).

Behavior: Plunge into water to catch fish. Elegants often in large, tight flocks; Royals found singly or in small, loose groups. Both breed in mixed colonies on islets within estuaries, harbors.

Similar Species: Caspian Tern (p. 205) larger, with deeper red-orange bill, black under wingtips, and (winter) peppered black-and-white forehead.

Where, When to Find: Both are found along the immediate coast, but Royal also occurs well offshore and around the Channel Islands. ROYAL: Uncommon visitor through the year; numbers are greatest in winter; a few nest in Elegant colonies. ELEGANT: Arrives in early to mid-March; common breeder (the Bolsa Chica colony can have up to 10,000 pairs), feeding widely along the coast. A post-breeding influx brings additional birds from the Gulf of California from June to October. Generally absent December through February. Elegant is casual, Royal accidental at the Salton Sea in spring and early summer, but neither species is expected inland.

Did you know? Elegant Terns did not breed in California until the 1950s.

Date & Location Seen:

Description: 18", wingspan 44". An unmistakable **black and white** seabird with bizarre **orange-red bill with black tip; lower bill longer than upper bill**. ADULT: Black above, white on forehead and underparts; winter adults have a broad white collar. Legs orange-red. JUVENILE: Gray-brown with white scaling above; legs pale orange, base of bill duller orange-red; black feathering on back and wings is attained through first winter. Males larger and longer-billed than females.

Voice: Calls include a barking *oww* or *arrr*, and shorter *yip* notes.

Behavior: Feeds (largely at dusk and into night) by skimming low over water, dragging long knife-thin lower mandible through the water to catch small fish. Flocks roost on beaches, tidal mudflats during the day, often sleeping and sunning in bizarre positions. Nests with terns on low islets within lagoons, harbors.

Similar Species: Unmistakable.

Where, When to Find: Locally common along the coast. Breeds at Bolsa Chica, Upper Newport Bay, Batiquitos Lagoon, south San Diego Bay and has nested in coastal Los Angeles County; winter flocks of up to several hundred birds are found in San Diego, Newport Bay, Seal Beach, Long Beach, and Santa Barbara with individuals or smaller groups often found elsewhere along the coast. Individuals may move back and forth between roost sites (e.g. in Long Beach and Santa Barbara) within a few days. A few move short distances up the major coastal river channels. Common from April to October at the Salton Sea, with nesting colonies at the south end.

Did you know? Skimmers first colonized California at the Salton Sea, first nesting in the early 1970s; the first coastal nesting was in south San Diego Bay in 1976.

Date & Location Seen: _____

Description: 13". The familiar domestic pigeon of cities and other areas of human habitation. "Wild type" birds are mainly gray with **white rump band, black wing bars, white wing linings**, and iridescent neck sides; tail has a black terminal band and white edges. The bill is black and legs are pink. An **array of other plumages** noted in city flocks, from pure white to reddish-brown or nearly black; many are pied and asymmetrically marked.

Voice: Gruff cooing notes; wingtips often make a clapping sound on take-off

Behavior: Abundant, tame, and ubiquitous. Feeds for scraps on ground, nests on building ledges, under bridges and other structures or (locally, as at Morro Rock, Pt. Dume and the Palos Verdes Peninsula) on sea cliffs. Rapidly flying flocks of "racing" varieties often seen overhead.

Similar Species: Our native Band-tailed Pigeon (p. 215) shows little plumage variation (unlike highly variable, rag-tag groups of Rock Pigeons). Band-taileds have orange-yellow feet and bill base, white hindneck crescent, and uniform gray plumage with darker flight feathers and pale gray terminal band to longer tail.

Where, When to Find: Ubiquitous introduced resident in towns, industrial and agricultural areas, ranch yards, harbors, beaches and nearly all other areas of human habitation.

Did you know? Although Rock Pigeons (also known as Rock Doves or Domestic Pigeons) are non-migratory, their remarkable homing ability has made them the subject of many pioneering studies of avian navigation and orientation, and popular with hobbyists.

Date & Location Seen: _____

BAND-TAILED PIGEON
Patagioenas fasciata

Description: 14". Our native pigeon, the large and relatively long-tailed Band-tail is nearly uniform gray, highlighted by a **white crescent** and iridescent green scalloping **on the hindneck** (absent in juveniles), and a **dark gray median and pale gray terminal tail band.** The underparts are tinged with purple. The **legs, feet and base of bill are yellow-orange**.

Voice: Deep, owl-like cooing notes: *hoo–whooOOOoo*; grating call given in display flights which cover long arcs with rapid, shallow wingbeats. Wingtips often make a clapping sound on take-off.

Behavior: Forages by picking seeds or berries (such as acorns, elderberries) from producing trees and shrubs; flocks may wander nomadically in search of these resources. Also visits seed feeders. Flocks congregate around water seeps in the mountains.

Similar Species: Citified Rock Pigeon (p. 213) usually shuns natural, wooded habitats. Rock Pigeon flocks show a variety of plumages and color morphs, unlike more uniform-appearing Band-tailed Pigeons. The Band-tail's deep hooting calls are often mistaken for those of owls (but are given only in daytime).

Where, When to Find: Common resident in oak and mixed oak-conifer woodlands throughout the coast range foothills and the higher mountains; also in many older residential areas with tall planted trees (e.g. pines, eucalyptus) and even locally in urban areas (e.g. Los Angeles Civic Center). Rare or absent along the immediate coast and in most coastal lowlands of Orange and San Diego Counties (but breeds locally in n. Santa Ana); a casual wanderer to the deserts and Channel Islands.

Did you know? This pigeon's spread into urban lowlands is a relatively recent phenomenon.

Date & Location Seen:

Eurasian Collared-Dove

Spotted Dove

Description: 12". Common and increasing introduced species. **Pale gray-brown** with **black hindneck collar**, grayish undertail, squared tail with black base, white corners. Dark flight feathers contrast with pale coverts, wing linings.

Voice: Clear or slightly gruff *coo-COO-coo*, often repeated for long periods; also a harsh grating scream.

Behavior: These doves feed mainly on the ground, but roost and nest in trees and often perch on wires, rooftops. Display flights involve quick climb with rapid wing-beats followed by long, curving glide.

Similar Species: Compare with White-winged Dove (p. 471). **Spotted Dove** (*Streptopelia chinensis*; 12"), an Asiatic dove introduced into Hollywood around 1915 and spreading to most of the Region's lowlands, is now scarce and local – most easily seen in Huntington Park and vicinity in L. A. Basin, and on Santa Catalina I. Darker than Eurasian with long, square-tipped blackish tail with broad white corners; broad necklace of black and white spots on hindneck of adults. Spotted gives gruff *coo-coo-ROO*. Domestic form of African Collared-Dove (*Streptopelia roseogrisea*; also known as "Ringed Turtle-Dove"), formerly established in central Los Angeles and a frequent escapee, is like small, cream-colored version of Eurasian Collared-Dove, with pale undertail, very different voice (but note that very pale Eurasians are often seen as well).

Where, When to Find: Generally tied to areas of human habitation. First established in coastal Ventura around 1990; birds spreading from e. United States (after accidental release in the Bahamas in the 1970s and subsequent spread to Florida) now found throughout the region and increasing; abundant in desert towns and Imperial Valley.

Did you know? The causes of the rapid decline of Spotted Doves since the 1970s remain unknown, but may include increases in urban predators such as Cooper's Hawks, crows, and introduced eastern fox squirrels.

Date & Location Seen:

Description: 12". One of the most widespread and abundant native birds in the Los Angeles Region, the Mourning Dove is a slender gray-brown dove with a **pointed, white-edged tail**, a black facial spot, and a few **black spots on the wing coverts**. Legs pinkish, bare orbital ring pale bluish. Juveniles show scalloped plumage due to whitish feather fringes.

Voice: Familiar song is a soft, cooing *hoo-OOOoo, hoo, hoo-hoo* with a distinctive rhythm; wings make whistling sound in flight.

Behavior: Abundant and tame, often visiting seed feeders. Nests may be placed in trees, shrubs and even planters or hanging baskets adjacent to houses. Often gathers in large flocks in fall, winter. Forages for seeds on the ground.

Similar Species: Smaller than pigeons and *Streptopelia* doves, with pointed tail. Small, scaly juveniles might suggest Inca Dove (p 471), a species of the southeastern deserts.

Where, When to Find: Found in nearly all terrestrial habitats, at all seasons. Perhaps the most widespread bird species in Southern California region and a familiar bird in urban and suburban areas.

Did you know? Remarkably widespread, Mourning Doves were found nesting in 400 of 411 blocks in the Los Angeles County Breeding Bird Atlas, 98 of 111 blocks in Orange County, and all but two of the 479 blocks in San Diego County.

Date & Location Seen: _____

Male

Description: 6″. A small dove found in southern desert valleys and locally in the coastal lowlands. **Tiny** and **short-tailed;** in flight shows **rufous wing flash**. Grayish head and pinkish breast of male show **scaly pattern;** female duller and more uniform but still shows scaliness. Bill pinkish at base.

Voice: Call is a soft, whistled *hoo-wup* which may be repeated for long periods.

Behavior: A shy, ground-inhabiting dove, retiring deep into shrubs or low trees when flushed. Flight rapid and direct.

Similar Species: Juvenile Mourning Doves show scaly plumage, but are larger with longer, pointed tails and lack rufous wing flash. See Inca Dove (p. 471).

Where, When to Find: Fairly common in towns, ranch yards and orchards in the Imperial, Coachella and lower Colorado River Valleys. Also found locally, but declining, in old orchards, shrubby borders of agricultural fields, and weedy areas in the southern San Joaquin Valley, coastal Ventura County (Camarillo, Oxnard Plain, Santa Clara River), and northern San Diego County; nearly gone from southeastern Los Angeles County and lowland Orange County. Wanders very rarely to the northern deserts.

Did you know? The related Ruddy Ground-Dove (*C. talpacoti*) now occurs rarely and irregularly in se. California and has been found in all the region's counties except San Luis Obispo.

Date & Location Seen:

Mitred Parakeet

Nanday Parakeet

Yellow-chevroned Parakeet

Rose-ringed Parakeet

Description: 13½"/13"/8½". **Bright green with pointed tails**. MITRED has thick ivory bill, white eye-ring, **red on forehead and face**, red flecks on neck; NANDAY has **black face**, pale blue breast, red "thighs"; YELLOW-CHEVRONED is small, grass-green with **yellow wing patch**.

Voice: MITRED gives harsh shrieks (often with nasal quality); NANDAY a harsh *kreeehh*; and YELLOW-CHEVRONED a scratchy *chree-chreet*.

Behavior: Fly in tight, noisy flocks. Feed in fruiting or flowering trees such as eucalyptus, coral trees, liquidambars; Yellow-chevroned partial to seed pods of silk-floss trees.

Similar Species: Larger, stockier Red-crowned Parrot (and other amazons; p. 224) have squared tails. **Rose-ringed Parakeet** (*Psittacula krameri*; 13"), is slender, pale green, with mostly red bill, very long pointed tail; males have thin pink and black collar; common in Bakersfield, with a few in Playa del Rey and elsewhere. Red-masked Parakeet (*Aratinga erythrogenys*; 13") like Mitred but smaller, with solid bright red head, red underwing linings; mainly San Gabriel Valley; some on Point Loma.

Where, When to Find: MITRED found year-round in the Los Angeles Basin, Malibu area, San Gabriel Valley, se. San Fernando Valley, Long Beach and western Orange County. NANDAY most numerous in canyons and residential areas near coast from Brentwood to Point Mugu (a few well into Santa Monica Mtns.). YELLOW-CHEVRONED mainly Los Angeles Basin, San Fernando and San Gabriel Valleys (easily found at Huntington Gardens in San Marino, Exposition Park, Sepulveda Basin, and L. A. Civic Center parks).

Did you know? All of these species (except Rose-ringed, from India) are native to South America and were imported to the United States in large numbers from the 1960s to the early 1980s.

Date & Location Seen: _____

Red-crowned Parrot

Lilac-crowned Parrot

Description: 12″. A large, chunky **square-tailed** parrot that is **mainly green** in color; **forehead and forecrown bright red**, sides of crown bluish. Red patch on secondaries shows in flight. Heavy ivory-colored bill.

Voice: Harsh cawing screeches and a downslurred *wheee-oh*; Lilac-crowned (see below) has similar screeches but also gives squeaky upslurred *kerleek?*

Behavior: Usually seen in flight when commuting between roosting and feeding sites; usually in pairs. Feeds (often quietly) on a variety of seeds and fruits. Huge and incredibly noisy flocks gather around roosting areas in the late afternoon.

Similar Species: Lilac-crowned Parrot (*A. finschi*, 12 ½″), in same areas as Red-crowned, is similar, but red forehead is darker and does not extend to crown, crown is washed with lilac-blue, and tail is relatively longer; gives upslurred *kwi-leeck?* in addition to harsh screeches. Other "amazon" parrots often seen in the San Gabriel Valley, in central Orange County, and elsewhere include the Red-lored Parrot (*A. autumnalis*; 12 ½″, yellow spot below red forecrown), Yellow-headed Parrot (*A.oratrix*; 14″, large, with entirely pale yellow head), and Blue-fronted Parrot (*A. aestiva*; 14″, blue forehead, yellow on face).

Where, When to Find: Year-round resident in San Gabriel Valley (up to 2,000 birds), San Fernando Valley, older urban areas of Orange County (600+), Malibu, Redlands area, and in San Diego's Ocean Beach/Point Loma and El Cajon. Huge evening roosts are found near the intersection of Baldwin Ave. and Live Oak Ave. in Temple City and near Fair Oaks Ave. and Monterey Rd. in South Pasadena.

Did you know? Red-crowned Parrots are native to northeastern Mexico, where their populations have declined severely. Lilac-crowneds are native to western Mexico.

Date & Location Seen: _____

Description: 23″. An unmistakable large **ground bird** with **streaked breast** and upperparts, **long** green-glossed **tail**, **bushy crest,** and (at close range) bare red and blue facial skin.

Voice: Call (delivered from atop a fencepost or shrub) is a slow, descending series of mournful cooing notes, suggesting a downtrodden, whimpering dog. Also gives a clacking rattle with the bill.

Behavior: Terrestrial, usually flying only when chased. Runs or walks, then raises and lowers tail slowly after stopping. Eats a variety of small reptiles, large ground insects, and even small birds.

Similar Species: Unmistakable. Thrashers are much smaller and have thin, decurved bills.

Where, When to Find: Uncommon but widespread year round resident throughout the deserts and fringes of the southern San Joaquin Valley, and in open brushy habitats of the foothills. Intolerant of urbanization and now absent from most of the coastal lowlands, but a few are still seen near the coast in undeveloped or rural areas. Most readily seen around desert campgrounds (e.g. Joshua Tree National Park, Borrego Springs) and in Imperial Valley.

Did you know? Roadrunners are ground-inhabiting cuckoos, and their footprints show the typical cuckoo pattern or two forward- and two backward-directed toes. The region's other regularly-occurring cuckoo, the Yellow-billed Cuckoo (*Coccyzus americanus*), is now a very rare summer resident in riparian zones, now mainly on the lower Colorado River and the South Fork of the Kern River.

Date & Location Seen: _____

Description: 15″. A medium-sized, very **pale buffy, gray and white** owl with **dark eyes** and **heart-shaped face**. Females usually deep buff on underparts, males usually white. Large, rounded head shows no "ear" tufts.

Voice: Commonly heard call is a rasping screech, often heard as birds undertake coursing flights in the evening.

Behavior: Active at night, when it hunts for rodents, often with long, coursing flights. Sits quietly during the day in trees or within structures (old barns and outbuildings, haystacks, bridges). Nests in large tree cavities, ledges, old buildings, haystacks or suitably large nest boxes.

Similar Species: No other owl in the Region combines dark eyes and very pale plumage. Among our owls, only the Short-eared (p. 237) is nearly as pale.

Where, When to Find: Fairly common (but secretive) year-round resident in suburban throughout the lowlands and foothills; most numerous at ranch yards and tree rows on the deserts and San Joaquin Valley portion of Kern County. A few penetrate heavily urbanized areas.

Did you know? Barn Owls have exceptionally keen hearing and can locate rodents and other prey in total darkness.

Date & Location Seen: _____

Description: 8″. A **small**, finely marked **grayish** owl with **yellow eyes**, short "ear" tufts (often not visible), **white spotted scapulars and coverts**. Like most of our small owls, it is best found and identified by voice.

Voice: An accelerating "bouncing ball" series of short, low whistles *hoo hoo hoo-hoo-hoo-oo-oo-oo*; also a rapid low double trill and some squealing notes.

Behavior: A nocturnal hunter of small rodents, large insects; almost never seen during the day, when it retreats to tree cavities (where it also nests). Usually found in pairs. Can often be lured into view at night by imitations of calls.

Similar Species: Uncommon Flammulated Owl (p. 457) of mountain forests is smaller, with dark eyes and different voice. Buff and brown Northern Saw-whet Owl (p. 457) lacks "ear" tufts and fine plumage patterning. Compare with larger Long-eared Owl (p. 237).

Where, When to Find: Widespread year-round resident in foothill, mountain and desert woodlands, though rarely seen unless searched for at night. Most common where live oaks predominate. Occurs in some well wooded residential areas and orchards, but generally absent from urban areas. Absent from Channel Islands.

Did you know? Western Screech-Owls do not have a red color morph (which occurs commonly in the eastern North American species).

Date & Location Seen: _____

GREAT HORNED OWL
Bubo virginianus

Description: 22". Our familiar **large, tufted** owl. Size of a Red-tailed Hawk, with **yellow eyes**, finely barred and streaked brown, gray and white plumage. Conspicuous **white throat collar**. Females are larger than males.

Voice: Often heard rhythmic hooting, higher-pitched in females than males: *hoo-HOO, HOO, HOO* or *hoo-hoo-HOO, hoo-HOO, hoo.* Fledged young give a rising shriek.

Behavior: Hunts nocturnally for rodents, snakes, large ground insects (such as Jerusalem crickets), and sometimes even smaller owls. Calling birds often sit conspicuously atop tall trees, utility poles.

Similar Species: Far larger than our other owls. Compare with two much rarer species: Spotted Owl (p. 457), which is dark brown, with dark eyes, lacks "ear" tufts) and Long-eared Owl (p. 237) longer and more closely-spaced "ear" tufts, warm brown facial disks, more streaked underparts.

Where, When to Find: Widespread resident in all mainland areas, from the coast to the high mountains and deserts; absent from the Channel Islands. Found in nearly all habitats that provide suitable nest sites (cliff ledges, broken tree trunks, old hawk nests). Found in many residential areas and large urban parks, but absent from the most heavily urbanized areas.

Did you know? This is the most widespread owl in the Americas, occurring from the sub-Arctic regions south to Argentina.

Date & Location Seen:

Description: 9 ½″. A **small**, **long-legged**, tuftless owl of open country. **Yellow eyes**, broad white chin and **white "eyebrows"** are distinctive. Body plumage spotted and barred, brown and white.

Voice: Rasping, barking notes, such as *kwik-kwik-kwik*.

Behavior: Often seen during the day, perching on earthen levees, fence posts, concrete cisterns, or on the ground; perched birds bob up and down when agitated. Nests in mammal burrows or artificial holes in the ground. Flight is low, with quick flaps and a glide; sometimes hovers when foraging (mainly at dusk, night).

Similar Species: Unmistakable; other small, yellow-eyed owls are woodland or forest birds and much shorter-legged. Rare Short-eared Owl (p. 237), also of open country and partly diurnal, is much larger and buffier, with long streaks below.

Where, When to Find: Common year-round resident in agricultural areas of the Imperial Valley; otherwise uncommon breeder and migrant through the remaining deserts. Coastal-slope populations have greatly declined with spreading urbanization; now extirpated from most of the coastal slope, but a few are resident at the Seal Beach National Wildlife Refuge, North Island Naval Air Station in San Diego, and a few other sites; small numbers of migrants reach the coastal and valley regions in fall and winter.

Did you know? Formerly a common breeding resident throughout the lowlands of the coastal slope, this species is now of considerable conservation concern in southern California west of the deserts.

Date & Location Seen:

Short-eared Owl

Long-eared Owl

Description: 15". A medium-sized owl with **yellow eyes, long "ear" tufts** (more closely spaced than in Great Horned), **pale orangish face**, and underparts with blackish streaks and crossbars.

Voice: Call, usually heard only on breeding territory, a single deep hoot; also moaning, wailing calls around nest.

Behavior: Often discovered roosting in conifers, tamarisks, or broad-leafed trees, sitting vertically not far from the trunk; small groups gather in winter roosts. Uses old nests of hawks, crows for breeding.

Similar Species: See Great Horned Owl (p. 233). **Short-eared Owl** (*Asio flammeus*; 15") is rare non-breeding visitor to grasslands, agricultural areas, marshes (including Channel Islands). It is paler and buffier, with very short tufts, long stripes below on buffy breast, whitish belly; prominent black "wrist" mark in flight. Perches on ground or clump of vegetation; floppy, coursing flight.

Where, When to Find: Very localized breeder in oak, riparian and conifer woodlands on the coastal slope and tree groves on the deserts. Most readily found at roosts in tree groves in deserts (e.g., in Antelope Valley, Anza-Borrego State Park). Populations in riparian woodlands in the coastal lowlands have almost entirely disappeared. Rare wanderer to Channel Islands.

Did you know? The "ears" of this and many other owls are simply feather tufts that signal species identity and behavioral state; they are not involved in the well-developed auditory abilities of owls.

Date & Location Seen:

**Lesser Nighthawk
Male**

**Common Nighthawk
Male**

Description: 9". With **long, pointed wings** and long notched tails, nighthawks are aerial feeders with a **white or buff band across the primaries**. Lesser is mottled gray-brown and buff, in a **"dead leaf" pattern**. Undertail coverts buffy; flight feathers have buffy spotting. Wing band white in males, buff in females (often hard to see in juveniles).

Voice: A quiet, low trill that may last several seconds, given in flight and while perched; also a nasal bleating series given in flight by displaying birds.

Behavior: Hides on ground or low branch during the day; foraging flights with erratic swoops and flutters, mainly at dusk and dawn. Nests on ground in gravel washes,

Similar Species: Common Nighthawk (*C. minor*, 9 ½"), an uncommon summer visitor (mainly June to August) in the eastern San Bernardino Mtns., is grayer, has bolder white wing bar closer to wrist joint of more pointed wings, lack buff on belly and undertail coverts, and gives distinctive loud, nasal *peeent* call. See Common Poorwill (p. 241).

Where, When to Find: Summer resident, mainly late March to September; abundant in the Imperial, Coachella and Colorado River valleys; more local in dry washes on the desert and very locally on coastal slope northwest to the Cuyama Valley. A few still nest in the Santa Clara, Big Tujunga and San Gabriel River washes, San Juan and Santiago Creeks in Orange County, the Santa Ana River from Redlands to Corona, and Miramar and Poway areas of San Diego. Migrants occur rarely on the coast and Channel Islands.

Did you know? Despite their name, nighthawks are not related to the hawks, nor are they especially closely related to the owls.

Date & Location Seen:

Male

Description: 8″. A small nightjar with a **large, flat-topped head** and **short, rounded tail**. Intricate **"dead-leaf" pattern** of brown, tan, gray, black and silver; throat black with white band below. **White** (male) **or buffy** (female) **tail corners.**

Voice: Distinctive, plaintive *poor-will* (*poor-will-ip* at closer range) is given repeatedly (about once every 1.5 sec), often for minutes on end. Gruff *wuk* or *wep* given in flight.

Behavior: Most vocal and active at dusk, but may feed and call much of the night when temperatures are warm. Roosts and nests on the ground; sallies up from ground in erratic, floppy flight to catch moths, beetles, etc.

Similar Species: Lesser Nighthawk (p. 239) has longer tail, white wing band, spends much time in flight (often in daylight). Very rare Mexican Whip-poor-will (*Antrostomus arizonae*, 9 ½″), which has summered in oak-conifer woods in the San Gabriel, San Jacinto and San Bernardino Mtns., has longer tail and very different voice (a gruff *prrip-prrRILLL!*)

Where, When to Find: Found in chaparral, dry woodlands, steep mountain slopes, and rocky desert hills throughout; resident in coastal and foothill regions, but generally quiet and inactive during colder months. Many birds from colder interior regions migrate, though some may hibernate. Migrants sometimes found in coastal urban regions in October and November.

Did you know? Winter hibernation in poorwills was first documented in the Chuckwalla Mountains of the Colorado Desert in 1946.

Date & Location Seen:

Description: 4 ¾". A tiny, dark gray-brown aerial bird with rapid twinkling wingbeats; like a "cigar with wings." **Dusky**, with **paler grayish throat, breast** and **rump**. **Short squared tail** has spiny tips to all feathers.

Voice: A very high, rapid chippering, often running into an insect-like trill. Very vocal around roost sites (and on northern breeding grounds), though migrants are usually silent.

Behavior: On the wing all day, frantic flight consists of rapid, stiff wing beats and short glides. Large evening roosting concentrations may occur in urban areas in spring and fall, with the swifts utilizing chimneys, building shafts – roost gatherings in Long Beach and downtown Los Angeles and San Diego may involve several thousand birds. Especially during inclement spring weather flocks may seek refuge at night in chimneys.

Similar Species: White-throated Swift (p. 245) is larger, with longer wings and tail; plumage more contrasting blackish and white. Chimney Swift (*Chaetura pelagica*, 5 ¼"), very rare visitor May to September mainly to urban Los Angeles area, is slightly larger and darker, with lower, staccato chippering calls. Swallows have looser flight on more flexed wings, are usually contrastingly pale on underparts.

Where, When to Find: Common and widespread migrant from mid-April to mid-May, and again from late August to early October; most often seen in numbers during stormy weather, when flocks often concentrate over lakes and reservoirs with swallows. Small flocks sometimes found in coastal lowlands in winter, but absent from early June to early August (when, in fact, Chimney Swift is more likely to occur).

Did you know? Although spectacular roosts may occur in our urban buildings, this species may also "roost" on the wing at night.

Date & Location Seen: _____

White-throated Swift

Black Swift

Description: 6 ½". An accomplished scythe-winged aerialist with bold patterning. **Blackish-brown** with **white throat** coming to a point on the lower breast, **white flanks and rump-sides**. **Long tail** has a shallow fork, but is **usually carried in a point**. White-markings often hard to see, so distinctive shape (long, thin wings, elongated rear body and tail) help identify it.

Voice: A long, descending series of rapid notes, *jee-jee-jee....*

Behavior: On the wing all day, often at great heights. Flight combines rapid wingbeats and glides. May fly low over freshwater ponds, lakes. Roosts throughout year and nests in spring, summer in crevices in cliff faces, but also crevices and weep holes in highway overpasses and bridges.

Similar Species: Black Swift (*Cypseloides niger*, 7 ¼") is **entirely blackish** (subtle white fringes on forehead, belly are hard to see), with **broad and squared tail**, broad wings angled at wrist; flight mainly long glides. Black Swift is a scarce migrant (mainly May, September), with a few pairs nesting behind waterfalls in rugged canyons (e.g. Big Santa Anita) in mountains; its winter grounds recently found to be in western Amazon region of South America.

Where, When to Find: Widespread; especially common in rugged mountains and coastal cliffs (including Channel Islands), but may be seen anywhere; least common in desert lowlands (Antelope Valley). More localized in winter; sightings of flocks often weather-dependent. Nests widely along freeway system, utilizing nest sites in overpasses.

Did you know? Swifts, though superficially similar to the unrelated swallows (which are songbirds), are closely related to the hummingbirds.

Date & Location Seen: _____

Male

Female

Description: 3 ¾". A spring and summer hummingbird, differing subtly in structure from our other common species (**bill long**, head small and squared, neck thin). MALE: **Chin black, throat violet** (looks black in most lighting); **white spot behind eye**; **broad white collar** below throat; sides and flanks olive, upperparts deep green; tail blackish, slightly forked. FEMALE: **Chin and throat whitish**, slight buff wash on flanks, tail with white corners.

Voice: Soft, squeaky *hew* or *tew* notes; soft, sputtering rattle. Wings of both sexes make dry reeling buzz in flight (most audible in male).

Behavior: Male's display flight is a rapid series of low, shallow arcs with an audible dry wing buzz. Distinctive nest is soft and smooth, often built from straw-colored fuzz from undersurface of sycamore leaves.

Similar Species: The gorget (iridescent area on chin, throat) of males of other species may look black under poor lighting conditions; sides of gorget of Anna's, Costa's are more elongated. Female Anna's is larger, dingier on underparts. Female Costa's has shorter bill and tail, lacks buff on flanks, has long grayish white eye-line connecting with pale gray neck sides. All differ in calls.

Where, When to Find: Breeds (April to August) in canyon woodlands (cottonwoods, alders, and especially sycamores), oak woodlands, well-wooded residential areas and parks. Spring migrants, widespread in desert, foothills and inland valleys) arrive by early April (mid-March on Colorado River); fall birds (often seen along coast) are gone by late September; only a few winter records.

Did you know? This highly migratory hummingbird winters in western and southern Mexico.

Date & Location Seen:

Male

Female

Description: 4". This abundant year-round resident is our largest hummingbird (though still diminutive). MALE: **Crown, chin**, and **throat brilliant rose red**; whitish ring around eye; upperparts iridescent green, underparts mostly olive-gray. FEMALE: Color on head is limited to **variable red patch in center of throat**; underparts dingy grayish; tail corners white. Juveniles lack red on throat.

Voice: Soft *chip* notes and scratchy *chicka-chicka-chika* series. Male song is a scratchy, squeaky series in a distinctive rhythm.

Behavior: Males perch conspicuously; display consists of slow, steep climb to 50-100', then a high-speed dive with a loud *peek* sound as the bird pulls out.

Similar Species: Smaller male Costa's has purple (not rose) gorget that is more elongated at rear sides; female Costa's is smaller and dumpier, and cleaner grayish-white below, with long white supercilium that joins white throat collar. Female Black-chinned is clean grayish-white below, has blackish lores and white spot behind eye, and shows a touch of buff on the flanks.

Where, When to Find: Common throughout the year in the coastal lowlands and foothills; widespread in the mountains in summer and fall; a few remain in the coldest areas (mountains, Antelope Valley) in winter where feeders or sufficient ornamental flowers are available. Found in urban areas, parks, chaparral, and woodlands; can be especially abundant around groves of winter-flowering eucalyptus.

Did you know? Ornithologists had disagreed whether the explosive popping sound at the bottom of the male's display dive is actually a vocalization, a mechanical sound produced by the tail feathers, or a combination of the two; recent studies aided by high-speed photography confirm that the sound is made by the spread tail feathers.

Date & Location Seen: _____

Male

Female

Description: 3 ½". A small, **short-billed**, short-tailed "pot-bellied" hummingbird of arid scrub areas and gardens. MALE: **Violet crown, chin and throat**, the sides of the **gorget long and pointed**. Underparts whitish, mottled green on sides. FEMALE: Lacks violet color; throat pale grayish white. **Long whitish supercilium** extends down behind ear coverts and connects with grayish white throat sides.

Voice: High, soft *pit* notes (suggesting a Bushtit) and a high, sputtering *pit-it-it-trrrrrr* series. Perched male give a very high-pitched, prolonged *ziinnggggggg*, rising then falling in pitch.

Behavior: Usually perches low, though territorial males select prominent perch. Male's display involves shorter climb than Anna's, with dive tracing a shallow "U" path.

Similar Species: See Black-chinned and Anna's, which female closely resembles. Beware effects of lighting angle on the iridescent crown and throat color (it sometimes looks close to Anna's rose red).

Where, When to Find: Found mainly in arid scrub regions, including chaparral and desert woodlands, but also fond of garden ornamentals (especially sages). Most numerous on the southern deserts (Joshua Tree National Park, Anza Borrego State Park, foothills surrounding the Coachella Valley). Also found through the Mojave Desert and in foothill chaparral in spring and summer, but small numbers are found year round in residential areas on the coastal slope; most or all birds depart the high desert in fall, returning in March. Usually not found high in the mountains, though some pass through mountain meadows in early fall.

Did you know? Many hummingbird hybrid combinations are known; in our region these include Costa's X Anna's as well as Allen's X Anna's.

Date & Location Seen: _____

Allen's Hummingbird
Male

Allen's Hummingbird
Female

Rufous Hummingbird
Male

Description: 3 ¾". Common resident coastal-slope hummingbird with rufous in the plumage. MALE: Gorget bright red to orange-red; crown and **back green, rump, tail, sides and flanks rufous**. FEMALE: throat and breast whitish; **sides and flanks washed cinnamon**; some **rufous at base of tail**. Immature male has some red on throat, more rufous than female.

Voice: Hard *tewk…tewk* calls and an excited *zeeeee-chuppity-chuppity*. Wings of adult male make musical trilling sound.

Behavior: Very aggressive, often commandeering feeders. Male's display involves back and forth arcs, then a climb and steep dive, ending with a breathy *pfvvvvvvvv* sound.

Similar Species: Rufous Hummingbird (*S. rufus*, 3 ¾"), migrant from mid-February through April and again July to September, almost identical, but adult male has completely or mostly **rufous back**. Pin-like outer tail feathers of Allen's are narrower than in Rufous. Females and immature nearly identical; few "identifiable" adult male Rufous are present after July.

Where, When to Find: Resident in gardens, urban parks, coastal sage, and willows on the Channel Islands and in the coastal lowlands from Malibu and the San Fernando and San Gabriel valleys south through coastal Orange County; more recently in Inland Empire and south on the coast to San Diego. Now outnumbers Anna's on coast. Migrant birds breeding near the coast from Ventura County north arrive in late January and February and depart by late summer. Southbound migrants move through the mountains from late June to August; casual migrant in deserts and Imperial Valley (where Rufous far more numerous).

Did you know? Resident birds formerly restricted to the Channel Islands, but have spread with the profusion of exotic plants such as cape honeysuckle, eucalyptus, and bottlebrush.

Date & Location Seen:

Male

Female

Description: 13". A distinctive, boldly plumaged waterbird with a **bushy crest** giving a large headed appearance. MALE: **Blue-gray above, white below,** with a blue-gray band across the upper breast; white patch on primaries shows in flight. FEMALE: Similar to male, but with additional **rusty band across lower breast** and onto sides and flanks. JUVENILE: Both sexes have single band (mixed blue and rust) across chest and rusty on flanks.

Voice: Loud, staccato rattle frequently announces the kingfisher's presence.

Behavior: Perches with very short legs on branches of waterside trees, shrubs (as well as utility wires). Flies with quick, irregular rowing wingbeats; when foraging hovers over water, then plunges in to catch fish, crayfish, and other prey. Nests in long burrows excavated in earthen river banks.

Similar Species: Our only kingfisher. Superficially suggests a jay, but behavior utterly different. Other plunge-diving waterbirds, such as terns, are very different in shape and plumage.

Where, When to Find: Widespread in migration and winter (late July to April) around ponds, lakes, reservoirs, rivers, and protected bays and estuaries (also sheltered coves on coast and Channel Islands). A very few remain to breed along rivers (e.g., Upper Salinas, Santa Ynez, Santa Clara, Santa Ana) and banks of some reservoirs and coastal creek mouths south to San Diego.

Did you know? Kingfishers make occasional visits to backyard fish ponds.

Date & Location Seen:

Acorn Woodpecker
Adult Male

Lewis's Woodpecker
Adult

Description: 9". A noisy and social inhabitant of oak woodlands, this medium-sized woodpecker is **glossy black above** with a **clown-like black, yellow and white face**, black chest, white underparts, and bold **white patches on the wings and rump**. MALE has white forehead, red crown; similar FEMALE has black bar on forecrown in front of the red patch.

Voice: Noisy. A repeated *ja-cob, ja-cob…*or *ratch-et, ratch-et…*along with a variety of grating or cawing calls.

Behavior: Social; nests in small communal groups. These groups harvest and store acorns in conspicuous "granary" trees (or utility poles), returning through the year to consume them. They also sally after flying insects and forage for ants on the ground or tree limbs.

Similar Species: Lewis's Woodpecker (*M. lewis*, 10 ¾") is a scarce and irregular winter visitor to open woods of oak and conifer; more numerous in San Luis Obispo Co., where a few breed. **Glossy greenish black** above with a red face and **pinkish belly; it lacks white** in the plumage.

Where, When to Find: Oaks are the key for finding this species; a conspicuous year-round resident in live oak woodlands and valley oak savannas throughout, as well as in mountain forests and riparian woodlands where oaks are present. Even urban areas with oaks, from Paso Robles and Santa Barbara south to the northern and eastern outskirts of San Diego, have these woodpeckers, though they've declined in some areas. Resident on Santa Catalina and Santa Cruz Islands.

Did you know? The antics and calls of Acorn Woodpeckers outside his honeymoon cabin near Lake Sherwood inspired cartoonist Walter Lantz to create the "Woody Woodpecker" character.

Date & Location Seen:

Red-breasted Sapsucker
Adult *ruber*

Hybrid Red-breasted X
Red-naped Sapsucker

Red-naped Sapsucker
Adult Male

Description: 8 ½". A mottled black and white woodpecker with **mostly red head** and **pale yellow belly**. Like all sapsuckers, it shows a **long white patch on the wings**. The back and central tail feathers are barred with white and the rump is white. Many birds, especially when worn, show some black and white markings on the face.

Voice: A querulous, descending *mew* or *kwirr,* but rather silent for a woodpecker. Territorial males in the mountains "drum" in a unique, broken rhythm.

Behavior: Drills distinctive horizontal rows of small holes in tree trunks and limbs, returning to eat sap that collects in these wells (as well as trapped insects). Look for such signs on Brazilian peppers, eucalyptus, various orchard trees, and oaks. Quiet and unassuming.

Similar Species: Red-naped Sapsucker (*S. nuchalis,* 8 ½") is an uncommon fall and winter visitor throughout the area; it closely resembles Red-breasted, but has **black bordering the red throat** and a **black bar from behind the eye across the hindcrown** (with a red patch behind this on the nape). Female Red-naped usually shows much white on the chin. Hybrids between these two closely-related species are not infrequently seen.

Where, When to Find: Widespread in small numbers from October through March, even in residential areas and city parks. Breeds in mixed oak-conifer woodlands and riparian groves in the mountains; departs highest mountain areas in winter.

Did you know? Despite the apparent damage sapsuckers inflict on trees, there is little evidence to suggest they are an important cause of tree death.

Date & Location Seen:

Male

Female

Description: 7 ½". This common small woodpecker has a **zebra-striped back**, black **spotting and barring on the sides**, **white spotted wings**, and thick black bars on the sides of the head. MALE has a red patch on the rear of the crown, lacking in FEMALE. As in all our woodpeckers of this genus, juveniles of both sexes have some red atop the crown.

Voice: Call is a short, staccato *p-r-r-t*, often drawn out as a long rattle *prt-prt-prrrrrrrrrrrt*; also a loud *quee-quee-quee* when birds interact. Birds on territory give a long steady drum with bill.

Behavior: Forages on trunks, limbs and small branches of a variety of trees (but especially oaks) and chaparral shrubs. Nest cavities are drilled in dead or dying limbs of oaks, sycamores, and other trees.

Similar Species: Ladder-backed Woodpecker (see p. 473) is closely similar, and both species are found around tree groves in the Antelope Valley; Ladder-backed has relatively wider white bars on the face and back, lacks the solid black uppermost back of Nuttall's, shows buffy cast on underparts, more black barring on outer tail feathers, and male has red extending farther toward forehead. Ladder-back's calls differ.

Where, When to Find: Year-round resident in oak and riparian woodland, low to middle-elevation mountain forests, and tall chaparral throughout; absent from Channel Islands, the southern and eastern deserts, and from many heavily urbanized areas.

Did you know? This species is nearly endemic to California, extending a short ways south into northwestern Baja California. It is known to hybridize with Ladder-backed on the western edge of the deserts, and very rarely with Downy from Santa Barbara to San Diego Counties.

Date & Location Seen:

Male

Female

Description: 6 ¾". Our **smallest woodpecker**, with **long white back stripe**, buffy-white underparts, and white-spotted wings. The **bill is very short**. MALE has red bar on nape, lacking in FEMALE.

Voice: Call is a soft *pik*; another distinctive call is a descending whinny, *dee-dee-dee-dee…* Territorial birds give a single drum roll, quieter than that of larger woodpeckers.

Behavior: An acrobatic woodpecker, foraging on small branches and twigs as often as on larger limbs. Drills a nest cavity with an entrance only 1 ¼" in diameter, often in a willow.

Similar Species: Nuttall's Woodpecker (p. 261) has black-and-white barred back and is more heavily marked below. Hairy Woodpecker (p. 265) is very similar but much larger, with a much longer bill and louder, sharper call note.

Where, When to Find: Year round resident in lowland and foothill willow woodlands, as well as in groves of other deciduous trees (including ornamental birches, liquidambars, plain trees in some urban areas). Formerly rare in Orange and San Diego Counties, it has now expanded over much of that region. It is absent from the Channel Islands; a few wander onto the desert and into the higher mountains.

Did you know? This woodpecker is found widely through North America, but its range gives out just south of our area.

Date & Location Seen: _____

Male

Female

Description: 9″. Like a **large version of the sparrow-sized Downy Woodpecker**; note especially the relatively **longer and stronger bill**. Outer tail feathers pure white.

Voice: Call is a loud, piercing *peek* or *pee-ik*. These calls may run into a long whinny, louder than Downy's and more on one pitch. Drum is a loud, strong roll.

Behavior: Bores into bark and wood with strong bill; often concentrates foraging on dead and dying trees.

Similar Species: Downy Woodpecker (p. 263) is much smaller, with short bill and softer call notes; Downy has black spots on white outer tail feathers (these are pure white in Hairy).

Where, When to Find: Year round resident in coniferous forests of the mountains, from big-cone Douglas-fir belt as low as about 2500′) to tree line. In Orange County just a few pairs occur high in the Santa Ana Mtns., and these have not been found in recent years. Formerly resident in cottonwood groves along major lowland rivers, but habitat loss now limits them to just a few sites, such as along the Santa Clara River in Santa Clarita. Almost never found in urban regions; very rare on deserts and along immediate coast (except in San Luis Obispo and northern Santa Barbara Counties), and unrecorded from the Channel Islands.

Did you know? This species has a huge range from Alaska and Canada south to Panama, and like many such widespread birds shows great geographical variation in size and plumage; the southernmost birds in Middle America are brown below and barely larger than a Downy.

Date & Location Seen: _____

_____

Male

Female

Description: 12". Large woodpecker. Our "Red-shafted" birds are generally **light brown above** with thin black crossbars and **white rump**; buffy white with **round black spots below**. **Black crescent across chest.** In flight shows **salmon-pink color in wings** and tail. MALE: red "whisker" mark, lacking in FEMALE. Rarely, late fall and winter birds show yellow wing color, red nape crescent, and (in males) black whisker mark; these are "Yellow-shafted" flickers; intergrades between red- and yellow-shafted birds show many "yellow-shafted" characters.

Voice: Common call is a piercing *keeeew* or *kleeew*; also gives a muffled *wur-wur-wu*r in flight and a *wick-a wick-a wick-a* series. Territorial birds give a long *wik-wik-wik-wik…* series, often followed by a drum.

Behavior: "Unwoodpecker-like"; often forages on the ground for ants, but also on trunks and limbs. Flashy wing color shows prominently in undulating flight.

Similar Species: Unmistakable, but see female Williamson's Sapsucker (p. 458), a smaller, uncommon species of conifer forests. Gilded Flicker (*Colaptes chrysoides*; 11"), a rare resident in easternmost Mojave Desert and Colorado River, has yellow wings and tail, broad black tail tip, head pattern like Red-shafted.

Where, When to Find: Resident in woodlands of foothills, mountains, and coastal regions, but has greatly decreased as a breeder in urban areas and is now gone from much of the coastal lowlands. Many migrants move into the area from late September through March, when seen almost anywhere (including the Channels Islands).

Did you know? Eastern/boreal "Yellow-shafted" and western "Red-shafted" flickers hybridize extensively where their ranges overlap on the Great Plains, and birds showing intermediate or combined characters are often seen in our region.

Date & Location Seen:

Description: 7 ½". A **bull-headed** flycatcher with faintly streaked **olive sides** and **white stripe down the center of the underparts** from the chin through the center of the breast and belly. Dark olive-gray above; white tufts may show above wings when perched. Wings long and pointed, even for a flycatcher; tail moderately short. As with nearly all of our flycatchers, the sexes are similar.

Voice: Song, usually only heard on the breeding territory, is a distinctive three-part whistle, with second note highest, last note downslurred: quick three beers! or whip wheee bew! Call a loud, measured *pip-pip* or *pilp, pilp.*

Behavior: Sits conspicuously with upright posture atop tallest available perch, often a dead treetop snag; undertakes long aerial pursuits for flying insects (and often returns to the same snag). Does not flick wings or tail.

Similar Species: Western Wood-Pewee (p. 271) is slightly smaller, slimmer, longer-tailed, and has a relatively smaller head and bill. The pewee shows a more muted in pattern (pale in center of underparts is not contrasting) and lacks streaks on the sides and flanks.

Where, When to Find: Summer resident (May to early September) mainly in conifer, mixed, and canyon woodlands of higher mountains, and very locally closer to coast where tall pines and eucalyptus augment native trees. Migrants scarce but widespread in lowlands from mid-April through May, and in September. Populations generally declining.

Did you know? This is one of our few landbirds to winter mainly in South America; only a couple have ever been found in winter in the our region.

Date & Location Seen: _____

Description: 6 ¼". A drab peak-headed flycatcher with dark olive gray upperparts, dull olive-gray breast with paler gray throat and belly. Wings are long and pointed, tail is moderately long. Indistinct grayish wing-bars; no eye-ring. In many ways seems intermediate between Olive-sided and smaller *Empidonax* flycatchers.

Voice: Quite vocal on breeding grounds. Common call is burry, descending *pee-ur*. "Dawn"-song more complex and monotonously repeated, e.g. *pee-ur pur-dil-ip*. Also gives cleared *pee-ye* and various sharp, sputtering notes.

Behavior: Perches upright, often on a conspicuous perch; aerial sallies for insects usually not as long or high as Olive-sided. Does not flick tail, but shivers wings briefly upon alighting. Usually in trees, but migrants may perch on low shrubs, fences.

Similar Species: See Olive-sided Flycatcher (p. 269). Compared with *Empidonax* (see especially Willow Flycatcher, p. 273), wood-pewee has larger head, longer wingtip that reaches nearer tail tip, darker plumage, and does not flick tail.

Where, When to Find: Summer resident (late April to early September) in oak, canyon riparian, and conifer woodlands. Most common in the higher mountains, but nests to near sea level on north coast, Santa Monica Mtns. Migrants widespread late April through early June, and August through September. Absent in winter, when they are in South America.

Did you know? In May and June wood-pewees on their breeding grounds may begin singing before dawn.

Date & Location Seen: _____

Spring

Fall Immature

Description: 5 ¾". The small look-alike flycatchers in the genus *Empidonax* are best identified by their calls, subtle plumage differences, bill size, and wing and tail length. Willow **lacks an eye-ring**, has relatively **long, broad bill** (orangish underneath). **Throat whitish**, **upperparts tinged golden-olive**; only a hint of yellow on belly. Dull whitish wing-bars. Larger and longer-tailed than most other *Empidonax*. JUVENILE: wing-bars buffy (dull whitish in adults).

Voice: Call is a rich *whit* or *pweet*. Song (often heard in spring migration) is a snappy, burry *witz-beeeur*!, also a rough *breeet*.

Behavior: The Willow flicks its tail quickly upward, like all our *Empidonax* except Gray Flycatcher. Migrants often perch on open shrubs, fence lines.

Similar Species: Our other small flycatchers have strong eye-rings. Pacific-slope (p. 279) more green and yellow; Hammond's (p. 275) has tiny bill, shorter tail; Gray (p. 277) dips tail downward. See also Western Wood-Pewee (p. 271).

Where, When to Find: Fairly common and widespread migrant from mid-May to early June, and again from August to early October. Formerly bred in wet willow thickets, but breeders are virtually gone from our region; remaining breeders are found on South Fork of Kern River, a few rivers in San Diego, Santa Barbara and Ventura Counties, and the lower Colorado River (where many breed in salt cedar thickets). Singing birds in our area in mid-June almost always prove to be migrants. Our migrants breed mainly from n. California to British Columbia.

Did you know? The breeding subspecies in southern California, *extimus*, is listed as endangered and has disappeared from most of its range in the region.

Date & Location Seen: _____

Hammond's Flycatcher

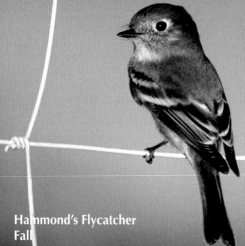

Hammond's Flycatcher
Fall

Description: 5 ½". Our smallest *Empidonax*, with **small, mostly dark bill**, relatively short tail, **olive-gray breast**, **grayish head**, long wingtip. White eye-ring broadest at rear. The large head, small bill and eye-ring give this small flycatcher a kinglet-like appearance. Fresh fall birds more yellow and olive overall.

Voice: Call, a soft *peep*, differs from calls of our other small flycatchers. Song not normally heard in our region.

Behavior: Flicks tail strongly upward, also flicks wings. Forages within canopy of shady woodlands, making quick sallies for insects; migrants may sometimes be found in more open habitats.

Similar Species: Dusky Flycatcher (p. 277) extremely similar; has slightly longer bill and shorter wingtip, paler head, very different call. Gray Flycatcher (p 277) is paler and grayer with longer bill that is mostly pinkish below, and longer tail that is dipped downward (not flicked up); call differs.

Where, When to Find: A fairly common and widespread migrant from early April to early May and an uncommon migrant from September to mid-October; winters very rarely in the region, with most heading south to Mexico and Guatemala. Breeds north of our region, from California's Sierra Nevada north to Alaska.

Did you know? Unlike the closely-related Dusky Flycatcher, Hammond's undergoes its complete annual molt before it leaves its breeding grounds and therefore migrates south later in the autumn.

Date & Location Seen:

Dusky Flycatcher

Gray Flycatcher

Description: 5 ¾"/6". Both very similar to Hammond's Flycatcher but slightly paler, longer-billed, longer tailed, and shorter-winged. DUSKY has olive back, grayish head with white eye ring and pale lores, pale underparts washed pale yellow on belly; medium-length bill variably pale below. GRAY is more olive-gray above, whiter below, with thin white eye ring; its relatively long bill has small blackish tip to pinkish lower mandible.

Voice: Both give soft *whit* call. On territory DUSKY also gives *dee-hic* notes and song of short phrases, e.g. *see-pit, gr-reep, seet*. GRAY's song two-parted, *chi-bit, greeep*.

Behavior: Typical *Empidonax* behavior, perching within or at edge of shrubs and low trees, with quick sallies for insect prey. Territorial birds may sing from high perches in conifers, oaks. DUSKY flicks tail upward; GRAY (unique among our small flycatchers) dips tail downward, then raises it.

Similar Species: Hammond's (p. 275) best told by unique *peep* call, small mostly dark bill, large head, and longer primary projection.

Where, When to Find: DUSKY is the common breeding *Empidonax* flycatcher of the high mountains (Big Pine Mtn., Mt. Pinos region and San Gabriel Mtns. south to Cuyamaca Mtns.), found late April to August where coniferous forest is broken by chaparral or meadows. Very uncommon spring and fall migrant through the northern deserts (late April to May, mid-August to early October); rarely detected on southern deserts; rare migrant on coast, with a very few winter records. GRAY breeds sparingly in arid conifers of northeastern parts of the San Gabriel and San Bernardino Mtns., and a few nest just west of the Mt. Pinos region in nw. Ventura Co.; uncommon migrant through lowlands (mainly April and early May, and September), with a few wintering throughout.

Did you know? Egg-laying dates of Dusky Flycatchers in the California mountains depend on the snowpack – in some large snowpack years eggs are not laid until July.

Date & Location Seen: _____

Description: 5 ½". **Yellowish** underparts (including throat) and yellow-tinged olive upperparts are usually distinctive, but the dullest birds may be told by **tear-drop shaped eye-ring** (pointed at rear), peaked crown, orangish lower bill, and hint of pale yellow on the throat.

Voice: Male gives a high, upslurred *psee-eeet!*, both sexes give a sharp, very high *seet*. Song, heard mostly in the early morning on the breeding territory, is a measured *psu-weeet, pit-ik, seep!*

Behavior: Flicks tail upward and sometimes shivers wings when perched. Forages within the canopy in shady canyon woodlands. The open cup nest is placed under loose bark, a root, or ledge on a shady bank (or sometimes under eaves or bridges).

Similar Species: The high-pitched call differs from *whit* or *peep* calls of our other *Empidonax.* Hammond's (p. 275) and Dusky (p. 277) have smaller, narrower bills, grayer heads and less yellow plumage (though in freshly fall plumage they can be strongly tinged yellow).

Where, When to Find: Our commonest nesting *Empidonax*, breeding from mid-March to August in shaded riparian and oak woodlands of canyons and even some well-wooded residential areas; a slightly duller subspecies nests on the Channel Islands. Migrants are found widely from March through May, and again (though less commonly) from August to early October. Rare in winter, mainly in wooded coastal areas.

Did you know? This species was formerly called the Western Flycatcher, but has been separated – perhaps questionably – from the nearly-identical Cordilleran Flycatcher of the Great Basin (including easternmost California), Rocky Mountains, and Mexican highlands.

Date & Location Seen: _____

Description: 7". This familiar, perky flycatcher is **blackish on the slightly crested head, breast and sides**, with dark gray upperparts and pale-edged blackish wings and tail; the **lower breast and belly are contrastingly white**. JUVENILE: differs from adult in having cinnamon-tinged wing-bars. Phoebes frequently **move and spread** their **tails in a strong arc**, and perch openly on wires, fence posts, open shrubs and buildings.

Voice: Call is a sharp, rich *chip*; song is a prolonged series of *fee-BEEE?, fee-BEER* phrases.

Behavior: A conspicuous, confiding species often found in close proximity to our dwellings, even in heavily urban areas. Phoebes make short sallies to the ground from an open perch to catch insect prey. The mud-lined nest is placed under building eaves, bridges, or natural sheltered sites.

Similar Species: Unmistakable; no other local flycatcher has strong black and white patterning; note that plumage pattern can resemble some juncos (p. 413), which are very different sparrow-like birds.

Where, When to Find: Common, though found singly or in pairs. A ubiquitous year-round resident, absent only from the higher mountains and desert scrub. Usually found near water, as around ponds, canyon bottoms, and irrigated areas (even gardens, small parks).

Did you know? Black Phoebes have a wide range from s. Oregon to n. Argentina but in the U. S. are mainly limited to the Southwest.

Date & Location Seen: _____

Description: 7 ½". An open-country flycatcher that is **grayish** above with a **salmon-colored belly** and contrastingly **blackish tail**. The head is flatter than that of the Black Phoebe, and the wings and tail are longer. JUVENILE has cinnamon wing-bars.

Voice: Call is a rich, down-slurred whistle *peeeew*. Song alternates downslurred *pdeeew* and rising *pi-di-reee?* Not as vocal as Black, and the song is usually only heard on breeding territories.

Behavior: Perches openly on fences, weed stems, and often even on bare ground. Most foraging takes place at ground level. The tail is dipped and spread in a broad, shallow arc when perched. Mud-lined nests are built under rock or building ledges.

Similar Species: See Ash-throated Flycatcher (p. 285) and kingbirds (pp. 287, 289). Females and immatures of rare Vermilion Flycatcher (p. 473) have lightly streaked breast, pale eye-line, and more limited pink or yellowish lower belly and undertail.

Where, When to Find: Fairly common winter visitor (September to March) to open fields, extensive park lawns and low scrub in the coastal lowlands. Fairly common year-round resident in open scrub and agricultural areas of the deserts; very common in winter in Imperial Valley. Also an uncommon breeding resident in dry, open valleys and foothills of the coastal slope (such as the Carrizo Plain, Simi Hills, Kenneth Hahn State Recreation Area in Los Angeles, and the interior foothills of Orange and San Diego Counties).

Did you know? Say's Phoebes have a huge latitudinal breeding range from near the Bering Sea shore in w. Alaska south to central Mexico. Our region hosts both breeding residents and migrants from well to the north.

Date & Location Seen: _____

Ash-throated Flycatcher

Brown-crested Flycatcher

ASH-THROATED FLYCATCHER
Myiarchus cinerascens

Description: 8 ½″. This medium-large, slender, bushy-crested flycatcher shows **rufous flashes in the wings and the long tail**, gray-brown upperparts, a **pale gray chest** and **pale yellow belly.** JUVENILE differs in its nearly entirely rufous tail.

Voice: Common calls include a sharp *bik* or *pip* and, on the breeding grounds, two-noted *ki-brick* and playground-whistle-like *pip-preeer*.

Behavior: Usually perches within the canopy of shrubs or trees, but sometimes more openly; perching posture is more horizontal than that of kingbirds or pewees. Does not dip or flick tail, but may crane its neck and bob the head when agitated. Nests in natural or woodpecker-excavated tree cavities or within open posts.

Similar Species: Brown-crested Flycatcher (*Myiarchus tyrannulus*; 9″), scarce and local summer resident in desert riparian (e.g. Kern River basin, Whitewater Preserve, Big Morongo Canyon, lower Colorado River), is larger, with heavier bill, more rufous in tail, different calls. Kingbirds lack rufous in wings and in their shorter tails, lack crested appearance. Say's Phoebe (p. 283) also lacks rufous in wings, has pinkish-orange (not yellow) belly, and frequently dips and spreads its black tail.

Where, When to Find: Fairly common spring and summer breeder, arriving late March or April (mid-March on southern deserts); most depart by mid-September, and only very rarely do individuals remain through the winter (most regularly in southeastern deserts). Breeds in a variety of open woodlands, from coastal oaks to open conifer forests and desert Joshua-trees.

Did you know? Three other closely similar species in Ash-throated's genus are casual or accidental visitors to our region; of these Dusky-capped Flycatcher (*M. tuberculifer*; 7 ¼″) is nearly as "expected" as Ash-throated in winter.

Date & Location Seen: _____

Description: 9". A boisterous and vocal flycatcher. Olive-gray above with a **yellow belly**. **Head and chest dark gray**, with **contrasting white chin patch**. **Dull blackish tail** has **narrow buff tip**. All of our kingbirds have a thin patch of orange-red in the center of the crown (lacking in juveniles), but this is almost always hidden.

Voice: Distinctive call is a loud *chi-BEER* or *CHEE-brrrr*, sometimes run into a series.

Behavior: Usually perches high in tall trees or on wires, sallying out to snatch flying insect prey. Very vocal. Often found in small flocks in winter, roosting in groups and spending the day eating berries as well as flying insects such as bees.

Similar Species: Western Kingbird (p. 289) is paler gray on head and chest, so white chin shows less contrast. Tail pattern differs, with Western's black tail bordered along the sides by white. Wings of Cassin's appear paler, with pale feather edges, and show more translucence in flight.

Where, When to Find: Locally fairly common and increasing year-round resident on the coastal slope; generally absent from the mountains and deserts, but some breed in eastern Mojave Desert woodlands. Best found in park-like settings with tall trees such as sycamores, eucalyptus; winter flocks easily found at El Dorado Park, Santa Fe Dam, and San Joaquin Marsh in Orange County, and around d Fallbrook and San Marcos in San Diego County.

Did you know? This is one of four North American bird species named for John Cassin, a renowned ornithologist in the mid-1800s.

Date & Location Seen: _____

Description: 8 ¾". Our most common yellow-bellied kingbird in spring and summer. **Upperparts pale gray** (sometimes slightly tinged with olive); the head and breast are also pale gray, with white throat showing little contrast. The **black tail has a thin white border** along the sides.

Voice: Common calls include a sharp *bik* and various sputtering notes; song is a *pik pik peek PEEK-a-loo* crescendo.

Behavior: Like all kingbirds, Westerns are pugnacious and are often seen harassing crows, ravens and hawks. Westerns generally perch lower than Cassin's, along fence lines and on tall weeds and shrubs (but also routinely perch in trees and on utility wires).

Similar Species: See Cassin's Kingbird (p. 287). Tropical Kingbird (*Tyrannus melancholicus*, 9 ¼"), rare fall and winter visitor from Mexico mainly to coastal areas, has much longer bill, yellow breast, brown tail with notched tip, and green-tinged upperparts.

Where, When to Find: A highly migratory kingbird, present in the Region mainly from mid-March to early September. A common migrant throughout the lowlands. Fairly common breeder in the open country that remains in the coastal lowlands, and a common breeder in desert agricultural regions and open rolling hills and valleys in other inland areas. Favors grasslands, agricultural fields and low scrub with scattered trees and shrubs. Westerns are rare after mid-September, and only a few have been noted locally in mid-winter.

Did you know? Males of Western (and other kingbirds) can be told from females by the slender, tapered tips to their outermost flight feathers (primaries).

Date & Location Seen: _____

_____

LOGGERHEAD SHRIKE
Lanius ludovicianus

Description: 9". A songbird turned bird of prey. Sleek but bull-headed; gray and white with a **bold black mask**. The black wings and tail show white patches. The thick **black bill is hooked at the tip**. JUVENILE: Like adults, but slightly barred brownish.

Voice: Generally quiet away from breeding territories, but sometimes gives a harsh scolding *jaahh jaahh jaahh*. The fairly unobtrusive song is a short series of gurgled or liquid two-note calls and musical bell-like notes.

Behavior: Perches openly on fence lines, wires, or the tops of shrubs or low trees, waiting to pounce on prey (large insects, lizards, small mammals and birds) with short flights. Flight is rapid and direct, often ending in a quick climb to a perch.

Similar Species: Northern Mockingbird (p. 355) similarly colored, but has thin bill, longer legs, lacks thick black mask, and shows more extensive white along the sides of its tail.

Where, When to Find: Found in open fields, grasslands and agricultural areas with scattered shrubs and trees. Only a few pairs of this once-abundant predator are still found in our coastal lowlands; small numbers of migrants augment this tiny population from July to March. Shrikes still breed uncommonly in the more rural inland areas, and shrikes are fairly common year-round residents in the deserts (with additional birds in winter). Channel Islands populations (of two island-endemic subspecies) much reduced; a few are still found on Santa Catalina I. and the northern islands, and the San Clemente I. subspecies is Endangered.

Did you know? Many species of shrikes are declining worldwide; pesticides, loss of prey populations, and modification of open country habitat may be among the causes.

Date & Location Seen:

Bell's Vireo

Gray Vireo

Description: 4 ¾". Vireos, small arboreal songbirds with slightly hooked bills, are less active than warblers or kinglets. Bell's is a **drab grayish** vireo with indistinct **thin whitish wing-bars**, **whitish line over the eye** and short whitish arc under the eye. Fairly thin bill is pale on lower mandible. Long tail is often held cocked slightly upward and waved about.

Voice: Breeding birds sing incessantly, a rough, feisty warble, with alternating songs inflected upward and downward. Call is a harsh, wren-like scolding *chee-chee-chee.*

Behavior: Flits about shrubs and low trees with an expressive tail, but usually hard to see in dense riparian growth. Feeds on caterpillars and other insects. Their cup nests, placed low in shrubs, are often parasitized by Brown-headed Cowbirds.

Similar Species: Gray Vireo (*Vireo vicinior*; 5 ¼") breeds rarely in arid scrub, junipers of interior San Diego County, Mojave Desert mountains (almost unknown in migration); all gray with short thick bill, thin white eye-ring, single faint wing-bar; also expressive with long tail. Warbling Vireo (p. 299) is larger but has a shorter tail held in line with body; Warbling lacks thin wing-bar, has olive-brown cast to upperparts. Hutton's (p. 297) and Cassin's and Plumbeous (p. 295) vireos show strong wing-bars and spectacles.

Where, When to Find: Summer resident (late March to early September) in extensive scrubby willow thickets; most are found in larger flood control basins (e.g. Prado Dam, Hansen Dam) and along unchannelized creeks and rivers (e.g., a few sites along the Santa Clara River, several creeks in Orange County, and the Santa Margarita, San Luis Rey and San Dieguito Rivers in San Diego Co.). Rarely seen in migration.

Did you know? The coastal California subspecies ("Least" Bell's Vireo) is listed as Endangered, having declined through loss of quality riparian habitat and low breeding success from brood parasitism by a burgeoning population of cowbirds. Localized cowbird trapping has allowed considerable recovery.

Date & Location Seen:

Cassin's Vireo

Plumbeous Vireo

Description: 5 ½". An **olive-gray** vireo with white throat, pale yellow sides, gray head with **bold white spectacles**, and **white wing-bars**. Rather stocky and short-tailed, with a heavy bill.

Voice: Song consists of well-spaced, short slurred phrases, some fairly clear, others harsh and burry. Common call is a descending scold: *shep, shep, shep, shep.*

Behavior: Forages sluggishly in tall shrubs and trees, sometimes quite high. Tail is held straight; no tail or wing flicking. Cup nest is suspended from twig fork.

Similar Species: Plumbeous Vireo (*Vireo plumbeus*; 5 3/4") larger, bigger-billed, gray above, with little or no yellow tint to flanks; scarce breeder in arid montane woodlands (e.g., ne. San Bernardino Mtns.), sparse winter visitor to coastal slope (often outnumbering Cassin's, especially southward). Hutton's Vireo (p. 297) lacks contrasting gray head and white throat; spectacle of Hutton's is interrupted above eye (complete in Cassin's). Warbling Vireo (p. 299) lacks wing-bars.

Where, When to Find: Uncommon summer resident (April to August) in oak and mixed oak-conifer woodlands of the higher mountains, mostly above 4000'. Most easily found in stands of canyon live oak, as slopes of Mt. Wilson or Mt. Pinos. Uncommon spring migrant (late March to mid-May) through foothills and lowlands; rather rare fall migrant and winter visitor in well-wooded parks.

Did you know? Cassin's and Plumbeous Vireos, along with the Blue-headed Vireo of eastern North America, were formerly considered the same species, called the "Solitary Vireo."

Date & Location Seen:

Description: 5". A small, compact **olive-green** vireo, **pale olive below** tinged slightly yellow. **White wing-bars**; thick **whitish eye-ring** (broken by olive above the eye) tends forward to bill as a broad spectacle. Legs blue-gray.

Voice: Song is a monotonous repetition of burry, slurred phrases, such as *dzuwee, dzuwee, dzuwee…* or *zweeu, zweeu, zweeu…* Calls include a scolding *ree-dee-dee-dee.*

Behavior: An arboreal gleaner, taking caterpillars and other insects from leaves and twigs. May flick wings, kinglet-fashion, but behavior still fairly sluggish as is typical of vireos.

Similar Species: Ruby-crowned Kinglet (p. 343) is closely similar, but more active and "nervous"; the kinglet has thinner blackish legs, a very thin pointed bill, and only one prominent wing-bar (bordered behind by blackish bar at the base of the flight feathers). See Cassin's Vireo (p. 295).

Where, When to Find: Year-round resident in oak woodlands and mixed oak-riparian or oak/chaparral interface, usually below 6000'. Although mainly a bird of coast live oaks, it breeds also in lowland riparian areas on the coastal slope, but is absent in most flat coastal lowlands except as scarce winter wanderer. Casual wanderer to the deserts.

Did you know? A unique subspecies of Hutton's Vireo found only on Santa Catalina I. is named *Vireo huttoni unitti* after Philip Unitt, long-time editor of the journal Western Birds and ornithologist at the San Diego Natural History Museum.

Date & Location Seen: _____

Description: 5 ½". A plain vireo **without wing-bars. Pale grayish olive** with a **pale eyebrow** and short pale line under the eye. Brighter birds, especially in fall, are tinged yellow on the sides. Bill and legs gray.

Voice: Song is a long rambling warble with many changes in pitch, e.g. *wilcheeweedeewhewcheweedeewill,* usually incorporating high fussy notes. Calls include a short *vit* and scolding *eeah.*

Behavior: Typical deliberate vireo gleaning behavior, working slowly through foliage gleaning insects; sometimes briefly hovers to pick food off leaves. Like most vireos, can sing incessantly while foraging.

Similar Species: Our other expected vireos have wing-bars (faint in Bell's). Vireos are told from warblers by theirs more sluggish behavior and heavier, hooked bills. Differ from small flycatchers in horizontal posture, gleaning behavior.

Where, When to Find: Rather common and widespread migrant March through May and mid-August to mid-October. Breeds (April to August) in streamside woodlands of sycamores, alders and cottonwoods, and in shady oak woodlands, from near the coast to about 7,000', but has declined greatly in recent decades.

Did you know? The Warbling Vireos in eastern and western North America may represent two different species; eastern birds are larger and their songs differ.

Date & Location Seen: _____

_____

Western Scrub-Jay

Island Scrub-Jay

Description: 11 ½". The familiar "blue" jay in the coastal lowlands and foothills of the region. Slender and long-tailed. **Deep blue above** with a **brown back patch,** pale gray underparts separated from white throat by a **partial blue collar. Lacks a crest.** JUVENILE: like adult but mostly gray-brown on head, collar gray and indistinct.

Voice: Main calls are a harsh, upslurred *jaaay?* or *jreeee?* and (usually in flight) a rapid series of *sheelp, sheelp…* notes. Interacting birds may give a dry rattle.

Behavior: Bold and familiar, scrub-jays are easily drawn to backyards with peanuts or sunflower seeds. Acorns form an important natural food, but these versatile omnivores also eat other seed, insects, and often eggs and nestlings of songbirds.

Similar Species: Steller's Jay (pp. 461) of mountain and foothill forests has conspicuous crest and is entirely blue below. **Island Scrub-Jay** (*Aphelocoma insularis*, 13") is found only on Santa Cruz Island, where it is the only jay; similar to Western but larger, heavier-billed, deeper blue.

Where, When to Find: Common resident through most of the region, being absent only in the highest portions of the mountains and the floor of the deserts. Found in a variety of scrubby and woodland habitats from sea level to about 6,000', and quite adaptable throughout our urban areas. A grayer, more slender-billed interior subspecies inhabiting oak and pinyon habitats in some of the higher mountains of the eastern Mojave Desert may best be considered a separate species (sometimes called "Woodhouse's Scrub-Jay".

Did you know? Scrub-jays have excellent spatial memory, and will return to retrieve acorns, peanuts, and other food items they have hidden away under leaves or in crevices.

Date & Location Seen: _____

Description: 17". Unmistakable **iridescent black** bird with **white belly and wing patches; very long pointed tail. Bill yellow**, as is variable bare skin patch below eye.

Voice: Nasal *meg? meg?* calls along with other harsh scolds.

Behavior: Found in loose flocks, foraging as they walk along ground or flying with deep buoyant wing beats. Nests, often in loose colonies, are deep stick piles high in trees.

Similar Species: Black-billed Magpie (*Pica hudsonia*; 18") similar but bill black, lacks yellow facial skin; found just north of us in Owens Valley and has wandered accidentally onto our northern deserts (and also as an escapee in coastal regions).

Where, When to Find: Localized in oak savannahs from the Santa Ynez Valley of Santa Barbara County north through interior San Luis Obispo County; often seen in the wine regions in these areas (though habitat conversion has led to declines here); rarely closer to coast (Morro Bay, Goleta) and until late in the 19th century found southeast to Los Angeles/Ventura County line. A few found in northwesternmost Kern County.

Did you know? Yellow-billed Magpies are found exclusively in California, mainly in the Central Valley and bordering foothills to the west.

Date & Location Seen: _____

Description: 17". Familiar large, chunky **all black** bird. **Heavy black bill, square or slightly rounded tail.** JUVENILE: plumage dull sooty; recently fledged young show pink on the base of the bill.

Voice: Harsh *cawwr* or *caw, caw caw* series, changing in quality with context. Interacting birds can give a loud dry rattle.

Behavior: Intelligent and inquisitive, crows forage in a variety of ways including scavenging dead animals, gleaning through trash, availing themselves of abundant seed or insect crops, and preying on small vertebrates or even intertidal invertebrates. Though bold and abundant, they are wary of people. Crows can gather into huge winter roosting flocks around tree groves in inland valleys and large coastal parks.

Similar Species: Common Raven (p. 307) is "like a crow, only more so." Raven has long, more pointed wings, longer wedge-shaped tail, heavier bill, and shaggy lance-like throat feathers. Crows almost never soar, unlike ravens. Also note deeper calls of raven. Male Great-tailed Grackle (p. 431) has much longer tail, whitish eyes.

Where, When to Find: Common year-round resident throughout the coastal lowlands and foothills, from the most urbanized areas through suburbs to a variety of open woodlands and orchards. Absent from the high mountains, and found only rarely on the deserts (a few have colonized cities in the Antelope Valley and elsewhere, and winter flocks sometimes found in the Imperial and Colorado River valleys). On the Channel Islands found only around Avalon.

Did you know? Crow populations have greatly increased since the 1970s, aided by ongoing tree planting, provision of food and garbage, and shooting bans; they have spread to south coastal San Diego County in the past twenty years.

Date & Location Seen: _____

Description: 24". Our largest songbird, being almost half again the length and twice the weight of a crow. **All black**, with long pointed wings, a **wedge-shaped tail**, **very heavy black bill**, and thin lance-like feathers on the throat. JUVENILE: like adult, but duller black, and with variable pink on the bill.

Voice: A deep, resonant croak, e.g. *craaaah* or *kronk*. Also a hollow knocking call and higher gurgling notes.

Behavior: Unlike crows, ravens routinely soar high in the air like hawks. Omnivorous, often seeking road kills along highways; many forage at landfills, around trash dumpsters. Effective predators, they also take rodents, reptiles, and eggs and young of many kinds of birds.

Similar Species: See smaller American Crow (p. 305). Soaring birds suggest hawks, but note pointed wings, wedge-shaped tail, and glossy black plumage (though reflected sunlight can make ravens look partly white in some lighting).

Where, When to Find: Common year-round resident in foothill and mountain areas, and abundant throughout the Mojave Desert (where increasing populations are impacting desert tortoises); less common on the Colorado Desert and scarce on the northernmost coast. Ravens are found in a variety of open and rugged mountain habitats, but are also found locally in urban areas (even downtown Los Angeles) and along the more rugged coastlines (including all the Channel Islands).

Did you know? Ravens are considered among the most intelligent of all birds.

Date & Location Seen:

Male

Juvenile

Description: 7 ¼". A flocking sparrow-like bird of open country. Pinkish-brown above, mostly white below. **Tail black with brown center and white edges**. MALE: **Black bib** on chest, black cheek patch, black bar across forecrown with small projecting feathers ("horns"). **Throat and eyebrow yellow**. FEMALE: Like male, but duller with less contrasting pattern. JUVENILE: Streaky, suggesting a sparrow or pipit. Desert birds are paler than coastal and Channel Islands birds.

Voice: Song starts with short *terp* notes, followed by a rising, tinkling flourish; often given in sustained flight. Flight calls include *tseep*, *tew*, and *zip* notes.

Behavior: A ground bird, but will perch on low shrubs, fence lines. Found in pairs in the breeding season, but gathers into large flocks (sometimes thousands) in fall and winter that wheel about low over open fields.

Similar Species: American Pipits (p. 361), which also flock in open country, are darker, more slender, streaked on breast. Sparrows have thicker, more conical bills.

Where, When to Find: Common breeder in open grasslands and sparse desert scrub in the deserts (including the Carrizo Plain and San Joaquin Valley) and adjacent rolling hills. Large flocks gather in these areas from September to March (especially in bare or closely cropped agricultural fields). Uncommon and declining in remaining open grasslands on coastal slope, with nearly all remaining sites threatened by urban development; winter flocks are now found only locally on coastal slope as open fields disappear. Common resident on the Channel Islands.

Did you know? This is our only true lark; the meadowlark is actually a relative of the blackbirds.

Date & Location Seen:

Male

Male

Female First-year

Female

Description: 5 ¾". A bi-colored swallow, **entirely dark above** (including through the eyes), **white below**. **Tail slightly forked**. MALE: Deep **iridescent steel blue** to blue-green above, pure white below; FEMALE: variable; usually much duller above than male, with slaty-brown cast. JUVENILE: brown above, variable tinge of gray across breast.

Voice: Calls have rich, liquid quality: *treep* or *chirp*. Song is a series of liquid chirps and whistles.

Behavior: Like all swallows, spends most of the day on the wing foraging for flying insects. Perches on wires, bare twigs, bulrushes, often over water. Nests in cavities in riparian trees; uses nest boxes near lakes, marshes.

Similar Species: See Violet-green Swallow (p. 313). Bank Swallow (p. 315) resembles juvenile Tree but has distinct brown breast band, pale brown rump, pale area behind cheeks. Purple Martin (*Progne subis*; 8"), now a rare migrant and scarce and local breeder in oaks and conifers in Tehachapi Mtns., north coast ranges, and San Diego County Mtns., is much larger than other swallows, with strongly notched tail; adult males are entirely shiny blue-black.

Where, When to Find: Common migrant (February to April) throughout, often concentrating around lakes, freshwater marshes. Fairly common fall migrant and uncommon and local winter visitor (mainly around coastal slope marshes, estuaries and Salton Sea, Colorado River). Uncommon to locally common breeder, especially where next boxes have been provided (e.g. Kern River Preserve, Saticoy and Santa Clara River mouth in Ventura Co., Ballona Freshwater Marsh in Playa del Rey, San Joaquin Marsh in Irvine, San Luis Rey River).

Did you know? This is the most common swallow in mid-winter in our area.

Date & Location Seen: _____

Male

Male

Description: 5 ¼″. A small, **short-tailed, green-backed** swallow with white underparts, **white on face over eye**, and **white sides to rump**. MALE: bright felt-green back and crown, violet rump. FEMALE: duller back and rump; face pattern more obscure. JUVENILE: even duller, little pattern to dusky face, dusky on back.

Voice: Most common call is a double-noted *tsew-tsip* or *chew-lip*. Song is a rhythmic series of *chip*, *tseep*, and *chew* notes.

Behavior: A swallow of wooded areas, spending more time perching in trees than other swallows. Nests in woodpecker-drilled cavities in conifers, sycamores or other trees; locally also nests in holes in cliff faces.

Similar Species: See Tree Swallow (p. 311), which is larger and longer-tailed, has dark crown down to eye, and lacks distinct white rump patches; beware that white on flanks of Tree can sometimes almost appear as rump patches.

Where, When to Find: Common spring migrant throughout the lowlands from February to April; less common in fall, and later than most other swallows (flocks of migrants are often noted in in October during storms). Common breeder in conifer and mixed forests in the foothills and mountains from April through August; a few nest closer to the coast, e.g. in Morro Bay, Santa Monica Mtns., and San Onofre. Rare and irregular winter visitor in the coastal lowlands, especially around wetlands in foothill regions.

Did you know? These swallows can be active and very vocal well before dawn in the mountains in summer.

Date & Location Seen: _____

Northern Rough-winged Swallow

Bank Swallow

Description: 5 ½". A **dull brown** swallow with mostly white underparts; **dingy gray throat and breast**. Tail squared or very slightly notched. JUVENILE: resembles adults, but with cinnamon wing-bars.

Voice: Calls are short, burry, e.g. *brrrt* or *prrrrit.*

Behavior: Flight buoyant, with floppy, swept-back wing beats. Often forages over water. Nests in holes in earthen banks, but in urban and suburban settings more typically in weep holes or drain holes in bridges, retaining walls or concrete river channels.

Similar Species: Dullest female Tree Swallows (p. 311) are slatier above, and show more contrast between the dark upperparts and whitish underparts. **Bank Swallow** (*Riparia riparia*, 5") is smaller, shorter-winged, paler backed, and shows a distinct dark breast band contrasting with white throat; it is an uncommon spring migrant (mainly April-May) and fairly common fall migrant (August-September) through the deserts (fewer in coastal area), and former breeder in coastal and river valley colonies.

Where, When to Find: Common migrant and breeding summer resident from February through August; found throughout the coastal lowlands, especially near canyon bottoms, creeks and flood control channels. Also breeds in the Coachella, Imperial and Colorado River valleys and locally elsewhere on the deserts. A few remain through the winter, mainly around lowland flood control basins.

Did you know? "Rough wing" refers to the sandpaper-like serrations on the outer edge of the outermost flight feathers.

Date & Location Seen: _____

At mud nest

Description: 5 ½". A **square-tailed** swallow with a **chestnut throat and cheek that contrasts with the white underparts**. **White forehead** contrasts with dark cap; upperparts with white back streaks and a distinct **deep buff rump** patch. JUVENILE: Duller and less strongly patterned, with variable white spotting in dull brown throat.

Voice: Calls include rough *vrrrt* or *veer* notes, a more musical *veeew*, and a prolonged song of grating, creaking notes.

Behavior: Often found in large flocks. Typical flight includes circling and steep upward climbs. The distinctive gourd-shaped nest, made of mud pellets, is placed under a protective ledge (commonly on highway overpasses, bridges over rivers or aqueducts, on dam faces, or under eaves of houses).

Similar Species: Distinct buff rump patch differs from all of our other swallows. Beware short-tailed juvenile of Barn Swallow (p. 319); it has dark forehead, noticeably forked tail. Wings broader and relatively shorter than Tree or Barn Swallows.

Where, When to Find: Common migrant and breeding summer resident throughout the region's lowlands, foothills and open areas in the mountains from late February to August; large flocks of these and other swallows are found in early spring around bodies of water. Winters mainly in South America; seen only very rarely after September in our region.

Did you know? This species' famous annual March 19th return to San Juan Capistrano Mission is simply a gimmick to promote tourism, but with some basis in the predictable annual cycles of migratory birds; urbanization has nearly eliminated swallow populations at the mission.

Date & Location Seen: _____

Description: 6 ½". A large, slender swallow with a **very long, forked tail**. MALE: Deep **steel blue above**, with a **chestnut forehead and throat**, **orangish underparts**. White spots show on the spread tail. FEMALE: resembles male, but tail shorter, underparts a bit paler. JUVENILE: Tail even shorter, but still strongly forked; underparts whitish-buff.

Voice: Common call is a scratchy *vit*. Song combines *vit* calls and other scratchy notes; also a strong upslurred whistle, e.g. *vit-wheeet?*

Behavior: Often found near water. Builds a mud cup nest on a ledge with a protective overhang; in our area nests are often under piers and other harbor structures, but also nests under bridges and building ledges near water in inland localities.

Similar Species: No other swallow combines the orangish underparts and very long forked tail. Shorter-tailed juveniles can suggest Cliff Swallow (p. 317), but have dark rump and prominent tail notch.

Where, When to Find: Common migrant and locally fairly common breeding summer resident in the lowlands mainly from March to September; fall migrants pass widely and commonly through the region as late as October. Small numbers remain through the winter around lowland lakes and flood control basins and at Salton Sea.

Did you know? Most of North America's Barn Swallows winter in South America, and in recent decades some of these have remained there to establish nesting populations.

Date & Location Seen: _____

Description: 5 ¾". A small, fussy woodland bird. **Plain gray**, tinged slightly brown, and sporting a **short gray crest**. The bill is gray and wedge-shaped; the stout legs are gray. Sexes and age classes are similar.

Voice: Scolding calls include *si si cheeh* and high *tsee* notes. Gives a bewildering variety of simple songs, such as *pee-doo, pee-doo, pee-doo* or *tu-wee, tu-wee, tu-wee*; also a bubbly trill.

Behavior: Found in pairs or family groups. Gleans insects and seeds from twigs, branches and trunks of oaks and other trees, shrubs. Often hammers audibly with the bill. Nests in cavities in trees, and will sometimes take to nest boxes.

Similar Species: Bushtits (p. 323) are much smaller and longer-tailed, travel in large flocks. Mountain Chickadee (p. 463) has strong black and white head markings and lacks crest. Another relative, the Chestnut-backed Chickadee (*Poecile rufescens*, 4 ¾"), is found in riparian groves and coastal conifers of western Santa Barbara and San Luis Obispo Counties; it shows a dark cap and bib contrasting with white cheeks, and rufous on the back and rump.

Where, When to Find: Fairly common year-round resident in live oak woodlands, and where oaks are mixed with chaparral, conifers; also in riparian woodlands with oaks or cottonwoods. Found in pinyon-juniper woodlands on the desert slopes of the higher mountains. Penetrates urban areas in larger parks and well-planted residential neighborhoods, but absent from urban coastal lowlands. Wanders casually onto the deserts, but has never been found on the Channel Islands.

Did you know? A closely related species, the Juniper Titmouse (*Baeolophus ridgwayi*; 5") is found very locally in pinyon-juniper associations in the higher mountains of the eastern Mojave Desert.

Date & Location Seen: _____

Male (Coastal)

Male (Interior)

Female (Coastal)

Description: 4". Bushtits are **tiny,** plump-bodied, **long-tailed, gray birds** that **travel in large, busy flocks.** The crown, sides and flanks are slightly tinged brownish. Bill is short, stubby and black. MALE: eyes dark; FEMALE: eyes creamy white. Juveniles of both sexes are dark-eyed. "Lead-colored" subspecies in eastern Mojave pinyon-juniper woodlands has gray crown and pale brown ear patch, lower-pitched calls.

Voice: Flocks keep up a constant light, rapid twittering *pit…pit…pit*, with a variety of other short notes such as *tsee* or *spik*. When a hawk or other aerial predator is sighted, many birds in the flock emit a high, trilling alarm call (often a birder's best hint that a hawk is in the vicinity).

Behavior: Acrobatic gleaning birds, often hanging upside down from small twigs. Flocks may consist of a dozen to several dozen birds, moving frantically through shrubbery and crossing gaps in single-file flight lines. The distinctive nest is a soft hanging pouch, 8-10" long, with a small entrance high on one side.

Similar Species: Unmistakable by virtue of tiny size, long tail, and flocking behavior. Juvenile Verdin (p. 473), found only on the desert, has sharply pointed bill with yellowish base, does not travel in flocks.

Where, When to Find: A very common and familiar year-round resident in woodlands and chaparral below 6,000'. Found in oak and riparian woodlands, chaparral, and urban parks and gardens. Also found on Santa Cruz Island.

Did you know? Bushtits are found from sw. British Columbia to Guatemala; their closest relatives live in Eurasia.

Date & Location Seen: _____

Male

Description: 5 ¾″. A small, stubby-tailed gray and white climbing bird with a **dark crown**, **white face** and underparts, rufous area under the tail. **Bill is long, slender and chisel-like**. The gray and black tail shows white patches near the corners. MALE: Black crown and hindneck. FEMALE: Crown and hindneck dark gray.

Voice: Common call is a nasal *airrhh* or *eehr*. Also soft *ht, ht* notes. Song is a rapid series of rich *twhee, twhee…* notes.

Behavior: Acrobatic, creeping head-first down trunks and branches. Hammers at bark or seeds with wedge-tipped bill. Often found in pairs or small family groups.

Similar Species: Red-breasted Nuthatch (p. 463) has black line through eye, pale rusty underparts; much smaller Pygmy Nuthatch (p. 463) has dark cap that reaches the eye.

Where, When to Find: Common year-round resident in foothill oak woodlands and in coniferous forests (including dry pinyon woodlands); small numbers are also resident in lowland valley oak savannas, riparian woodlands with mature cottonwoods and sycamores, and some well-planted suburban parks. Wanders rarely in fall and winter to the deserts and the immediate coast. An interior subspecies (with very different stuttering call) breeds just north of us and rarely wanders to the northern, eastern deserts in fall and winter.

Did you know? Head-first creeping by nuthatches down trunks and branches is aided by an especially long and strong hind claw.

Date & Location Seen:

Rock Wren

Canyon Wren

Description: 6". A **pale gray-brown** wren with a **buffy belly**. Back speckled with white; the whitish **breast** is **finely streaked**. The barred tail is held in line with the body (not angled upward as in many wrens). Bill is long and thin.

Voice: Song is series of repeated cricket-like notes, *tr-ree, tr-ree, tr-ree…* or *jeer, jeer, jeer…* Calls include a trilled *pd-zeeee* and various scolding notes.

Behavior: Perches almost exclusively on rocks, talus slopes, and rocky desert soils, foraging for insects and spiders. Nests are built deep within rock crevices. Bobs up and down when agitated.

Similar Species: The **Canyon Wren** (*Catherpes mexicanus*; 5 ¾") is rich rusty, with a contrasting white throat and very long, slender bill. Its song is a beautiful cascade of clear whistled notes; call a loud, buzzy *zeep*. It is an uncommon and local resident in shaded canyons with granitic boulders or steep rock cliffs (e.g. Morro Rock, Kern River Canyon, Mission Canyon in Santa Barbara, Malibu Canyon, Big Santa Anita Canyon, and Orange County's upper San Juan Creek, Mission Gorge in San Diego).

Where, When to Find: Fairly common resident on rocky desert flats and slopes, talus slopes in mountains, and other rocky areas; locally inhabits artificial rock surfaces (such as face of Hansen and Santa Fe Dams). In winter additional migrants arrive in the region, sometimes occurring in less typical habitats.

Did you know? Rock Wrens have successfully colonized all of the California Channel Islands.

Date & Location Seen: _____

House Wren

Pacific Wren

Description: 4 ¾". A **plain brownish** wren with **fine black barring** on the wings, flanks, undertail and tail. Shows only a thin, indistinct eyebrow. The tail is moderate in length and often held cocked upward.

Voice: Calls include a rolling, trilled *aairrrrr,* a harsh, scolding *jihhhh, jihhhh,* a thinner *shhhihhh,* and mewing notes. The lively, bubbly song is a pleasing set of trills, sputters and fussy notes; it is one of the characteristic spring sounds in riparian and oak woodlands.

Behavior: Often delivers its song energetically from an exposed perch, with tail vibrating. Forages for insects, spiders, and grubs along branches, trunks, and in tangles. Nests in cavities, which may be aggressively commandeered from other birds.

Similar Species: See Bewick's Wren (p. 333), which has bold white eyebrow. **Pacific Wren** (*Troglodytes pacificus;* 4"), like a tiny, stub-tailed House Wren with deep rusty plumage tones, is a scarce winter visitor to damp, tangled woodland understory; more numerous (and nesting locally) in north coastal San Luis Obispo County.

Where, When to Find: Summer resident (March to September) in oak and riparian woodlands and mountain thickets; uncommon through the winter in thickets and well-planted parks and gardens in the foothills and coastal lowlands. Fairly common in winter along the Colorado River and at the Salton Sea; otherwise mainly a migrant in the desert regions.

Did you know? House Wrens are known to puncture the eggs of other songbirds and sometimes take over nest cavities.

Date & Location Seen: _____

Description: 4 ¾". A small, busy denizen of extensive marshes of cattails and bulrushes (tules). Well-marked, with a dark crown, **whitish eyebrow**, **black and white striped back**, and **rusty wings and rump**. Dull whitish breast, with tan sides and belly. The **short tail is often cocked vertically** or even forward over the back. JUVENILE: patterning more subdued than adult.

Voice: Common call is a hard *chet-chet*. The energetic song, given endlessly in the breeding season (and often even at night), is a variable set of rattles, gurgles and *tik* notes, such as *tuk, tik, jrrrrrrrr*.

Behavior: Perches on vertical reed stems, gleaning for insects. Often stays well hidden, but singing birds sometimes sit more openly. Nest is a woven structure attached to reeds.

Similar Species: Bewick's Wren (p. 333) lacks rusty tones and has a plain brown back.

Where, When to Find: A fairly common but localized year-round resident in some of the larger coastal estuaries such as Upper Newport Bay and freshwater marshes (abundant at Salton Sea, Colorado River, and Piute Ponds on the Edwards Air Force Base north of Lancaster). Much more widespread in winter, when found in a great variety of wetlands.

Did you know? The Marsh Wrens of eastern and western North America have different vocal repertoires (much more extensive in western birds) and differ slightly in appearance; they are considered separate species by some taxonomists.

Date & Location Seen: _____

BEWICK'S WREN
Thryomanes bewickii

Description: 5 ¼". A slender wren with a long tail that is often cocked upward at an angle and flipped from side to side. **Brown above** with a distinct **white eyebrow, grayish white below**. Undertail and upper surface of tail finely barred with black. White tail corners sometimes visible.

Voice: Quite vocal. Common calls include a buzzy, scolding *bzzzzz* and a scratchy *vvit* or *jik*. The complex and varied song starts with short introductory notes and buzzes and ends in a musical trill; individuals have a variety of different songs.

Behavior: A curious and often confiding bird of dense brush, constantly moving about and waving its long tail. Feeds on insects and spiders, often probing into loose bark, root tangles and crevices in stone walls. The nest is placed in a crevice, among exposed roots, or in an artificial cavity.

Similar Species: House Wren (p. 329) lacks the distinct white eyebrow, has a slightly shorter tail, and is more evenly gray-brown above and below. Marsh Wren (p. 331) has striped back, shorter tail, and rusty on wings and rump; usually only in marshes.

Where, When to Find: Common year-round resident in coastal scrub, chaparral, and dense desert scrub and in the brushy understory and edges of oak and riparian woodlands throughout. Mainly found below 5,000'. Absent from heavily urbanized areas, but found in suburban gardens and parks with enough shrubby growth.

Did you know? Bewick's Wrens are resident on most of the Channel Islands, but a subspecies found only on San Clemente I. is now extinct.

Date & Location Seen: _____

_____

Description: 8 ½". An **overgrown,** long-billed **streaky** wren with **chestnut crown**, **white eyebrow**, and **black spotted throat and chest**; black and white barring on wings and tail. White tail corners show in flight. Sexes of all wrens similar.

Voice: Call is a repetitious, low *kur-kur-kur…* or *kruh-kruh-kruh…* Also harsh grating calls, kek-kek-kek.

Behavior: Territorial males can be conspicuous as they sing from yuccas, ocotillos, or other taller plants; foraging birds are found on or near the ground. Nest (built for breeding and for roosting) is a large ball of twigs, grasses in cactus or other spiny plant.

Similar Species: Not likely to be confused with other wrens (all much smaller, plainer); compare with Sage Thrasher (p. 475).

Where, When to Find. Resident in Joshua trees, cactus scrub, and washes on the deserts, including Imperial (where local) and Colorado River valleys. On the coastal slope, small and declining populations persist in alluvial washes and dry hillside scrub with cactus in the Camarillo and Moorpark areas of Ventura County, at Big Tujunga Wash, and locally east in the foothills from the San Gabriel River to Pomona (e.g. Bonelli Regional Park) and San Bernardino. A population remains on the Palos Verdes Peninsula, and small populations occur in a few areas of coastal and interior Orange and San Diego Counties.

Did you know? Along with the California Gnatcatcher, this species is emblematic of the loss of hillside scrub habitats to urban development on the coastal slope; birds from southeastern Orange County though coastal San Diego County are considered a separate subspecies (*sandiegensis*) from the other southern California populations.

Date & Location Seen:

Breeding Male

Non-breeding

Description: 4 ½". A small, slender, and very active songbird; **blue-gray above**, **whitish-gray below** with a **white eye ring**. Long **black tail shows much white along the sides** (looks mostly white from below). MALE: black stripe on sides of forehead in breeding plumage, lacking in winter birds and immatures. FEMALE: Lacks black forehead mark; tinged slightly brownish above.

Voice: Call is a thin, peevish *speeeeee* or *speeee-peee*. Unimpressive song is a series of squeaky, wheezy notes and chips.

Behavior: Very active, flitting around low shrubs and mid-levels of trees while flipping the long tail from side to side. Makes frequent short sallies for flying insects as well as gleaning twigs and foliage.

Similar Species: See California (p. 339) and Black-tailed (p. 475) gnatcatchers. Bell's Vireo (p. 293) lacks black and white in its gray tail.

Where, When to Find: Uncommon to fairly common in winter (mainly September to March) in riparian woodlands, coastal sage scrub, chaparral and other brushy habitats in the coastal lowlands; fairly common in scrubby thickets in the Imperial and Colorado River Valleys. Breeds uncommonly in oak-riparian woodlands and dry coniferous forests (mainly pinions) in the foothills. Uncommon migrant in spring and fall through the deserts.

Did you know? Though widespread in the lowlands in winter, Blue-gray Gnatcatchers generally avoid urban habitats.

Date & Location Seen:

Breeding Male

Female

Description: 4 ½". A dirty grayish gnatcatcher with a **mostly black tail** that shows just a bit of white on the edges and tips of the outer tail feathers. The **underparts are medium gray**. MALE: has dark gray back and shows a **black forehead and crown** from late winter and to mid-summer (just a small black streak over the eye in non-breeding season); FEMALE: **strongly tinged with brown** on the back and flanks, lacks black on the head.

Voice: Call is a rising then falling *meeeew*, varying from nasal and kitten-like to harsh and scratchy. Also a scolding *chih chih chih*.

Behavior: Typical active gnatcatcher foraging, working low through scrubby growth. The nest is a small, soft cup in low shrub.

Similar Species: Blue-gray Gnatcatcher (p. 337) is cleaner gray and white, and shows much more white in the tail (best seen from below or when tail is spread). Blue-gray never shows a black cap or strong brown tones to the plumage.

Where, When to Find: Uncommon year-round resident in remnant tracts of coastal sage scrub in the coastal lowlands from se. Ventura County south. Most readily found on the coastal side of the Palos Verdes Peninsula, O'Neill Regional Park and various other localities in Orange County (e.g., Upper Newport Bay and Crystal Cove State Park), coastal San Diego County (e.g., Lake Hodges and many other sites).

Did you know? This gnatcatcher is found only in coastal southern California and the Baja California Peninsula; the subspecies in California (*californica*) is classified as Threatened because so much of its habitat has been lost to suburban sprawl.

Date & Location Seen: _____

Description: 7 ½". A **chunky dark gray semi-aquatic songbird** of rushing mountain streams with long pinkish legs and short tail (often cocked upward). JUVENILE: paler below, with yellowish beak.

Voice: Loud *zeet* or *zeet-zeet* call is audible about roaring of creek water. Loud song, often given in flight, includes paired whistles, buzzes.

Behavior: Perches on boulders along creeks, frequently bobbing up and down and "blinking" conspicuous white eyelids. Submerges into flowing water to forage on aquatic invertebrates, small fish. Flight is rapid and whirring. Nest, a ball of mosses, placed in spray zone of cascades.

Similar Species: Unmistakable. Black Phoebe (p. 281) also perches on rocks in creeks, but has white belly, very different shape.

Where, When to Find: Uncommon and localized resident along fast-flowing permanent mountain and foothill streams; typical localities include the Kern River in the vicinity of Lake Isabella, Sespe Creek, Big Santa Anita Canyon in the San Gabriel Mtns., the upper Santa Ana River in the San Bernardino Mtns., and the north fork of the San Jacinto River. Casually wanders to non-breeding streams, and to lower elevations, in winter, and breeding sites and numbers vary with rainfall and stream conditions.

Did you know? Adaptations for an aquatic existence include very dense plumage, extra-large oil glands for waterproofing, nasal flaps to keep water from entering the nostrils, and short, well-muscled wings for underwater propulsion.

Date & Location Seen: _____

Male Displaying Crest

Ruby-crowned Kinglet

Golden-crowned Kinglet
Female

Description: 4 ¼". This tiny, plump "neurosis with feathers" is a common winter visitor. **Olive** with a **white eye-ring** (broken above), **one bold white wing-bar bordered behind by a black bar** at the base of the flight feathers. Tiny thin bill, short notched tail and slender black legs with yellow feet. MALE: bright red crest, hidden except when bird is agitated. FEMALE: lacks red crest.

Voice: Call is a husky *ji-dit*, often run into an agitated series. Song starts with high, thin notes then builds into rich, warbled repeated phrases, amazingly loud for so tiny a bird.

Behavior: Extremely active, constantly flitting about and often flicking its wings. Often feeds by hovering briefly to pick insects off foliage. Found singly or in small, loose groups. Often forms the core of mixed-species groups of small insectivorous birds in winter.

Similar Species. Hutton's Vireo (p. 297) has very similar plumage; the vireo is more sluggish, has a thicker bill, heavier blue-gray legs, and two strong wing-bars with no black bar behind them. **Golden-crowned Kinglet** (*Regulus satrapa*; 4") sometimes visits the region's woodlands and parks in winter (and is a scarce breeder in the higher mountains); it differs in having black and white head stripes, a yellow or (male) yellow and orange crown patch, and very high, thin *see see see* call notes.

Where, When to Find: Common winter visitor throughout, mainly from late September to early April; found in woodlands, tall chaparral, thickets and gardens. A few have summered recently in fir forests high in the highest mountains, where formerly more numerous.

Did you know? Breeding populations in California's mountains have declined greatly.

Date & Location Seen:

Description: 6 ¼". A **fluffy-bodied**, **long-tailed brown bird** of dense brush, heard far more often than seen. **Breast is pinkish with indistinct thin streaks**. **Eyes whitish**. Bill short, stout, slightly curved.

Voice: Song, a characteristic sound of chaparral and brushy riparian habitats, is a series of *peep* notes, accelerating into a rapid trill, *peep, peep, peep-peep-pee-pee-pee-prrrrr*. Song of female is slower, with notes often doubled and no terminal trill. Call is a dry purring chatter.

Behavior: Flits about within dense brush, the thin, loose tail often angled upward. Gleans insects, also eats small berries. Found in closely associated pairs, the male and female frequently trading calls.

Similar Species: Wrens have thinner bills, dark eyes, very different calls.

Where, When to Find: Common year-round resident in chaparral and coastal sage scrub in foothills and lower mountains (to about 6,000'). Absent from most of the Los Angeles Basin, the Palos Verdes Peninsula, and coastal northwestern Orange County; unrecorded on the Channel Islands. Found locally on the desert slopes of the mountains, but otherwise absent from the arid interior. Very sedentary and rarely crosses tracts of unsuitable habitat.

Did you know? The Wrentit has no close relatives in the New World; DNA studies suggest its relationships lie with a group of Asian babblers known as parrotbills.

Date & Location Seen:

345

Western Bluebird
Male

Western Bluebird
Female

Mountain Bluebird
Male

Mountain Bluebird
Female

Description: 7". A plump thrush with short tail and long pointed wings. **Head, wings, rump and tail blue. Breast, sides, and variable patch on back rusty-brown.** MALE: blue areas deep, vibrant. FEMALE: plumage paler, more subdued. JUVENILE: spotted above and below with white.

Voice: Calls include a musical *phew* (often given in flight) and a rough chatter. Song consists of short warbled phrases.

Behavior: Versatile; hops on ground for insects, sallies into the air for flying insects, and picks berries from mistletoe, junipers, toyon, etc. Nests in tree cavities, nest boxes.

Similar Species: Mountain Bluebird (*Sialia currucoides*; 7 ¼") is an irregularly common winter visitor to open alfalfa fields and grasslands in the interior valleys; they nest in open habitats high in San Bernardino Mtns., Mt. Pinos. Males are uniformly bright sky blue; females are grayer with slight tan wash to breast. See Lazuli Bunting (p. 421).

Where, When to Find: Fairly common year-round resident in oak, conifer and riparian woodlands of foothills and mountains; now also widespread in large coastal lowland parks where nest boxes have been provided. Small flocks may be more widespread in winter, feeding on berries, insects in park-like situations.

Did you know? In winter in the lowlands Western Bluebirds often flock with Yellow-rumped Warblers and Lark and Chipping Sparrows.

Date & Location Seen:

Russett-backed group

Description: 6 ¾". *Catharus* thrushes are plump, thin-billed birds with spotted breasts and buffy wing stripes which show in flight. Swainson's is **uniformly russet brown on upperparts, wings, tail**. Broad **buff eye-ring; throat and breast buffy with brown spots;** sides and flanks brownish, belly white.

Voice: Song begins with querulous *queee*, followed by beautiful, fluty phrases that spiral upward. Calls include a liquid *whit* or *pwip*, and a rich *queee?*

Behavior: Feeds on insects deep within shady woodland understory, sometimes more openly on pathways, lawn borders. Migrants sometimes feed in small groups, and often visit fruiting shrubs. Does not flick wings or cock tail. Territorial birds sing from mid-story. This nocturnal migrant is often heard overhead in spring and fall, giving a distinctive *queee?* flight call.

Similar Species: Hermit Thrush (p. 351) shows contrast between brown or gray-brown upperparts and rusty tail, has whitish eye-ring, and blackish spots on creamy breast. Hermit frequently flicks wings and cocks tail, unlike Swainson's. Call notes differ.

Where, When to Find: Common spring migrant (late April and May) and generally uncommon fall migrant (September, early October) throughout the lowlands. Fairly common breeder (May to September) in riparian thickets north of Pt. Conception. Farther south, an uncommon and declining breeder in alder groves and tall willow woodlands in shady canyons (e.g. Big Santa Anita Canyon, Trabuco Canyon) and more rarely in extensive willow woodlands in the coastal lowlands (Harbor Regional Park, Villa Park Dam flood basin). Winters in Central America.

Did you know? Our Pacific Coast "Russet-backed" birds may well be a separate species from "Olive-backed" birds in the rest of North America (Olive-backeds winter in South America).

Date & Location Seen: _____

_____

349

Description: 6 1/2". Plain **grayish brown** to **brown above, with rump and tail contrastingly reddish brown.** Buffy-white on **breast with blackish spots**; sides and flanks grayish, belly white. Complete, **thin white eye-ring**. Breeding subspecies in mountains is slightly grayer, larger and longer-billed than our small, dark wintering birds.

Voice: Beautiful song begins with long whistle, then cascading fluty phrases; successive songs on different pitches. Calls include *chup* or *chup-chup*, a clear descending whistled *tew*, and a wheezy, rising *zhweee*.

Behavior: Hops on ground for insects, usually remaining in shade; often visits fruiting shrubs in winter. Usually seen singly. Rapidly flicks wings and slowly raises and lowers tail when perched.

Similar Species: Swainson's Thrush (absent in winter) is more uniform russet-brown above, with broad buff eye-ring, brown spots on buffy breast; doesn't flick wings or cock tail. Thin bill separates thrushes from sparrows.

Where, When to Find: Common from October to early April in parks, gardens, chaparral and woodlands in coastal lowlands and foothills; migrant and scarce winterer on the deserts. Our only spotted thrush normally present from November to early April. Small numbers breed in white fir forests above about 7,000' in the highest mountains (such as Mt. Pinos and high zones of San Gabriel and San Bernardino Mtns.).

Did you know? Many consider this species the finest songster in North America.

Date & Location Seen:

Male

Juvenile

Description: 10". A familiar large, plump thrush with gray-brown upperparts, **rufous-red breast**, and **white markings around the eyes**. MALE: Head blackish, breast deep reddish-orange; FEMALE: paler and duller, with gray-brown head. JUVENILE: heavily spotted with dusky on the breast, and with whitish on the wings and back.

Voice: Song is a pleasing carol of two- or three-noted rich whistled phrases. Calls include a hard *pup-pup*, a squealing *kli-kli-pup*, and a high, lisping flight call.

Behavior: Much of the time feeds mainly on the ground, often probing into moist soil for earthworms and grubs. Runs on the ground, with sudden stops. The nest is a mud-lined open cup. Winter flocks seek sources of berries, including toyon, mistletoe, and planted fruiting trees and shrubs such as pyracantha, olives, and palms; they often flock with waxwings.

Similar Species: Varied Thrush (*Ixoreus naevius*; 9 ½") is an irregular winter visitor to shaded woodlands, mainly in foothills and north coast; it is more furtive than robins, and differs in long orange eyebrow, gray or black breast band, and orange patterning on wings. See Black-headed Grosbeak (p. 417) and Spotted Towhee (p. 387).

Where, When to Find: Robins breed fairly commonly in moist woodlands of the mountains and foothills, and also in well-watered residential areas and urban parks in the lowlands. In winter they travel in nomadic flocks and can be very common where fruits and berries are available.

Did you know? Robins were not known to nest in the lowlands of the region until tree planting and irrigation afforded them suitable habitat.

Date & Location Seen:

Description: 10″. This familiar large and long-tailed songster is **gray** above and grayish-white below, with **large white patches on the wings** and **extensive white along the sides of the tail**. Eyes yellowish. The slender bill is slightly curved. JUVENILE: differs from adults in brown spotting on the underparts, dark eyes.

Voice: Famous song is rich, loud and varied; it consists of a huge variety of simple notes or phrases, each usually repeated 3-6 times. Many of these phrases are copied from other birds (or other familiar ambient sounds). Frequently sings at night in spring and summer. Calls include a harsh *chack* and a drawn-out scolding *shrrrrr*.

Behavior: Feeds on insects and berries. Often runs a few steps on the ground, then stops and flashes wings open in jerky fashion (which may serve social functions as well as flush up insect prey). Aggressive when protecting nest and fledglings.

Similar Species: Much scarcer Loggerhead Shrike (p. 291) has thicker, hooked bill, bold black mask. See female Phainopepla (p. 365), Townsend's Solitaire (p. 465).

Where, When to Find: Common year-round resident in urban areas, suburbs, orchards and ranch yards. Much less common in natural scrub and desert woodland habitats, though still widespread (including several Channel Islands). Absent from the higher mountains.

Did you know? Mockingbirds have thrived in human-modified landscapes, benefiting from irrigation and the planting of fruiting trees and shrubs. Even by the early 1900s famous ornithologist Joseph Grinnell had noted a five-fold increase in numbers in the Los Angeles region.

Date & Location Seen:

Description: 12". A large, long-tailed **brown** bird with a remarkable **long, decurved bill**. Brown plumage enlivened only by a whitish chin, dark "whisker marks" and **orangish-buff undertail coverts** and suffusion on belly.

Voice: Song is rich and varied, with phrases (including mimicry) repeated 2-3 times; it is choppier than a mockingbird's song, with harsher phrases and less repetition. Calls include a harsh *chelk* and a gurgling *gr-lik*.

Behavior: Terrestrial, scratching through the leaf litter with its long, curved bill for seeds, insects. Runs on the ground; flight is labored, low. Hard to see except when vocalizing, when it often perches atop a shrub or low tree.

Similar Species: California Towhee (p. 391) has similar plumage, but a very different short, conical bill. Range overlaps slightly on the western edges of the deserts with paler Le Conte's Thrasher (p. 475). Similar Crissal Thrasher (p. 475) is restricted to southeast and easternmost deserts.

Where, When to Find: Fairly common year-round resident in chaparral, brushy riparian thickets throughout coastal slope. Extends to western edge of deserts around Palmdale, Morongo Valley, Yaqui Well in Anza-Borrego, and upslope to about 5000'. Scarce or absent from the coastal lowlands and urbanized areas. Unrecorded from the Channel Islands.

Did you know? This thrasher is almost exclusively found in California, extending just a short ways into northwestern Baja California.

Date & Location Seen:

Juvenile

Breeding
Adult

Non-breeding

EUROPEAN STARLING
Sturnus vulgaris

Description: 8 ½". A stocky **blackish** songbird with a **short, squared tail** and pointed brown wings. **Straight, pointed bill**; dull pinkish-orange legs. BREEDING: Body plumage **iridescent black, bill bright yellow** (base bluish in males, pinkish in females) WINTER: Plumage **heavily spangled with whitish** spots, bill blackish; white spotting wears away in late winter to reveal breeding dress. JUVENILE: gray-brown throughout, with dark bill and lores, but shows distinctive starling shape.

Voice: Extremely varied; song incorporates much mimicry (including entire songs of species such as Western Meadowlarks and California Quail). Buzzes, clicks, rattles and high squealing characterize the prolonged song. Calls include a buzzy *dzeeer*, harsh *shurrr*, and sharp *vit* predator alarm call.

Behavior: Waddles on ground, using gaping motion of bill to probe lawns, soil. Flocks also exploit fruit (grapes, olives, palm fruits, etc.), grain, and even tidal wrack and estuarine mudflats. Flies with rapid wingbeats, flight silhouette appearing triangular. Nests in cavities in trees or structures, often aggressively usurping other species from cavities.

Similar Species: Blackbirds have longer tails, never show yellow bills.

Where, When to Find: Very common year-round resident throughout the region; most numerous in urban, suburban and agricultural areas, but also invasive in natural riparian and conifer woodlands. Large flocks gather in the winter in open parks, fields, and agricultural areas.

Did you know? This species was introduced from Europe to New York in the late 1800s; the first birds reached the Los Angeles region in the late 1940s.

Date & Location Seen:

Non-breeding

Description: 6 ½". A slender ground bird with a **thin bill**, gray-brown upperparts, pale, **buff-tinged underparts** with **streaks on breast**, and **white edges to the tail**. BREEDING birds are grayer above and richer buff below, with breast streaks reduced or absent. WINTER birds more heavily streaked below, faintly streaked on back.

Voice: Calls include a thin *tseep* and doubled *tsi-sip*. Jingling song, given in flight, is rarely heard in our area.

Behavior: Walks on ground, **constantly bobbing the tail** up and down. Gathers in large flocks in open fields, sometimes mixing with Horned Larks. Sometimes sits on fence lines, wires, tree branches but usually seen on the ground.

Similar Species: Many sparrows are superficially similar but have short, conical bills and do not bob tails. A secretive relative, the Sprague's Pipit (*Anthus spraguei*; 6 ½") winters in very small numbers in bermuda grass fields in the Imperial Valley, and the Red-throated Pipit (*Anthus cervinus*, 6") of Eurasia is seen regularly along the coast in fall.

Where, When to Find: Common winter visitor, mainly from October to early April, to agricultural areas of the desert valleys and sod farms, other open fields, extensive lawns and even lakeshores and beaches in the lowlands of the coastal slope.

Did you know? This species, formerly known as the Water Pipit, nests in tundra areas above timberline (including rarely on our highest mountain, Mt. San Gorgonio) and in the Arctic.

Date & Location Seen:

Adult

Juvenile

Description: 7 ¼". A **sleek, crested** bird that travels in tight flocks. **Soft brown, tinged yellow on the belly**. **Black chin and mask**. Lower back and rump gray. Blackish **tail has yellow band** at the tip. Small **wax-like red spots** are found on the tips of the secondaries of many adults. JUVENILE is duller, with broad indistinct streaking below.

Voice: Call is a very high-pitched *sreeee*, unassuming but creating quite a din in large flocks.

Behavior: Nomadic visitors, descending on fruiting trees and shrubs such as toyon, elderberries, mistletoe, and pyracantha to consume berries. Flies in tight flocks, often of dozens or hundreds of individuals; often flocks with American Robins. In warmer weather often sallies from treetops for flying insects. Within flocks birds may perch in close proximity, sometimes even passing berries to one another.

Similar Species: Flocking behavior and triangular flight shape can suggest European Starling (p. 359).

Where, When to Find: Irregularly common visitor from September through May, with the largest numbers often occurring in late winter and spring. Found throughout the region where berry crops can be found, including urban parks, residential areas, and native woodlands. On the deserts found mainly around towns, large ranch yards, but also where mistletoe is abundant.

Did you know? No other local wintering species remains so late in spring (waxwings sometimes even linger to early June).

Date & Location Seen: _____

Male

Female

Description: 7 ¾". A sleek, long-tailed **crested** bird with **red eyes**, short thin bill. MALE: **Shiny black**, with **large white wing patches** (usually visible only in flight). FEMALE: **Dark gray**, with indistinct **pale gray wing patches**. JUVENILE: Like adult female, wing patches virtually lacking; male acquires black plumage by first winter.

Voice: Common call is a soft, upslurred *pooee*; also a harsh *churr*. Song consists of disjunct, scratchy warbles. Captured birds expertly mimic a variety of other birds' calls when handled.

Behavior: Perches upright atop shrubs, low trees. During warmer months sallies after flying insects; in fall and winter feeds mainly on mistletoe and other berries. Often found in small loose flocks.

Similar Species: Northern Mockingbird (p. 355) is larger, lacks crest, and has much white in the tail.

Where, When to Find: Common on the southern deserts in fall, winter, and spring, breeding in early spring. Fairly common spring and summer visitor (mainly mid-April to mid-September) to coastal and foothill canyons with oaks, sycamores, and chaparral; also in arid woodlands on the desert slopes of the mountains. Winters irregularly around mistletoe sources, commonly on the southern deserts but also in arid interior woodlands and in small numbers in the coastal lowlands (where a bit more widespread in migration).

Did you know? Phainopeplas can digest mistletoe fruits in as little as 20 minutes, excreting the sticky seeds and aiding the plant's spread.

Date & Location Seen:

lutescens

orestera

Description: 4 ¾". Warblers are small, active insect-gleaning birds of shrubby and wooded areas. Orange-crowned is **plain olive-yellow throughout** with an indistinct yellow eyebrow, a **yellowish eye-ring broken by a thin dark line** through the eye, and faint olive breast streaking. Olive-gray tail lacks white markings. MALE: dull orange crown patch, nearly always hidden; body plumage brighter yellow-olive. FEMALE: duller; head tinged grayish in some birds. JUVENILE: shows indistinct buffy wing-bars. Channel Islands birds (also breeding from Palos Verdes Peninsula south locally to San Diego) are slightly larger-billed, with more extensive blurred olive streaking below.

Voice: Song is a colorless trill, usually rising then falling slightly in pitch. Call is a sharp *tik*; also a thin *seet* in flight.

Behavior: Gleans and probes twigs, leaves for insects; often feeds low in shrubs. Nests on or near ground, but territorial males may sing from high perches.

Similar Species: Yellow Warbler (p. 375) lacks dark eye-line, has shorter tail with pale yellow areas, pale yellow edges to wing feathers. Dullest gray-headed Orange-crowned females (mainly *orestera*, found as migrants and scarce winter visitors) can suggest Nashville (p. 369) and MacGillivray's (p. 371) warblers.

Where, When to Find: Common spring (March to early May) and fall (late July to October) migrant throughout the region. Winters fairly commonly in planted shrubs and riparian thickets in the coastal lowlands; common in winter in Imperial, Colorado River valleys, but scarce elsewhere in the arid interior. Breeds in oak woodlands, willow thickets and tall chaparral in coastal and foothill canyons.

Did you know? These warblers and many other small gleaning species probe into eucalyptus blossoms in the winter and often stain their faces black as a result.

Date & Location Seen: _____

Nashville Warbler
Male

Virginia's Warbler
Male

Description: 4 ¾". A small, rather short-tailed warbler with a **complete white eye-ring** on a **gray head**, olive upperparts, **yellow underparts including throat**; bright yellow undertail. Male has clearer gray head; brighter yellow underparts. As with most warblers, young female in fall is dullest. Like Orange-crowned, bill is especially sharply-pointed.

Voice: Call is a soft *plink*, subtly but distinctly different from calls of our other warblers. Song, a few *see-pit* notes followed by a quicker series of sweet notes.

Behavior: Frequently bobs tail up and down while foraging. Gleans for insects, spiders in foliage of low trees, shrubs, and even weed stems. Typical of warblers, singing males on territory may sing for many minutes from a high perch.

Similar Species: Female Orange-crowneds with grayish heads (p. 367) differ in split (not complete) eye-ring, duller and faintly streaked breasts. Female Common Yellowthroat (p. 373) has longer tail, brown tinge to plumage, skulking habits. Closely-related **Virginia's Warbler** (*Vermivora virginiae*; 4 ¾"), rare but regular visitor to coast mainly in September and rare breeder in arid woodlands of eastern San Bernardino Mountains and east Mojave ranges, lacks green on wings and has yellow mainly limited to undertail.

Where, When to Find: Fairly common spring migrant (late March through April) through the lowlands and foothills, especially in live oak woodlands. Uncommon in fall (mid-August to early October), though many move through the mountains; a very few may winter in coastal areas. Small numbers breed in mixed conifers and black oaks around 6-7,000' on Mt. Pinos and Greenhorn Mtns., more rarely in the San Gabriel, San Bernardino Mtns.

Did you know? The scientific name *ruficapilla* refers to the largely hidden rufous crown patch of males.

Date & Location Seen: _____

Male

Fall Immature

Description: 5 ¼". A skulking warbler of dense thickets. **Olive-green above** and **yellow below**. **Head and chest gray** with **white arcs above and below the eye**. The bill is rather long and bicolored (blackish above, pinkish below); the long legs are pinkish. MALE has black in front of eye, black mottling on the throat; FEMALE and immatures lack black, have pale gray to whitish throat.

Voice: Call is a hard, sharp *tik* or *tsik*. The song is a short chanting series, e.g. *tr-ree, tr-ree, tr-ree, sweet-sweet*.

Behavior: Generally keeps well within low, dense thickets, but migrants may be in more open areas. Rarely forages high, though territorial males sing from perches well up in trees.

Similar Species: Nashville Warbler (p. 369) is smaller and shorter-tailed, has a complete eye-ring and yellow throat. Some female Orange-crowned Warblers (p. 367) have grayish heads, but they are duller and more uniform in plumage, show indistinct breast streaks, and have grayish legs.

Where, When to Find: Uncommon spring (mid-April through May) and fall (mid-August to late September) migrant through the lowlands; more common on the desert than in coastal lowlands. Breeds in willow thickets in the Greenhorn, San Gabriel and San Bernardino Mtns. from about 6,000' to 7,500' (the stream at Buckhorn Campground along the Angeles Crest is a consistent spot). Winters from nw. Mexico south to Central America; there are only a few winter records for our area.

Did you know? "Squeaking" or "pishing" sounds made by the observer will often bring this skulking warbler (as well as various wrens, sparrows and other birds) into view.

Date & Location Seen: _____

Adult Male

Female

Description: 5". A wren-like warbler of wet thickets and marshes. **Bright yellow throat** contrasts with duller underparts (**sides washed with brownish**). Upperparts olive-green; undertail yellow. MALE: **Bold black mask and forehead** bordered behind by white. FEMALE: Lacks mask, has indistinct whitish eye-ring; pale yellow throat contrasts with brownish cheeks and sides. Young males have a hint of a black face mask.

Voice: Call is a husky *jip* or *tidge*. The distinctive, loud song repeats several two- to four-note phrases, e.g. *wichety, wichety, wichety...* or *wee-wee'chu, wee-wee'chu, wee-wee'chu...*

Behavior: Skulks in cattails, tules, or moist, shrubby vegetation, feeding on insects. Males may sing from an open perch, and they sometimes give songs in short flights.

Similar Species: The black-masked male is unmistakable. Females can resemble dull females of other plain-winged warblers, such as Yellow (p. 375), Nashville (p. 369), Orange-crowned (p. 367), and MacGillivray's (p. 371), but note yellowthroat's long, rounded tail, contrast between pale yellow throat and dull pale brownish underparts, and indistinct complete eye-ring.

Where, When to Find: Common resident in marshes and wet understory of riparian woodlands, including Salton Sea and Colorado River; numbers are augmented in winter. Migrants (mainly April-May and August-October) may be found in a variety of brushy and weedy habitats, including on the deserts.

Did you know? Along with the Yellow Warbler, this is the most widespread breeding warbler in North America.

Date & Location Seen:

Adult Male

Immature Female

Description: 5". A fairly stocky, **short-tailed** warbler that is **mainly yellow throughout**. Plain head lacks markings except for **bold dark eye** and indistinct pale eye-ring, MALE: bright yellow, with **thin red streaks on breast**. FEMALE: duller, paler, lacking red streaks. Immature females can be very dull, nearly lacking yellow. All birds show yellow patches in tail (so **tail appears all yellow below**), yellow or whitish edges to wing feathers.

Voice: Call is a down-slurred *chip*. Sprightly song starts with high *sweet* notes, then a short high twitter and emphatic *see-see-whew*! ending. In flight gives a buzzy *zzeet*.

Behavior: Bobs tail up and down while foraging. Typical warbler gleaning behavior, often quite high in deciduous trees. Nest is a soft cup well up in a tree.

Similar Species: Other mostly yellow warblers (Orange-crowned, Wilson's) have longer, all dark tails. Duller females with more evident eye-rings can suggest Nashville Warbler or Common Yellowthroat.

Where, When to Find: Common spring (late April through May) and fall (August to mid-October) migrant throughout the lowlands; a very few remain to winter in willow thickets, exotic growth. Fairly common breeder (late March to August) in tall foothill woodlands of cottonwood, willows or alders near watercourses; some breed in lowland willows (even along the Los Angeles River near Elysian Park). Pale subspecies *sonorana* breeding on lower Colorado River now greatly reduced in numbers.

Did you know? As with many of our riparian species, Yellow Warbler nests are often parasitized by Brown-headed Cowbirds, though they do show some ability to recognize cowbird eggs and re-nest.

Date & Location Seen: _____

_____

**Audubon's
Breeding Male**

**Audubon's
Non-breeding**

**Myrtle
Non-breeding**

**Audubon's
Immature Female**

YELLOW-RUMPED WARBLER
Setophaga coronata

Description: 5 ½". Our abundant wintering warbler. Always shows **bright yellow rump patch**, patch of **yellow on sides**, and **white patches near corner of tail**. Gray to gray-brown, with white wing-bars, whitish belly. "Audubon's" subspecies has **yellow throat patch** (throat may be whitish in immature females); breeding male has black chest, large white wing patch. "Myrtle" subspecies has white throat which extends back to point behind ear region and thin whitish eyebrow; breeding male has mottled black chest and bold white wing-bars.

Voice: *Chip* call of Audubon's has strong "ch" quality; Myrtle call is flatter *tup*. Song is a loosely-patterned warble.

Behavior: Varied in feeding habits, gleaning foliage, sallying after flying insects, or probing eucalyptus blossoms for nectar. Often forages in the ground in loose flocks (may associate with bluebirds and with juncos and other sparrows).

Similar Species: The yellow rump patch distinguishes even the dullest winter immatures from our other regularly-seen warblers.

Where, When to Find: Very common winter visitor (October to April) throughout the lowlands in a variety of habitats. Attracted to groves of winter-flowering eucalyptus, but also in riparian woodlands, chaparral, parks and gardens. "Audubon's" race predominates; "Myrtle" is much less common, constituting only about 5% of our Yellow-rumpeds (and mainly found in riparian habitats). "Audubon's" breeds (May to September) in pine-fir forests above 6,000' in all of our high mountain ranges.

Did you know? The "Audubon's" and "Myrtle" subspecies groups were formerly regarded as separate species, and some still consider them such although there is an extensive hybrid zone.

Date & Location Seen: _____

_____

Male

Immature Female

Description: 5". A warbler that is **gray above** and **white below**, with black markings and much white in the outer tail feathers. The dark ear patch connects to gray hind-neck; two strong **white wing-bars**. The **tiny yellow spot in front of the eye** is hard to see. MALE: **Black ear patch and throat**, and **bold black streaks on the sides**. Adult FEMALE has dark gray ear patch, some black on lower throat; immature female lacks black on throat.

Voice: Call is a dull *tup*. Song is a series of high, buzzy notes, e.g. *zeea-zeea-zeea-ZEE-zee*.

Behavior: Actively gleans insects from leaves and twigs of oaks and other trees. Often joins other warblers, kinglets and other small insectivorous birds in migration and winter.

Similar Species: Townsend's Warbler (p. 381) is similarly patterned but has extensive olive and yellow coloration. Mountain Chickadee (p. 463) lacks side streaking and wing-bars, and has white ear patch.

Where, When to Find: A fairly common to common migrant throughout, moving earlier in spring (beginning in late March and mainly in April) and later in fall (mid-September through October) than most other warblers. Breeds in mixed pine and oak woodlands from about 5,000 to 7,000' in the mountains (possibly including the Santa Ana Mtns.), especially where canyon live oaks predominate. A very few remain to winter in riparian thickets and park-like woodlands in the coastal lowlands.

Did you know? Like most of our warblers, but unlike the Yellow-rumped Warbler, there is little seasonal change in plumage.

Date & Location Seen: _____

Townsend's Warbler
Male

Townsend's Warbler
Female

Hermit Warbler
Adult Male

Hermit Warbler
Immature Female

TOWNSEND'S WARBLER
Setophaga townsendi

Description: 5″. Patterned much like the Black-throated Gray Warbler, including **bold white wing-bars**, but the **upperparts** are **olive-green** and the pale areas of the head and **breast** are **yellow**. Adult MALE is **black on throat**, **ear patch**, and much of the crown. Immature males are similar but with slightly less black on the head and throat. FEMALE duller, with little black on the throat; immature females can lack black on the throat and are pale yellow on the throat and breast.

Voice: Call is higher than Black-throated Gray's, a light *tip*. Song is also higher, a modest crescendo of high, wheezy buzzes.

Behavior: Actively gleans for insects, particularly moth larvae. Like many warblers, it travels about woodlands in mixed-species flocks in winter.

Similar Species: Hermit Warbler (*Setophaga occidentalis*; 5″) shares white wing-bars and outer tail feathers, but is gray above, unmarked white below; male has a bright golden-yellow head and black throat; female and immatures have little or no black on the throat and a duller yellow head. Status as migrant similar to Townsend's, but less common, rare in winter; a few breed in pines around 7000′ from Greenhorns, Mt. Pinos to San Bernardinos. Hybrid Townsend's X Hermit Warblers are sometimes noted in our area in migration.

Where, When to Find: A common migrant through live oak woodlands, lower mountain forests and other wooded areas in spring (mainly mid-April through May); fall migrants (September to mid-October) are common in mountain forests, less so in coastal lowlands. Uncommon in winter in extensive riparian and oak woodlands and well-planted parks and residential areas on coastal slope (more common from coastal Ventura County north). Strictly a migrant through the interior.

Did you know? Forty-five species of warblers, most of them rare migrants or vagrants, have been found in southern California.

Date & Location Seen: _____

Male

Female

Description: 4 ¾". A small, very active warbler that is **bright yellow-olive above** and **bright golden-yellow below**. The yellow forehead contrasts with a **shiny black cap** (males) or mixed black and olive cap (most females; some females show only olive). The dark eye stands out on the blank yellow face. Wings and tail are unmarked olive-green.

Voice: Call is a distinctive soft *timp*; also gives a slurred *tsilp*. The song is a rapid series of *chip* notes, building in volume and speed, but often trailing off at the end.

Behavior: Intensely active, gleaning, hovering, and making short sallies for flying insects. The tail is flipped about as the bird flits about.

Similar Species: Orange-crowned Warbler (p. 367) is much duller yellow, shows a thin dark line through the eyes, and is shorter-tailed. Yellow Warbler (p. 375) is plumper and shorter-tailed, has yellow tail spots and edges to wing feathers.

Where, When to Find: Common spring (late March through May) and fairly common fall (mainly late August through September) migrant throughout; often one of the most common and conspicuous migrating songbirds in oak woodlands and on the deserts in spring. Breeds fairly commonly in willow thickets on the north coast (south to northern Santa Barbara County); a very few breed in willow thickets in steep ravines in the higher mountains in summer (formerly bred more widely in the lowlands). Rare but regular in winter in willow thickets of the coastal lowlands.

Did you know? Along with the phalarope, snipe, plover and storm-petrel, this is one of five birds named for famed late 18th and early 19th century American ornithologist Alexander Wilson.

Date & Location Seen: _____

Description: 7 ½". A **large**, **thick-billed** warbler-like bird with a **deep yellow throat and breast**, **white spectacle** around the eyes, olive upperparts, whitish belly, and **long olive tail**. The sexes are similar, but female has less black in front of the eye and a less intensely yellow breast.

Voice: Distinctive. The loud, rich song is a measured, loose collection of chatters, rattles, caws, and whistles, with notes sometimes repeated rapidly. Call is a nasal *airrh* and a snappy *cheew*.

Behavior: Skulks in dense brush and thickets, where surprisingly hard to see. Territorial males may perch openly for prolonged periods while singing, and often sing exuberantly in flight with deep, snappy wingbeats. Feeds on insects and berries.

Similar Species: Unmistakable; Common Yellowthroat (p. 373) is much smaller.

Where, When to Find: Uncommon and local breeder (mid-April to August) in extensive riparian thickets in the lowlands; consistent sites include Sepulveda and Hansen Dam basins, Whittier Narrows, and a few creeks in Orange County (e.g. Villa Park flood basin). Also fairly common along the Santa Ynez River, South Fork of the Kern River, Prado Dam basin, Mojave Narrows area, many creeks in western San Diego County, and along the lower Colorado River.

Did you know? The relationships of the chat to other wood-warblers continue to be studied and debated; it now appears that this chat is only distantly related to the more typical warblers.

Date & Location Seen: _____

Male

Juvenile

Description: 8″. A large sparrow with a **black head**, **white-spotted black wings** and back, and white corners on the black tail. Bright **rufous sides**, flanks and undertail, contrasting with white center breast and belly. **Eyes red**. Females are slightly duller, with slaty heads. JUVENILE: is brownish and heavily streaked, but shows distinctive wing spotting and white tail corners.

Voice: Call is a scratchy rising mew, *reee-eeh?* Song is a simple, loud buzzy trill, sometimes with a short whistled introductory note.

Behavior: Towhees are large sparrows that scratch about with their feet in the leaf litter for seeds and insects. Spotteds usually forage well within dense brush, but may often be seen at open edges. Singing males may perch openly atop shrubs.

Similar Species: Male Black-headed Grosbeak (p. 417) is superficially similar but has a much thicker bill, shorter tail, more extensive orange color, and arboreal habits. Much smaller Dark-eyed Junco (p. 413) lacks white spotting.

Where, When to Find: Common year-round resident in chaparral, oak woodlands, and riparian thickets from sea level (including Santa Catalina, Santa Cruz Islands) to about 7,000′. Scarce in urban areas. Migrants pass uncommonly through more open, desert areas, and a few winter around tree groves and brushy thickets on the deserts.

Did you know? The "double-scratch", a quick forward and backward two-step maneuver, is a unique foraging behavior of towhees and some other sparrows.

Date & Location Seen: _____

Description: 6". A softly-colored gray-brown sparrow with a **rufous crown, black and white streaks bordering the sides of the throat,** rufous streaks on the back, and a white eye-ring. Lacks wing-bars. JUVENILE (usually seen with adults) is finely streaked below.

Voice: Call is a plaintive *dear dear dear*; also a soft *tseeet* and a dry chatter. The song is a jumbled series of notes, recalls a House Wren song but thinner and scratchier.

Behavior: Usually found in pairs. Feeds inconspicuously on the ground, where generally secretive; however it is often very responsive to "pishing," approaching the observer closely. Singing males perch openly atop a shrub or yucca stalk.

Similar Species: Chipping Sparrow (p. 393) is more cleanly marked, whiter below, with white wing-bars and a black line through the eye; Chippies flock in open areas.

Where, When to Find: Fairly common but unobtrusive year-round resident in open coastal sage scrub and steep rocky hillsides with tall grasses, from sea level to about 4,500'. Avoids continuous chaparral and wooded areas, and absent from urban habitats. Although virtually restricted to natural habitats (and therefore declining in some coastal areas), they do occupy large road cuts planted with sparse scrub and also extensive grassy hillsides with exotic artichoke thistle. Resident on Santa Cruz, Anacapa Islands.

Did you know? The chatter call, rusty crown, and DNA sequence group this species with two close relatives in Mexico and set it apart from Cassin's, Botteri's and other sparrows formerly in *Aimophila* but now placed in the genus *Peucaea*.

Date & Location Seen: _____

Description: 8 ½". A familiar **large, plain brown** sparrow. **Undertail is rusty orange;** the throat is tinged with orange and bordered below by short, faint streaks. Thin orangish eye-ring. JUVENILE resembles adult but has fine streaking on the breast.

Voice: Call is a sharp *chink*. Song is a series of *chink* notes strung into a loose, accelerating series. Also gives a descending series of rough, squealing notes.

Behavior: Usually found in pairs. Scratches in the leaf litter and on open ground for seeds, insects. Like many seed-eating species, towhee feed mainly grubs and other invertebrates to their nestlings.

Similar Species: California Thrasher (p. 357) is somewhat similar in plumage, but has long, thin down-curved bill. Fox Sparrow (p. 403) is whiter below, with heavy spotting. Range does not overlap with similar Abert's Towhee (p. 479) of Salton Sink, Colorado River.

Where, When to Find: Common year-round resident in brushy habitats throughout the coastal lowlands and up to about 5,000' in the mountains. Occurs in chaparral, coastal sage scrub, open woodlands and residential areas, but absent from the most heavily urbanized areas. Absent from the deserts and the Channel Islands.

Did you know? This and other ground-inhabiting birds suffer heavily from predation by feral cats in urban areas and populations cannot survive around the many sanctioned "feral cat colonies" in the region.

Date & Location Seen:

Non-breeding Adult

Breeding Adult

Juvenile

Description: 5 ½". A small, slim, long-tailed sparrow with gray underparts and rump, streaked brown back, and distinctive face pattern: **black line through the eye**, **white or buffy eyebrow**, and **rich brown crown** (bright **rusty** in breeding adults). Bill black in breeding adults, otherwise dull pinkish. JUVENILE: Like dull non-breeding adult, but extensively streaked below.

Voice: Calls include a rich *tseet* and soft *tik*. Song is a colorless dry trill, usually faster and less musical than the trilled song of a junco.

Behavior: In fall and winter found locally in flocks of 10-50 birds in park-like areas with lawns or weedy fields and scattered trees, in open orchards, and sometimes on residential lawns. Flocks flush up into trees when disturbed. Flocks may mix with other species such as juncos, Yellow-rumped Warblers, and Lark Sparrows.

Similar Species. Immature White-crowned Sparrow (p. 409) is much larger with bright pinkish-orange bill. Brewer's Sparrow (p. 477) has finely streaked crown, pale area between bill and eye, and thin white eye-ring.

Where, When to Find: Fairly common but rather local from September to April in open park-like areas, including residential areas and orchards in inland valleys and lowlands of the coastal slope; widespread as a migrant on the deserts, where a few winter at ranch yards, towns in the southern areas. Breeds (April to August) in open, dry coniferous or pine-oak forests in the mountains, and locally in the higher coast ranges and oak woodlands in the foothills.

Did you know? Chippies are among the most widespread sparrows in North America, breeding from Alaska to Nicaragua.

Date & Location Seen: _____

Adult Breeding Male

Female

Description: 5 ¾". A slender, long-tailed sparrow of mountain chaparral with **gray head and underparts**. **Back streaked rusty brown**, and wing feathers also edged with rusty. **Pink bill** stands out against the gray or (breeding male) **black face and chin**.

Voice: Call is a high, weak *tik*. The beautiful song is a series of sweet upslurred or downslurred notes, accelerating to a very rapid trill.

Behavior: A bird of dense chaparral cover, best seen when males are singing from the top of a low shrub. Feeds on the ground for seeds, insects.

Similar Species: Juncos (p. 413) show extensive white in the tail; no other sparrow is so extensively gray on the head and underparts.

Where, When to Find: Fairly common breeder (late March to August) in extensive tracts of chamise and other low chaparral on mountain slopes, usually above 3,000' and in the coast range from Ventura County north. A few also breed in coastal sage scrub in the highest Santa Monica Mtns. (e.g. Castro Crest) and (now very rarely) in the San Joaquin Hills of Orange County. Migrants found only casually away from breeding habitat, and there are just a few winter records.

Did you know? Juveniles of this species and most other plain-breasted sparrows are streaked below for a few weeks after fledging.

Date & Location Seen:

Adult

Description: 6 ½". A large, handsomely marked sparrow of open country with scattered trees. **Bold face pattern** includes chestnut ear patch with white spot at rear, black "whiskers", white markings around the eyes, and chestnut and white crown stripes. Whitish below with **black spot in center of breast**. Long **tail has a bold white outer edge** and corners. IMMATURE: slightly duller on the head; juveniles are lightly streaked below.

Voice: Call is a soft, warbler-like *tsip*. The song consists of varied short phrases, often repeated two to four times, that include sweet notes and rough, burry trills.

Behavior: Flies with strong, undulating wingbeats. Easy to see, flocks feed on lawns and short-grass fields, retreating into trees or onto fences or wires when flushed.

Similar Species: Vesper Sparrow (p. 477) has more subdued head pattern with white eye-ring, streaked breast, narrower white edge to tail.

Where, When to Find: Fairly common but local through the year in open areas of the lowlands and foothills where trees and shrubs are interspersed with open, grassy areas; most numerous in interior valleys. Flocks are more widespread in fall and winter (September to April). Large numbers occur in pasturelands and on fence lines along Hwy 138 between Quail Lake and Neenach.

Did you know? The "harlequin" head pattern and brown, black and white tail suggest some species of larks, but this bird is a true sparrow.

Date & Location Seen:

Adult *belli*

canescens

nevadensis

Description: 6". A **gray-headed** sparrow with **black and white whisker marks**, a **white eye-ring** and **white spot in front of the eye**, and a black tail. **Black spot in the center of the whitish breast**; lightly streaked tan sides and flanks. Birds of coastal slope hills (subspecies *belli*) are plain dark gray and unstreaked above and have broad black whiskers; birds of Mojave Desert, southern San Joaquin Valley (subspecies *canescens*) are paler gray and faintly streaked above, with narrow whiskers. JUVENILE: more extensively streaked below, head browner and less strongly patterned than adult.

Voice: Calls are soft, tinkling notes. The song, variable among populations, is a short, mechanical series of notes delivered in jerky, sing-song pattern, such as *chee chuppa-chee chuppa-chee*.

Behavior: Terrestrial, running with tail held upward, like a tiny thrasher. Males sing from atop low shrubs; best brought into view by "pishing".

Similar Species: Juvenile Black-throated Sparrow (p. 477) differs from juvenile Sage in having bold, long eyebrow and more limited streaking below.

Where, When to Find: Common resident (subspecies *canescens*) in sparse saltbush scrub and other arid, low scrubby habitats from Antelope Valley north and east through Mojave Desert; also arid western Kern County and Carrizo Plain. The darker *belli* an uncommon resident on chamise-covered slopes from 2,000 to 5,000' in coast ranges, lower slopes of San Gabriel Mtns. and the hills above Santa Clarita, and much of interior San Diego County; tiny populations remain elsewhere.

Did you know? A larger, slightly paler subspecies with stronger back streaking (*nevadensis*) nests in the Great Basin and visits the interior of our Region in winter. It may be a species distinct from our "Bell's" Sparrows.

Date & Location Seen: _____

_____

Adult *beldingi*

Adult *nevadensis*

Adult *rostratus*
"(Large-billed)"

Grasshopper Sparrow

Description: 5 ½". A small sparrow of open areas with **streaked back, breast and flanks**; often shows a yellow tinge in front of the eye. They have a **small bill**, a **short, notched tail**, and **bright pink legs**. Belding's" subspecies (*beldingi*) of coastal salt marshes has darker streaking and a thinner bill; "Large-billed" subspecies (*rostratus*) has plainer grayish back, diffuse streaks on head and breast, and much larger pinkish bill.

Voice: Calls include a sharp *tip* and a high *tsee*. Large-billed gives buzzier *zink* note. Song is high and buzzy.

Behavior: Feeds in loose flocks on the ground in open grassy areas; usually perches on weed stems, fences or wires (less often in trees).

Similar Species: Song Sparrow (p. 405) has a longer rounded tail and grayer face, and inhabits wet brushy areas. **Grasshopper Sparrow** (*Ammodramus savannarum*; 5"), rare and declining in open tall-grass hillsides with scattered shrubs, is unstreaked buffy below, has a larger bill, spikier tail, and an eyebrow that is orangish in front and gray behind.

Where, When to Find: Subspecies *nevadensis* is a common winter visitor (August through April) to grasslands and agricultural fields in interior and desert valleys and where open space remains in the coastal lowlands; a few breed in open mountain meadows (such as Baldwin Lake). Endangered "Belding's" is a fairly common resident in coastal pickleweed marshes from Morro Bay to San Diego. "Large-billed", breeding in Colorado River delta region, is uncommon fall and winter visitor to Salton Sea and rare winterer on the coast (e.g. San Diego Bay, Bolsa Chica Ecological Reserve, Seal Beach National Wildlife Refuge, Pt. Mugu, Morro Bay).

Did you know? More than one species may be involved in this complex.

Date & Location Seen: _____

"Sooty"

"Thick-billed" *stephensi*

"Slate-colored" *schistacea*

Description: 7". A **large** sparrow, variable in bill size, shape, and plumage color. Our breeding "THICK-BILLED" birds have **thick, swollen bills**, **gray heads** and upperparts, **rusty on wings and tail**, and white underparts with breast spots like inverted Vs. In winter and migration we also have "SOOTY" birds, which are more uniformly **dark brown above** (including wings, tail; sometimes grayer on the head), **densely marked with brown spots below**, and have smaller bills, and "SLATE-COLORED" birds which resemble Thick-billeds but have smaller bills.

Voice: Variable song combines clear slurred whistles and short trills, and often includes mimicry of other birds' calls. Calls vary: Thick-billed a metallic *chink*, Sooty a smacking *thick*, and Slate-colored a more slurred *tewk*.

Behavior: Scratches on the ground, towhee-like, for seeds and insects. Singing birds tee up on the tops of shrubs or low conifers.

Similar Species: Song Sparrow (p. 405) is much smaller, with bold face pattern and streaked back. Compare with thin-billed Hermit Thrush (p. 351).

Where, When to Find: Thick-billed is a common breeder (April to September) in thickets of ceanothus and willows about 6,000' in the San Gabriel Mtns.; they winter in dense chaparral in the foothills and mountains. Sooty is a common winter visitor (October to March) to chaparral (and uncommon in coastal lowlands); status of Slate-colored is similar but on average they occupy more open chaparral. All groups are uncommon in migration on the deserts (Thick-billed scarcest).

Did you know? Each of the three groups of Fox Sparrows noted above comprises several subspecies; a fourth ("Red") group, bright rufous and gray birds of the boreal regions, occurs here as a rare winter visitor.

Date & Location Seen: _____

Description: 6". A common and familiar long-tailed sparrow of wet brushy or marshy areas. **Boldly streaked below**, with a blackish **central breast spot**. Strongly patterned face with **broad gray eyebrow** and **black whisker stripe**. The **wings and tail are tinged rusty**. JUVENILE: more lightly streaked, with buffy wash below. Birds of Salton Sea, lower Colorado River paler, more reddish.

Voice: Sprightly but variable song starts with a Beethoven-like motif of piping notes, followed by lower husky notes and short trills. Call is a distinctive *chemp*.

Behavior: Singing males may perch openly for many minutes, but otherwise these sparrows forage low, often on wet ground. Flight is relatively weak, with the tail pumped up and down.

Similar Species: Lincoln's Sparrow (p. 407) is smaller, more finely streaked, and is strongly buffy across the breast. Savannah Sparrow (p. 401) has shorter, notched tail, bright pink legs, and (often) yellow eyebrow.

Where, When to Find: Common year-round resident in marshes, riparian woodlands, and other wet, densely-vegetated habitats throughout the region (including well-planted suburban yards); also in oak woodland understory and coastal sage scrub, but not found in drier chaparral. On the deserts mainly limited to marshes and riparian oases, though migrants and winter visitors from more northerly breeding areas are sometimes found more widely.

Did you know? Of some 25 subspecies of Song Sparrows throughout North America, only one (*heermanni*) is widespread in southern California; endemic subspecies on San Clemente and Santa Barbara Islands are now extinct.

Date & Location Seen:

Description: 5 ½". A skulking, **finely streaked** sparrow of damp brushy and weedy areas. The **breast is washed with buff** and has fine streaks (and usually a small central spot). Also note the broad gray eyebrow, narrow buff eye-ring, and **buffy whisker**. The wings are tinged rusty. Slender and long-tailed shape, with **peaked crown**.

Voice: Song is a hurried warble, usually rising then falling in pitch. Calls include a sharp *thik* and buzzy *zzeeet*.

Behavior: Moves furtively through low, dense weedy growth and damp brushy areas, though "pishing" will often bring birds into view.

Similar Species: Song Sparrow (p. 405) is more boldly streaked and lacks buffy breast, but beware close similarity of Lincoln's to juvenile Song. If it's in the lowlands from late May through August, it's almost certainly a juvenile Song.

Where, When to Find: Fairly common winter visitor (September to April) in damp, weedy fields, riparian understory, freshwater marshes, and woodland edges throughout the lowlands. Migrants are noted widely (mainly September-October and March-April). A few pairs breed in wet meadows of willow, corn lily and other damp growth on Mt. Pinos, around Big Pines in the San Gabriel Mtns., south of Big Bear in the San Bernardino Mtns.

Did you know? This sparrow was named by Audubon in 1833, not for Honest Abe but for Thomas Lincoln.

Date & Location Seen:

Adult *gambelii*

Immature *gambelii*

Adult *pugetensis*

Adult *oriantha*

WHITE-CROWNED SPARROW
Zonotrichia leucophrys

Description: 6 ½". A cherished and familiar winter visitor, large and long-tailed with **bold black and white crown stripes**, **plain gray underparts**, streaked back, and **orangish bill**. In immature crown stripes are dark brown and creamy. Most are "Gambel's" subspecies (*gambelii*), which breed in the Alaska and Canada taiga regions. Coastal breeders (*pugetensis* and *nuttalli*) on the coast from n. Santa Barbara County to sw. British Columbia, have yeller bills, streaked black and tan backs, and a brown tinge below. "Mountain" birds (*oriantha*) differ from Gambel's in having black between the eye and the darker pink bill.

Voice: Song (heard all winter) consists of wheezy whistles and trills in a distinctive pattern, such as *dzew, zeedle zhee-jee dzu*; songs of *pugetensis* and *oriantha* includes sweet repeated trills. Common calls include a sharp *pink* and high *seet*.

Behavior: Feeds in flocks on the ground near or within brushy areas, flying into bushes or low trees when flushed. They readily visit backyard feeders.

Similar Species: Golden-crowned Sparrow (p. 411) has duller grayish bill, duller and browner underparts, and different crown pattern. Compare immatures with much smaller Chipping Sparrow (p. 393).

Where, When to Find: Common winter visitor (late September to April) in brushy areas, weedy fields, chaparral, desert scrub, and gardens throughout. "Puget Sound" birds (*pugetensis*) mainly winter on the immediate coast, especially from Los Angeles County north; similar "Nuttall's" (*nuttalli*) is year-round resident on coast north of Pt. Conception. "Mountain" subspecies (*oriantha*) is a scarce migrant (May, September) through the deserts; a few breed in high San Bernardino Mtns.

Did you know? This well-known species has been the subject of many pioneering studies of song learning and dialects, physiology, and migration.

Date & Location Seen:

Breeding Adult

Non-breeding

Immature

Description: 6 ¾". A large sparrow, **dull gray below** and striped on the back, with a dull pinkish-gray bill and **yellow suffusion on the forecrown**. ADULT: **crown bordered with black; forehead bright yellow** (pattern is stronger and bolder in breeding plumage, with black extending down to the eyes). IMMATURE: head plainer, with dull yellow tinge to forecrown.

Voice: Song is a series of 2-5 long, plaintive whistles, usually going down the scale (as if singing "*I'm sooooo sad*"). Calls include a sharp *chewp* and a drawn-out *tseeet*.

Behavior: Feeds in small flocks in dense brushy areas, usually avoiding open areas; will flock with White-crowned Sparrows, but often in pure groups.

Similar Species: Immature White-crowned Sparrow (p. 409) has creamy white eyebrow and central crown stripe, pinkish bill, "cleaner" gray underparts.

Where, When to Find: Common winter visitor (late September to April) in tall dense brush, woodland understory, and woodland edges throughout the foothills and lower mountain slopes. Less common but still widespread in the coastal lowlands (including Channel Islands) where dense brushy areas and wooded riparian corridors remain. Only a few are found on the deserts and in the most urbanized lowland areas.

Did you know? Golden-crowneds breed as far north as northwestern Alaska and winter birds usually come only as far south as southern California and northwestern Baja California.

Date & Location Seen: _____

Description: 6". A **dark-hooded** sparrow with a **light pink bill** and **flashing white outer tail feathers**. In our common "Oregon" birds MALE has **black head**, contrasting with **pinkish-brown back**, white chest, and **pinkish sides**. FEMALE: Head slaty-gray to pale gray. JUVENILE: Streaked on the back and breast. "Slate-colored" birds have slaty to gray-brown backs and slaty gray sides (paler and washed with brown in females). "Gray-headed" (*caniceps*) have a pale gray head, blackish mask in front of the eyes, gray sides, and a reddish brown back. Pink-sided (*mearnsi*) have head like Gray-headed, extensive pink wash on underparts, brown back.

Voice: Song is a simple, slightly musical trill, usually quite rapid, but sometimes with distinctly spaced notes. Calls include a sharp *tik* and high twittering.

Behavior: Winter birds flock in open areas with nearby trees and brush for cover. They hop on the ground and picking for seeds. Winter flocks often mix with other sparrows, bluebirds, Yellow-rumped Warblers and goldfinches.

Similar Species: Streaky juvenile may suggest Vesper Sparrow (p. 477). Slate-colored's resemblance to Black Phoebe (p. 281) is purely superficial.

Where, When to Find: "Oregon" breeds commonly in conifer and mature oak woodlands of mountains and north coastal areas, and locally in well-wooded canyons to near the coast (as in Malibu); increasingly, they are breeding in wooded parks and residential areas of lowlands south to San Diego. They are common and widespread in winter (mid-October to March). A few Slate-coloreds occur with winter Oregon flocks, and Gray-headed, Pink-sided are found rarely but annually in winter.

Did you know? Juncos are among our hardiest songbirds, wintering even in the high mountains.

Date & Location Seen: _____

Western Tanager Male

Western Tanager Female

Summer Tanager Male

Summer Tanager Female

Description: 7". **Bill stout** compared to slender, pointed bills of orioles, but not conical like those of grosbeaks. MALE: Red to **orange-red head**; otherwise **bright yellow** with **black back, wings and tail**; two **wing-bars** (front yellow, rear white). FEMALE: olive-green above, pale yellow below, with **two white wing-bars**; some show only limited yellow on the underparts. Winter and immature males show only limited orange on face.

Voice: Call is a rising *pr-d-dik*; also a soft *whee?* (also given in flight). Song is a series of hoarse, scratchy robin-like phrases: *pr-rit, pree-ur-rit, pree-u,* etc.

Behavior: Gleans insects with sluggish movements through foliage, often high in trees; also sallies after flying insects. Feeds largely on berries and nectar in winter.

Similar Species: Male unmistakable. Female's heavy bill distinguishes her from similar female orioles such as Hooded (p. 435) and Bullock's (p. 437). **Summer Tanager** (*Piranga rubra,* 7 ½") breeds locally in interior riparian woods from South Fork of the Kern River to Colorado River and western edges of deserts; male entirely bright red with pale bill; female all mustard-yellow, lacking wing-bars.

Where, When to Find: Common spring migrant (mid-April through May) throughout; fall migrants noted as early as late July, but mainly in late August and September. Common breeder (May to August) in conifer and pine-oak woodlands throughout, mainly above 4,000' but locally in shady canyons as low as about 2,500'. Winters in very small numbers in coastal-slope parks and residential areas, especially around flowering eucalyptus.

Did you know? Genetic studies show that the "tanagers" of this genus are more closely related to our grosbeaks and buntings than to the diverse tanagers of the New World tropics.

Date & Location Seen:

Male

Female

Description: 8 ¼". The **very thick bill**, **white wing patterning** and **yellow underwing linings** are distinctive in all plumages. ADULT MALE: **Head mostly black**; back streaked; **collar, breast, sides and rump rich orange**; black wings and tail have bold white markings; immature male duller, with striped head. FEMALE: **Brown crown stripes** and eye-line; **tawny, streaked breast**; brown wings with limited white markings.

Voice: Song is a rollicking and varied series of rich whistled notes. Calls include a sharp *eek* and (usually in flight) a wheezy *wheet?* Begging juveniles give an incessant *wheee-u.*

Behavior: Arboreal foragers, they take fruits, berries and seeds as well as insects; often visit sunflower seed feeders. The energetic song is sometimes given in flight in spring.

Similar Species: American Robin (p. 353) is very different in shape and behavior, and lacks white in the wings. Compare with Spotted Towhee (p. 387).

Where, When to Find: Common breeding visitor (early April to mid-September) in woodlands (oak, conifer, and riparian) of the mountains and foothills, including some well-planted suburban residential areas. Spring migrants (early April through mid-May) are common and widespread throughout; smaller numbers of migrants pass through in August and September, but this species remains only very rarely in winter.

Did you know? The Rose-breasted Grosbeak (*Pheucticus ludovicianus*) is the Black-headed's eastern North American relative, yet grosbeaks in our Region from October through winter are as likely to be Rose-breasted as Black-headed.

Date & Location Seen:

Male

Female

Description: 6 ¾". MALE: **Bright, deep blue** on the head, underparts and rump; the black face sets off the **thick, silvery beak.** Two **thick, cinnamon wing-bars.** FEMALE: Tawny-cinnamon on the head, underparts and rump; cinnamon wing-bars. The thick bill is distinctive. Immature males resemble females but have patches of blue coloring.

Voice: The song is a continuous rich, scratchy warble. Calls include a sharp *penk* and a buzzy *zzzzt*.

Behavior: Forages on weed stems, on the ground, and in low shrubs, taking both seeds and insects. The habit of switching the tail from side to side is distinctive.

Similar Species: Female Lazuli Bunting (p. 421) is smaller with a shorter tail and much smaller bill. Males in poor light may look all black, resembling a cowbird.

Where, When to Find: Uncommon breeding visitor (mid-April to September) in brushy riparian edges, willow bottomlands, and wet weedy fields. Least common in north coastal areas; more numerous on coastal slope from Ventura County south through San Diego County; also on South Fork of Kern River and lower Colorado River Valley. Flood control basins (e.g. Sepulveda, Hansen and Prado Dams) are good places to find this colorful bird. Migrants are noted very uncommonly throughout the lowlands as late as October.

Did you know? Though called a grosbeak, this species is, in fact, an outsized bunting closely related to the Lazuli.

Date & Location Seen: _____

Breeding Adult Male

Female

Description: 5 ½". A finch-like bird with **wing-bars**. MALE: **Head and upperparts bright blue**, **breast tawny-orange**, belly and wing-bars white. Immature males have more limited blue, and blue of winter adults is partly hidden by brown feather tips. FEMALE: **Plain** gray-brown head and upperparts, **tawny breast**, **narrow white to buffy wing-bars**. JUVENILE: resembles female, but breast is finely streaked.

Voice: Song is a rapid, jumbled warble, with many notes given in pairs. Call is a sharp *pit*; in flight gives a distinctive buzzy *zzzitt*.

Behavior: Forages for seeds on weed stems; also feeds in shrubs and on the ground. Agitated birds "switch" their tails from side to side.

Similar Species: Blue Grosbeak (p. 419) is larger and heavier billed. Indigo Bunting (*Passerina cyanea*, 5 ½"), a rare migrant and summer visitor, is similar to Lazuli in size and shape; male Indigo is entirely deep blue, female is rich cinnamon-brown with blurred breast streaks and no wing-bars. Compare female to juvenile Nutmeg Mannikin (p. 455).

Where, When to Find: Common spring (April-May) and fall (August-September) migrant throughout; numbers in coastal lowlands are smaller. Fall migrants may concentrate in damp, weedy flood control basins and river channels. Breeds (late April to August) on brushy hillsides and riparian borders in the foothills and lower mountains. Winters mainly in western Mexico.

Did you know? These buntings can be "fire followers" in that they are often common in the years following a chaparral burn.

Date & Location Seen: _____

Male

Female

Description: 8 ¾". A familiar dark-eyed blackbird of marshy areas and open fields. MALE: **Black** throughout, with a **bright red wing patch** (at the "wrist") that is usually bordered behind by creamy yellow. In fresh fall plumage the black back feathers are edged with rusty. FEMALE: **Striped above and below**, with a buffy eyebrow and throat, and usually a reddish-brown tint to the wings and back. The young male is like a dark female with a limited red wing patch.

Voice: Song is a loud, semi-musical *cong-ka-REEE*. Calls include a harsh *check*, a harsh, slow rattle, and a high whistled *teeew*.

Behavior: Males sing from atop reeds or other emergent vegetation in marshes and wet meadows; displaying males flare out the red wing patch, but the red appears more limited on the folded wing of a resting bird. The nest is woven around reed stems. Large flocks (often mixed with starlings and other blackbirds) occur in winter. These blackbirds walk on the ground, and often hold the tail high when feeding.

Similar Species: See Tricolored Blackbird (p. 425), which is closely similar but more localized. Female might be confused with a large sparrow or finch, but note longer, sharper bill, walking behavior.

Where, When to Find: Common breeder around freshwater marshes, lake margins, and wet, weedy pastures and meadows. Widespread in winter in open fields, agricultural areas and marshes, and some open urban parks.

Did you know? Some consider this to be the most abundant bird in North America.

Date & Location Seen: _____

Male

Female

Description: 8 ¾". A close relative of the Red-wing, breeding very locally in dense colonies. MALE: Shiny black throughout, with a **deep red wing patch bordered by a broad white stripe**; at rest usually only the white stripe is visible. FEMALE: **Sooty gray** (often appearing almost blackish), with **whitish streaking on the breast** and a pale eyebrow, whisker mark and chin.

Voice: Song is a harsh, nasal version of Red-winged's; a colony of singing males can be quite an acoustic experience (bringing to mind strangled cats). Calls are lower and more nasal than those of Red-winged.

Behavior: Breeds in dense colonies of dozens or hundreds of birds in cattail and bulrush marshes; also patches of nettles or thistles near water. Breeding birds may travel miles to forage in fields, grasslands.

Similar Species: Red-winged Blackbird (p. 423) very similar. Tricoloreds have more pointed wings and longer, more slender bills; males differ in their glossier plumage and darker, more limited red wing patch with a broad white border. Female Tricolored is sootier (lacking rufous); the streaking is more limited, so belly is solid sooty-black.

Where, When to Find: Breeding colonies are found around lakes in the Kern River Valley, Antelope Valley, San Jacinto Valley, and north-central San Diego County and locally elsewhere, but now few breed in coastal lowlands. Winter flocks occur in variable numbers in open grasslands and agricultural areas, and in some urban parks (e.g. Sepulveda Basin, El Dorado Park, Huntington Central Park). Absent from the eastern and southern deserts.

Did you know? Tricolors, largely limited to California and rapidly declining, are the most colonial of all North American songbirds.

Date & Location Seen: _____

Breeding

Non-breeding

Description: 9″. Not a lark, but a relative of the Red-winged Blackbird. Stocky and short-tailed, with a long, pointed bill. **Cryptic streaked brown above**; head with bold stripes. **Bright yellow below** with **black "V" on chest** and streaked white sides. **Tail bordered with white**. Winter birds and especially immatures are less boldly marked.

Voice: Loud, bubbly song is a burst of fluty whistles; calls include a harsh *chuck*, a low rattle, and in flight a high *wheet?*

Behavior: Found in pairs or small groups on open ground, foraging for insects and seeds. Males sing from atop shrubs or on fence lines or utility wires. Walks on ground, flicking open white-edged tail.

Similar Species: Stocky, triangular shape may suggest a starling in poor light. Pipits and larks are slimmer, lack extensive yellow below.

Where, When to Find: Uncommon to fairly common year-round resident in agricultural lands, grasslands and open desert scrub in the interior valleys and locally in coastal lowlands where suitable grassland habitat remains. An influx of wintering birds occurs from September to March in open areas on the coastal slope, including extensive lawns, pasturelands and open weedy fields; common in winter in the Imperial and lower Colorado River valleys.

Did you know? Meadowlarks were once very common breeders in the coastal lowlands, but urbanization has greatly diminished their populations.

Date & Location Seen:

Male

Female

Description: 9″. A familiar blackbird, often common in urban areas, with a fairly short, pointed bill and medium-long tail. MALE: **Shiny black** throughout, with iridescent green and purple highlights; glaring **pale yellow eyes**. FEMALE: **solidly dull gray-brown**, with **dark eyes**.

Voice: Song is an unmusical, forced *k-squeesh* or *tz-squee*. Call is a hard, wooden *check*.

Behavior: Male delivers song while fluffing plumage and spreading tail. Often tame around outdoor eateries, parking lots, parks where they walk on the ground and pick up seeds, insects, and food scraps. Gather in large flocks in winter, often with other blackbirds and starlings. Nests in loose colonies in dense foliage of trees, hedges (and aggressive in defense of nesting area).

Similar Species: Male Great-tailed Grackle (p. 431) is much larger, with longer keel-shaped tail; female grackle is warm brown and tan (not cold gray-brown). Smaller Brown-headed Cowbird (p. 433) has smaller, thicker bill and shorter tail. Female Red-winged (p. 423) and Tricolored (p. 425) blackbirds have streaks.

Where, When to Find: Common year-round resident in open lowland areas, including urban areas, agricultural regions, stables and open woodlands; numbers increase in winter. Also breeds around clearings, lakes and meadows in the mountains, withdrawing in winter.

Did you know? Though common and seemingly adaptable, Brewer's Blackbirds appear to be declining in our region.

Date & Location Seen: _____

_____

429

Male

Female

Description: 17″ (male), 14 ½″ (female). A very large and noisy blackbird that has become established in our region only in the last fifty years. MALE: **glossy black** with **very long, oddly shaped tail**; eyes whitish. FEMALE: Warm sooty-brown above, paler **tan-brown below**; **eyes whitish** (light brown in young birds).

Voice: Male's song is a loud, mechanical utterance including whistles and harsh grating sounds. Calls include a harsh *chuck* and wooden *cut-a-cut-a-cut.*

Behavior: Singing males fluff plumage, spread keel-shaped tail. Grackles nests in loose colonies, especially in marshes, but also in other vegetation near water. They walk on the ground, probing for grubs, seeds; also take bird eggs, small fish, and other prey.

Similar Species: Brewer's Blackbird (p. 429) is smaller with a shorter, more standard-looking tail. Nearly the size of an American Crow (p. 305), but very different in shape (with much longer tail, shorter wings, more slender bill).

Where, When to Find: Locally common year-round resident in lowlands; a conspicuous resident in desert towns and agricultural areas, but also on the coastal slope in urban parks with lakes that have marshy borders or islands. Easily found at Lake Balboa (Sepulveda Basin), Echo Park, Harbor Regional Park, Legg Lake, San Joaquin Marsh, Laguna Niguel Regional Park, and many other areas.

Did you know? These grackles spread northward into California from Arizona and Mexico in the early 1960s; the first nesting records for the coastal areas were in the late 1970s and early 1980s.

Date & Location Seen: _____

Male

Female

Juvenile

Description: 7 ¼". A small, short-tailed blackbird with dark eyes and a **stubby, finch-like bill**. MALE: **Black** throughout, with a **dark brown head**. FEMALE: Plain gray-brown. JUVENILE: Resembles female, but paler, faintly streaked below, and with pale scalloped edges to wing and back feathers; molting young male in first fall has patches of black.

Voice: Male's song a gurgling *glug-glug-gleeee*, delivered with bowed head and partly spread wings and tail. Calls include a sharp rattle and (in flight) high whistles.

Behavior: Cowbirds feed mainly on the ground for seeds and insects. Gather in large flocks in winter, often with other blackbirds, starlings. In the breeding season males display and chase females; females sneak through woodlands looking for open cup nests of other songbird species in which to deposit their eggs. "Brood parasites," cowbirds leave it to foster parents to care for their eggs and young.

Similar Species: Brewer's Blackbird (p. 429) has a thinner bill, longer tail; male has pale eyes and shiny black head, female is darker, sootier. Streaked juveniles suggest sparrows or a female House Finch.

Where, When to Find: Year-round resident in the Region. Widespread and fairly common in spring and summer in woodlands in the lowlands and mountains; common but localized in winter, when flocks occur in open areas and park lawns (also dairies and agricultural fields in the Antelope, San Jacinto and Imperial Valleys).

Did you know? A huge increase in cowbirds with agriculture and urbanization has had severe impacts on many species (e.g. flycatchers, vireos and warblers) that they parasitize; intensive cowbird trapping efforts have aided these host species in many areas.

Date & Location Seen: _____

Adult Male

Adult Female

Juvenile

Description: 8″. A slender, long-tailed oriole with a **thin, slightly curved bill**. ADULT MALE: **Deep yellow** with a **black face and throat**, back, and tail; wings black with white wing-bars. Bill black above, bluish at base. FEMALE: Olive-gray above, uniformly yellow below; two thin white wing-bars. JUVENILE: like female, but bill shorter, plumage tinged buffy. First-spring male resembles female but has black throat.

Voice: Calls, a rising whistle, *eeek?*, and a staccato chatter. Unimpressive song is a jumble of short whistles and chatters.

Behavior: Probes in foliage and flowers for insects and nectar; often visits hummingbird feeders. Nest is a woven pouch suspended from the underside of a palm frond or other broad leaf.

Similar Species: Female Western Tanager (p. 415) is stockier, with thicker bill. Female Bullock's Oriole (p. 437) has grayish-white belly, straighter bill.

Where, When to Find: A sure sign of spring is the arrival of these colorful birds in mid- to late March. Fairly common breeder (March to August) in lowland parks, residential areas and canyon woodlands; very partial to fan palms. Adult males have usually departed by early August, but females and immatures continue to mid-September. Very rare in winter. Generally scarce on the northern deserts, and absent from the mountains.

Did you know? The abundant plantings of palms in the Region have undoubtedly allowed Hooded Orioles to increase in numbers.

Date & Location Seen:

Adult Male

Female

Immature Male

Description: 8 ¼″. Stockier than a Hooded Oriole, with shorter tail and a **straight, sharp bill**. ADULT MALE: **Bright orange** or yellow-orange on underparts, rump and face. **Black crown**, eye-line, and stripe on chin. **Large white patch on wing** coverts. **Tail orange-yellow with black center and tip**. FEMALE: Gray back, pale grayish-white belly. Head and breast yellow-orange. Rump and tail dull yellowish. First spring male resembles female, but with black chin and eye-line.

Voice: Song is a rollicking *chick-chicky, tew, tew* (may be more complex). Calls include a dry chatter (lower and slower than Hooded's) and a soft *hyew*.

Behavior: Forages for insects within the foliage of broad-leafed trees; takes nectar from flowers of eucalyptus, silk oaks and other trees and shrubs. The woven nest is suspended in a deciduous tree.

Similar Species: Female Hooded Oriole (p. 435) is more slender, has a thinner decurved bill, longer more graduated tail and is more olive above and entirely yellowish below. Male Black-headed Grosbeak (p. 417) is also black, orange and white but has a very thick bill and differs in pattern.

Where, When to Find: Fairly common breeding visitor (March to August) to oak and riparian woodlands and well-planted parks and residential areas of the coastal lowlands and foothills. Local breeder in riparian habitat on the deserts, but a widespread migrant there (late March-early May and July-August). Adult males have usually departed to Mexico by mid-July; fall migrants are rare after early September. A few winter in well-planted coastal parks, especially around flowering eucalyptus groves and bottlebrush plantings.

Did you know? In many areas nests are woven from green plastic Easter basket "grass" or monofilament fishing line.

Date & Location Seen: _____

Adult Male

Female

Description: 6″. A red finch of foothill and mountain woodlands with a stout bill and **notched tail**. ADULT MALE: Washed with **raspberry red through the head, breast and rump**. The brown back and wings are also washed pinkish; a few blurry streaks on the sides. FEMALE (immature male similar): **Patterned head** shows dark ear patch and crown, indistinct whitish eyebrow and whisker stripe; **blurry brown stripes below**; olive-brown back with indistinct blurry streaks.

Voice: Song is a rich rapid warble with a few inflections and short trills. Calls are a sharp *pit* (given in flight) and *cheer-i-lee*.

Behavior: Feeds on buds and catkins in spring, berries and seeds in winter; rarely visits feeders in our region. Found singly or in small, loose flocks in winter.

Similar Species: House Finch (p. 441), much more abundant in lowlands, has smaller bill (slightly curved on top), smaller head, longer tail, and sharper and more extensive streaking on belly and flanks; male's more restricted color is more orange-red, female has patternless head. See Cassin's Finch (p. 465).

Where, When to Find: Fairly common resident in oak-conifer woodlands in the mountains, and in mature oak and oak-riparian woodlands in the foothills; breeding range extends to sea level in canyons of Santa Monica Mtns. and in coastal Santa Barbara and San Luis Obispo counties. Irregular (usually uncommon) winter visitor more widely in the lowlands, but rare on the southern coast and mainly a rare fall migrant through the deserts.

Did you know? Unlike House Finches, male Purple (and Cassin's) Finches do not attain their red color until a year old.

Date & Location Seen:

Male

Female

Description: 6″. Perhaps the most common and familiar native bird in the southern California lowlands. The **stubby bill** is slightly curved along the top; long tail is only slightly notched. MALE: Variably **red to orange-red** (or even orange or yellow) on the forehead, eyebrow, chin, throat, breast and rump (brightest males have more extensive red wash). **Sides and belly with long, distinct streaks.** FEMALE: **Long gray-brown streaks below; head relatively unpatterned**, with only slight thin eyebrow.

Voice: Song is a cheery, musical warble, descending slightly and usually ending with a long burry note. "Happy" sounding calls include a variety of bright, inflected chirp notes.

Behavior: Abundant and confiding, often nesting in planters, porches and under eaves; Feeds on seeds, buds; commonly visits seed feeders. Often found in flocks in fall and winter.

Similar Species: See Purple (p. 439) and Cassin's (p. 465) finches. In flight House shows smaller head, shorter wings, longer tail than those species. Females are told from various streaky sparrows by curved bill, blurred streaking, plain head, and sweet chirping calls.

Where, When to Find: Common and ubiquitous year-round resident in woodlands, grasslands, deserts and urban areas; absent only from dense mountain forests and extensive tracts of chaparral.

Did you know? Formerly restricted to Mexico and the western states, this species was introduced in the East and now occurs over all of the United States and southernmost Canada.

Date & Location Seen: _____

Description: 4 ¾". A streaky goldfinch relative with short notched tail, long wings, and slender pointed bill. **Streaked above and below**, with **yellow fringes to flight fe**athers. Brightest birds, usually adult males, have **broad yellow wing-bar**, a **yellow stripe on the spread wing**, and yellow wash on breast. Dull birds have whitish wing-bars but still show traces of yellow wing stripe. All show dark rear portion of ear patch with pale neck sides curving behind.

Voice: Calls include scratchy *sheee-u*, rough *pit-pit* notes, and a buzzy, rising *zzhreeee?* Song is a rambling mix of calls notes, trills.

Behavior: Siskins feed on seeds, catkins, buds and insects; when winter flocks "invade" lowlands they often frequent thistle feeders. Nests high in conifers.

Similar Species: Goldfinches lack streaking. House, Purple and Cassin's Finches are much larger and heavier-billed, lack yellow in wings.

Where, When to Find: This small finch is erratic in its occurrence. Every few years large numbers occur in the lowlands (even onto the deserts) in fall and winter, feeding at seeding trees, weedy fields, and thistle feeders. Smaller numbers occur other winters, and many years siskins are virtually absent. Breeds uncommonly (to commonly) in coniferous forests in the highest mountains, with numbers and timing of nesting varying from year to year.

Did you know? The siskin's irregular comings and goings are typical of the species' range throughout North America.

Date & Location Seen:

Male

Female

Description: 4 ½". A tiny green and yellow finch with a dark gray bill. ADULT MALE: **Olive-green above**, bright **yellow below**; forehead and cap black. Black **wings and tail have large white patches**. FEMALE: Dull olive above and pale yellow below; dull whitish wing-bars and a small white patch at the base of the wing's flight feathers. Dullest females are nearly gray above and show just a hint of yellow wash below. Immature male resembles a bright female, but has a touch of black on the cap.

Voice: Song is a rambling collection of the species' call notes, sweet inflected notes, and imitations of the calls of many other species. Calls include high, slurred whistles (e.g. *teeey-yee?* or *teee-yur*), a scratchy *shik-shik*, and high twittering notes.

Behavior: Feeds low on buds, catkins, weed seeds (especially dandelions and other composites); visits thistle feeders. Nest is a tiny, soft cup in a low shrub or willow.

Similar Species: Slightly larger American Goldfinch (p. 449) lacks green tones to upperparts and always shows white under-tail coverts; winter birds are strongly brown-tinged. American shows a single broad wing-bar, but lacks patch at base of flight feathers.

Where, When to Find: Common resident in chaparral, riparian woodlands, and well-planted residential areas of the lowlands and foothills, especially near water. Generally absent from the high mountains, and restricted to well-watered areas on the desert.

Did you know? This is the only goldfinch that breeds on the Channel Islands.

Date & Location Seen:

Male

Female

Description: 4 ¾". One of our most sought-after birds, this goldfinch is largely limited to California. MALE: Pale **gray** throughout, with a **black cap, face and chin**, **yellow patch on breast**, and **extensive yellow markings on the wings**. Bill pale pinkish gray. FEMALE: Like male, but gray back is tinged brown, lacks black on head, yellow on wings and breast reduced. All show white spots on the underside of the tail.

Voice: Song is a tinkly jumble of call notes of both this species and a great variety of others; a careful listening reveals that most of the notes are copied from other species. Most common call is a very high, tinkling *tink-u*; flying birds are often detected high overhead by this distinctive call.

Behavior: Feeds on seeds of annuals; especially fond of fiddlenecks in the spring. Usually found in small, loose groups, even nesting in small "colonies."

Similar Species: Dullest females differ from dull female Lesser Goldfinch (p. 445) in white undertail coverts, yellow wing edges, and longer tail. All goldfinches differ from warblers in their thicker, conical bills.

Where, When to Find: Erratic but fairly common breeder in dry woodlands and brushy areas with some water and riparian vegetation nearby. Favorite spring and early summer localities include Placerita Canyon/Walker Ranch near Santa Clarita, Hansen Dam, Big Rock Creek near Valyermo, Butterbredt Spring, Morongo Valley, and much of interior San Diego County. Small flocks occur irregularly in fall and in winter, most predictably in chamise chaparral; generally rare on the eastern and southeastern deserts.

Did you know? Outside of California, this species breeds regularly only in nw. Baja California.

Date & Location Seen: _____

Breeding
Male

Non-breeding
Adult Male

Non-breeding
Female

Description: 5". Our largest goldfinch, but still a small bird. BREEDING MALE: Bright, **clear yellow** with black forehead, black wings with one white wing-bar, **white rump and undertail**, and **pink bill**. WINTER ADULT MALE: tan above, pale gray below with yellow face, throat; **black wings show broad white wing-bar** and yellow "shoulder." FEMALE: **tan and pale yellow**; dark wings who two wing-bars; breeding female has pink bill. Immature males resemble females, but get yellow at shoulder and some black on forehead by spring.

Voice: Song is a rapid jumble, faster and shorter than songs of our other goldfinches and lacking mimicry. Calls include *yip-yip* (or "*potato chip*"), given in flight, light twitters and soft whistles.

Behavior: Forages in trees at catkins and seed-pods, in low, weedy growth, and at thistle feeders. Winter flocks may occur with juncos, other goldfinches, Chipping Sparrows, and Yellow-rumped Warblers.

Similar Species: See Lesser Goldfinch (p. 445).

Where, When to Find: Fairly common but local breeder in willow groves throughout the coastal lowlands and foothills; especially numerous in the larger dam basins and watercourses where willows are extensive. More widespread in the lowlands in winter, when found in parks and residential areas with seed-producing trees such as sycamores, birches, alders, and Chinese elms and dandelion-infested lawns. Uncommon to fairly common migrant and winter visitor (late October-April) on the deserts.

Did you know? In our area, adult males rarely attain immaculate yellow and black breeding plumage.

Date & Location Seen: _____

Male

Female

Description: 6 ¼". This urbanite is an Old World sparrow introduced from Europe. A dumpy bird with a stout bill. MALE: **Black bib** (partly obscured by gray feather tips in fall, winter), **gray crown**, pale gray cheeks, **rufous neck sides** and rufous areas on striped back and wings, and one thick white wing-bar. Bill black in breeding season, otherwise yellowish. FEMALE: dingy gray-brown with tan and brown back stripes, broad creamy eyebrow; dull yellowish bill.

Voice: Incessant chirping calls, *chillip, churp, shrillip, shur...* These also repeated monotonously as male's song. Also, various twangy chatters.

Behavior: Bold and tame, picking seeds, scraps from the ground; also takes insects. Nest is a messy ball of grasses or straw jammed into a cavity, roof tile, or even street sign or old Cliff Swallow nest; nest is sometimes as a free-standing structure in a tree. Roosting flocks in dense evergreen trees make a din at dusk.

Similar Species: Our native sparrows (classified in a different family) are slimmer, have shorter and more sharply-pointed bills, and differ in face pattern.

Where, When to Find: Abundant year-round resident in all urban areas, and around ranch yards, dairies and almost any other area with plenty of people or livestock. Generally forsakes natural habitats and absent from the mountains except around settlements and towns, such as Wrightwood and Big Bear Lake.

Did you know? A century and a half of evolution since this species' introduction to the eastern U. S. from Europe has led to measurable differences among populations in size, shape and plumage pigmentation.

Date & Location Seen: _____

Orange Bishop
Male

Orange Bishop
Female

Pin-tailed Whydah

Description: 4 ½". A **stubby-tailed** African finch established in some lowland riverbottoms of Los Angeles and Orange Counties. BREEDING ADULT MALE: **Brilliant orange to orange-red** with **black forehead, crown, breast and belly**; long colorful rump and undertail feathers obscure most of the short tail. FEMALE: Buffy below, streaked brown above; crown streaked with dark, indistinct pale eye-ring. Non-breeding male (December to May) and juvenile similar to female.

Voice: Call a soft *tsit*; displaying male gives sharper, incessant *tsit, tsit, tsit…*

Behavior: Displaying males call from open perches atop reeds or shrubs and often give bouncing flight displays punctuated by calls. Otherwise inconspicuous, feeding on grass seeds and other seeds; sometimes visits seed feeders.

Similar Species: All but breeding males suggest sparrows such as Grasshopper (p. 401); note bishop's stubby tail, plainer face. **Pin-tailed Whydah** (*Vidua macroura*; 4 ¾") is another African finch sometimes seen in weedy areas of coastal slopes; spectacular black and white breeding male has very long central tail feathers (adding 8" to length) and red bill. Female, non-breeding male suggest female bishop, but whiter below, with strong dark stripes on sides of crown and reddish bill.

Where, When to Find: Year round resident along river systems and larger urban parks in the coastal lowlands. Easily found in late summer and fall (when males are conspicuous) along the San Gabriel River around Whittier Narrows, the Los Angeles River near Glendale, Long Beach and the Sepulveda Basin, Ballona Freshwater Marsh, Huntington Central Park, and other areas with extensive tall grasses and weeds. Inconspicuous and hard to find from late winter through spring.

Did you know? The male bishop is polygynous, weaving several nests on his territory and attracting several mates.

Date & Location Seen: _____

Adult

Juvenile

Description: 4". A tiny southern Asian finch now locally established in coastal southern California. **Thick, conical black bill**, short pointed tail. ADULT: **Deep chestnut** head and upperparts, **white underparts with fine black scaling**; the upper tail coverts are tinged orange-yellow. Sexes are similar. JUVENILE: Rich tawny head and upperparts, becoming slightly paler buff on the belly and undertail; a few incoming scaly feathers often visible on the underparts.

Voice: Common call is a bugling *ki-bee*.

Behavior: Found in flocks in damp, weedy growth where it mainly eats grass seeds. The nest is an untidy ball in a tree. The flight is fast and direct, usually in tight flocks.

Similar Species: Adults are distinctive, but the plain juveniles might be mistaken for a female Lazuli or Indigo Bunting (p. 420); note the mannikin's short, very thick bill, thin tail, and short rounded wings lacking wing-bars. Several other species of mannikins and waxbills (all in the estrildid finch family) are sometimes seen as escapees.

Where, When to Find: Year round resident along river systems and larger urban parks in the coastal lowlands. Easily found at Huntington Central Park, but also Goleta, along the Los Angeles River near Glendale, Sepulveda Basin, Whittier Narrows, the San Diego River, and other areas with extensive tall grasses and weeds.

Did you know? Also known as "Spice Finch" or "Spotted Munia", this bird was imported for the pet trade and has been established in our area since the 1980s. It is not yet accepted to the "official" California bird list.

Date & Location Seen: _____

Flammulated Owl

Northern Pygmy-Owl

Spotted Owl

Northern Saw-whet Owl

Flammulated Owl *(Otus flammeolus)*

6 ¾". A very uncommon small migratory owl found May to September in mixed coniferous forests at 5,500-7,500'in the higher mountains. Dark eyes, nearly tuftless head and mottled gray and warm tan plumage. Call a soft, low *hoo*, often doubled. Found along Angeles Crest Hwy. from Buckhorn Campground to Dawson Saddle; also Mt. Pinos, Greenhorn Mtns., Big Pine and Pine Mtns, San Bernardino and San Jacinto Mtns., Clark Mtn.

Northern Pygmy-Owl *(Glaucidium gnoma)*

6 ¾". This uncommon to rare small, long-tailed owl suggests a tiny falcon or shrike as much as an owl. Most active in the morning and early evening. Call (given in early morning; less often later in day and at night) is a piping *toot*, given at 2-3 second intervals (beware similar call of Merriam's chipmunks); also a rapid trill. Resident in shaded canyons of oaks, alders, conifers from San Bernardino and San Gabriel Mtns. north; also Coast Range from Ventura County north.

Spotted Owl *(Strix occidentalis)*

17 ½". A rare and declining owl of shaded oak-conifer canyons at 2,500-5,500' from the Santa Barbara County high country east through the Transverse Ranges and south through the mountains of San Diego County; a pair or two continue to be found in the Santa Ana Mtns. Crestless, with dark brown, mottled plumage, dark eyes. Active and vocal at night; call a barking *hoo, hu-hu, HOOO*.

Northern Saw-whet Owl *(Aegolius acadicus)*

8". A small nocturnal owl with puffy, crestless head, yellow eyes, white eyebrows, white spotting on wings, and long reddish-brown streaks below. Call is a low, whistled *toot*, given monotonously at intervals of less than one second. Also squirrel-like barks and a soft rising screech. Resident in fluctuating numbers in all mountains from the canyon live oak and big-cone Douglas-Fir zone around 5,000' up to mixed pine and fir forest at 6,000-7,500'. Also resident on Santa Cruz, Santa Catalina Islands. Casual migrant and winter visitor in the lowlands.

Date & Location Seen:

Mountain Quail

White-headed Woodpecker
Male

Calliope Hummingbird
Male

Calliope Hummingbird
Female

Williamson's Sapsucker
Male

Williamson's Sapsucker
Female

Mountain Quail *(Oreortyx pictus)*

11″. A large, retiring quail of foothill and mountain chaparral and open coniferous woodlands. Long straight head plume, chestnut throat, and chestnut and white bars on the sides. Often heard, but hard to see; look for family groups along roads in late summer. Call a loud, mellow *t'wook*; also a conversational *kew-kew-kew-kew...* series. Resident above 1,500′ in the Coast Ranges and all higher mountains west of the deserts (including Santa Ana Mtns.); also in mountains of Joshua Tree National Park.

Calliope Hummingbird *(Selasphorus calliope)*

3 ¼″. Our smallest hummingbird; short-billed and short-tailed. Male has purplish red rays on throat; female has buff-tinted sides and sides of neck, tail tip shorter than wing-tip. Calls very high-pitched. Breeds (May to August) very locally in willow thickets within coniferous forest high Mt. Pinos Region, San Bernardino Mtns., rarely in other high mountains. A few found irregularly in spring migration (late March to early May) along the foothills, mainly at feeders and around flowering citrus groves and patches of golden currant.

Williamson's Sapsucker *(Sphyrapicus thyroideus)*

9″. Male is a striking black woodpecker with yellow belly, red chin, white head stripes, and large white wing patch; female has brown head, barred brown and black back, yellow belly and black chest patch. Uncommon resident in high pine-fir forests above 7,000 from Mt. Pinos and Greenhorns s. to San Jacinto Mtns.; a bit more widespread in mountains in winter (in yellow pine belt), when also found rarely in conifer plantings in foothills and lowlands.

White-headed Woodpecker *(Picoides albolarvatus)*

9″. Unmistakable black woodpecker with white head; large white wing patches show in flight. Male has red crescent on hindneck. Call is a sharp *pee-dink* or *peek-it*. Fairly common year-round resident in all mountains (except Santa Anas and desert ranges) in pine forests around 5,000 to 8,000′, especially Jeffrey, Coulter, ponderosa and sugar pines. Easily found at Mt. Pinos, Charlton Flat, Chilao, Big Bear L. Found very rarely at planted pines in lowlands in winter.

Date & Location Seen:

Pinyon Jay

Steller's Jay

Clark's Nutcracker

Pinyon Jay *(Gymnorhinus cyanocephalus)*

10 ½". Entirely dull blue, crestless jay, shaped like small long-billed crow. Walks on ground; nasal, laughing *ha-a-a* calls distinctive. Found locally in flocks in pinyons and open pine forests of eastern Mojave Desert ranges, Piute Mtns., ne. San Bernardino Mtns., Garner Valley area in San Jacinto Mtns., and very locally elsewhere. Rarely and erratically, flocks wander more widely in fall, winter.

Steller's Jay *(Cyanocitta stelleri)*

11 ½". Bold, deep blue crested jay; raucous calls include a *shook-shook-shook*… series and harsh *jeaahhh*. Often confiding around mountain campgrounds, picnic areas and residential areas. Found commonly from tree line down to foothill canyons with oaks, big-cone Douglas-firs (even into bordering residential areas above Pasadena, Arcadia, etc.); absent from the Santa Ana Mtns. Resident in coastal conifers of nw. San Luis Obispo Co. Casual visitor elsewhere in coastal and desert lowlands.

Clark's Nutcracker *(Nucifraga columbiana)*

12". A raucous crow-like bird of open coniferous forests above 6,500 on Mt. Pinos, high San Gabriel, San Bernardino, San Jacinto Mtns. Gray overall with a white patch on black wings, broad white borders to black tail, and white undertail. Long pointed black bill. Call is a harsh grating note. Eats conifer seeds; also walks on ground for seeds, insects. Numbers erratic; in very rare invasion years a few may be found in the lowlands in winter.

Date & Location Seen: _____

Mountain Chickadee

Red-breasted Nuthatch Male

Pygmy Nuthatch

Brown Creeper

Mountain Chickadee *(Poecile gambeli)*

5 ¼". Confiding, active pale gray bird with white cheeks and a black throat, crown, and line through eye. Feeds acrobatically in conifers, oaks. Calls, a hoarse *chi-dee-dee*, high *seep* notes and descending gurgle; haunting song of 3-7 clear whistles, e.g. *dee-dee, doo* or *dee-de-dee, du-du-du*. Common in mountains (uncommon in Santa Ana Mtns.); regular in fall, winter in foothills, more rarely and erratically in coastal and desert lowlands.

Red-breasted Nuthatch *(Sitta canadensis)*

4 ½". Our only nuthatch with a black line through the eye and white eyebrow above that. Male has black crown, rich orangish underparts; female has gray crown, paler underparts. Call, nasal "tin horn" *eenk eenk eenk*. Breeds in fir forests of the highest mountain ranges, above 6,500'. Found irregularly in planted conifers in the lowlands in fall and winter (rare or absent some years, fairly common others; breeds rarely and very locally in this habitat).

Pygmy Nuthatch *(Sitta pygmaea)*

4 ¼". Smallest nuthatch, and our only one dark from crown to eye. Blackish eye-line, gray crown, buff tinge to underparts. Hyperactive in small, noisy groups, feeding at tips of pine boughs or on branches. Call, a high *peep*, often running into an excited series. Found in pines from 5,000 to 8,500' in the higher mountains; also resident in coastal pines around Cambria. Casual around planted pines in lowlands in winter.

Brown Creeper *(Certhia americana)*

5 ¼". A slender, cryptic trunk-creeping bird, using long tail as a prop. Streaked black and brown above; grayish-tan below. Long buffy wing-stripe visible in flight. Unobtrusive, usually found by very high *tseeee* note; song is a rhythmic *see-see-seee, seedly-see*. Fairly common resident in conifers above 5,000'; also in coastal conifers from Morro Bay north. Rare migrant and winter visitor to lowlands.

Date & Location Seen:

Townsend's Solitaire

Green-tailed Towhee

Red Crossbill
Adult Male

Red Crossbill
Female

Cassin's Finch
Adult Male

Cassin's Finch
Female

Townsend's Solitaire   *(Myadestes townsendi)*

8 ½". A slender, long-tailed thrush; perches upright, often on high, conspicuous perch. Gray with white eye-ring, buff wing patch, white tail sides. Call, whistled *heep*; long, rambling fluty song is sometimes given in flight. "Flycatches" in summer; eats mistletoe and juniper berries in winter. Breeds above 6,000', south to Santa Rosa Mtns. Uncommon in fall, winter in pinyon-juniper of desert foothills; rare winter visitor to coastal lowlands.

Green-tailed Towhee   *(Pipilo chlorurus)*

7 ¼". Large sparrow with olive upperparts, reddish cap, white throat, gray underparts, and green-tinged wings and tail. Call a kitten-like *mew?* Lively song of buzzy trills and short whistles suggest Fox Sparrow. Breeds (late April to early September) in ceanothus thickets and other mountain chaparral within conifer forests above 6,000' (absent as breeder in Santa Barbara County). Uncommon migrant in desert lowlands; rarely seen in coastal lowlands (mainly in migration).

Red Crossbill   *(Loxia curvirostra)*

6." Flocking finch that specializes on conifer seeds, extracted (often audibly) with unique crossed mandibles. Males orange-red to brick red, females olive; variable in size, bill size. Distinctive *jeep-jeep* calls in flight, where it appears large-headed, short-tailed. Breeds irregularly in pine forests (rarely in planted pines in coastal lowlands, deserts); erratic wanderer to planted pines of lowlands (widespread some years, absent most others).

Cassin's Finch   *(Haemorhous cassinii)*

6 ¼". A close relative of the Purple Finch, breeding in pine-fir forests above 6,000' in high mountains from Mt. Pinos south to Santa Rosa Mtns. Bill longer and more sharply pointed than Purple's. Adult male has red cap, deep pink wash to breast, rump, fine streaks on flanks, and pale back streaks. Female and immature male like Purple, but with finer, sharper streaking, more pointed bill. Song longer, more varied, flutier than Purple's; call *tr-dlip*. Erratic visitor (mainly spring) to desert slope; casual (mainly fall) on coastal slope.

Date & Location Seen:

Gambel's Quail
Male

Gambel's Quail
Female

Sandhill Crane

Mountain Plover

Stilt Sandpiper
Breeding

Gambel's Quail
(*Callipepla gambelii*)

11". Replaces California Quail (p. 67) on deserts from Victorville and San Gorgonio Pass east and south to Borrego Valley, Imperial Valley and lower Colorado River (but beware overlap, hybrids, and translocations). Introduced on San Clemente I. Chukar (*Alectoris chukar*, 14"), a large partridge with black necklace, red bill, black bars on sides, also introduced on San Clemente and San Nicolas Islands, and in rocky hills on Mojave Desert (such as Butterbredt Spring).

Sandhill Crane
(*Grus canadensis*)

35-45". This stately, tall pale gray bird has a distinctive "bustle" of long curved feathers on the hind quarters; adults show bare red crown. Flies with neck outstretched. Flocks winter locally in agricultural fields in Imperial Valley (especially just se. of Brawley and Unit 1 of Salton Sea National Wildlife Refuge); also in agricultural areas of Colorado River, and sometimes found on Carrizo Plain. Compare with Great Blue Heron, often mistakenly called a "crane" (p. 89).

Mountain Plover
(*Charadrius montanus*)

9". A plain sandy-brown plover with no strong markings that winters (October to early March) in flocks in bare, recently burned, and heavily grazed agricultural fields in the Imperial Valley, with smaller numbers in Antelope, San Jacinto Valleys, Carrizo Plain. A few formerly occurred in open grasslands near the coast; a few rarely winter at Seal Beach Naval Weapons Station. Restricted to western North America, where rapidly declining and seriously threatened.

Stilt Sandpiper
(*Calidris himantopus*)

8 1/2". Appears intermediate in size, shape between Dunlin and a dowitcher; longer-legged than either. Bill long, distinctly drooped. Grayish color, white supercilium, white rump in flight. Breeding plumaged adults strongly barred below, rusty on crown, cheek. Small groups (up to 100+) found in shallow water at south end of Salton Sea, usually with dowitchers, mainly August to April. Casual spring and rare fall transient elsewhere.

Date & Location Seen:

_____

_____

Laughing Gull
Breeding

Laughing Gull
Non-breeding

Laughing Gull
First Winter

Yellow-footed Gull

Gull-billed Tern
Breeding Adult

Black Tern
Breeding Adult

Laughing Gull
(Leucophaeus atricilla)

16". Medium-small long-winged gull with dark gray back blending to black wingtips, blackish legs, slender red (in adults) or black bill. Breeding adults have black head; winter adults and juveniles have dark smudge behind eye. Fairly common post-breeding visitor from Mexico to Salton Sea, mainly July to September along shoreline and in flooded fields; casual along coast. Franklin's Gull (*Leucophaeus pipixcan*), scarce spring and fall migrant at Salton Sea (a few elsewhere) is slightly smaller with white in wingtips, shorter bill; winter birds and juveniles have blackish half-hood.

Yellow-footed Gull
(Larus livens)

27". Large dark-backed gull much like Western but with bright yellow legs, heavier bill; juvenile with whitish belly, unlike darker Western. Deep call suggests a sea lion! Post-breeding visitor from Gulf of California to Salton Sea, where uncommon to fairly common (southern end) along immediate shoreline from late June to September (rarely through the winter); a few coastal records.

Gull-billed Tern
(Gelochelidon nilotica)

14". Distinctive mid-sized whitish tern with heavy black bill, long black legs. Breeding adults have black crown; winter adults and juveniles have whitish heads with small dark spot behind eye. Swoops to catch fish, insects, lizards, crabs; does not plunge-dive. Declining breeder at Salton Sea, mid-March to early September; since 1980s also breeding at s. San Diego Bay, but casual elsewhere on coast.

Black Tern
(Chlidonias niger)

9 ¾". Small and short-tailed. Breeding adult mostly black with white undertail, gray back and wings; non-breeders and immatures have gray back and wings, white underparts with gray patch on sides of breast, black markings on head; juveniles shaded brown on back, sides, flanks. Catches prey at water surface and in the air. Common spring, abundant fall migrant (mainly late April through May, August through October) at the Salton Sea; many non-breeders remain through summer. An uncommon migrant through northern deserts in May and late July to early September), rare in fall (August to early September) and casual in spring (May) on coast.

Date & Location Seen:

_____

_____

Ferruginous Hawk Adult

Prairie Falcon Juvenile

White-winged Dove

Inca Dove

Ferruginous Hawk *(Buteo regalis)*

23". A large hawk with a wide yellow "gape." Light morph birds are mostly white below (including underwings) with dark feathering on the legs (adults); gray and rusty (adults) or brown (juveniles) above, with mostly whitish tail. Scarce dark morph is dark chocolate brown throughout, with whitish flight feathers. Uncommon winter visitor (late September to March) in grasslands, agricultural fields in interior valleys (e.g., Carrizo Plain, Cuyama, Antelope, San Jacinto and Imperial valleys, Lake Henshaw area); generally rare on coast.

Prairie Falcon *(Falco mexicanus)*

16". Large pale brown falcon of open deserts, rocky hills and grasslands. Underparts white with brown streaks, spots; flanks and "armpits" blackish. Uncommon to fairly common in fall and winter in dry interior valleys such as Carrizo Plain, Antelope Valley, San Jacinto Valley, and through Mojave Desert; local breeder. Uncommon to rare in fall and winter in coastal lowlands, Imperial Valley.

White-winged Dove *(Zenaida asiatica)*

12". Stocky desert dove with distinctive large white patch half way out upper wing. Shortish squared tail with white corners. At close range shows bare blue skin around eye. One distinctive song is *who-cooks-for-you?* Common from April to mid-September on southern deserts, Imperial and Colorado River valleys; rare, mainly as a migrant, on northern deserts, and rare wanderer to coast, islands.

Inca Dove *(Columbina inca)*

8". A small, long-tailed dove that appears scalloped throughout; flashes rufous in wings and much white in outer tail feathers in flight; call is mournful, repeated *no hope*. Ground-doves (p. 221) have much shorter tails; beware fledgling Mourning Doves (p. 219) which also appear scaly. Towns and ranch yards of Imperial and Colorado River Valleys, rarely in Mojave Desert.

Date & Location Seen:

Gila Woodpecker

Ladder-backed Woodpecker

Vermilion Flycatcher Male

Vermilion Flycatcher Female

Verdin Male

Verdin Juvenile

Gila Woodpecker   (*Melanerpes uropygialis*)

9 ½ ". "Zebra-barred" back, unmarked grayish-tan head and underparts, round red cap in males; whitish patch on outer wing in flight. Noisy; gives a rolling *churrrr* and a yipping series. Restricted to se. deserts, where found locally in woodlands and towns of Imperial Valley and Colorado River. Compare to smaller Ladder-backed and to female Williamson's Sapsucker (p. 458).

Ladder-backed Woodpecker   (*Picoides scalaris*)

7 ½". Desert relative of Nuttall's Woodpecker which is resident in Joshua tree woodlands, ranch yards and desert riparian woodlands in Mojave, Colorado Deserts west to Antelope Valley, San Gorgonio Pass, Anza-Borrego Region, and very locally farther west. Differs from Nuttall's in longer bill, dingier head with broader white areas, broader white bars on back (including uppermost back), and more extensive barring on outer tail feathers; male Ladder-backed has more extensive red on crown. Call a sharp *pik* like Downy Woodpecker, and grating *jee-jee-jee-jee-jee*.

Vermilion Flycatcher   (*Pyrocephalus rubinus*)

6". Glowing red crown and underparts make male unmistakable; note blackish mask and upperparts; female suggests Say's Phoebe (p. 283), but shorter-tailed, finely streaked on whitish breast, clear pinkish or yellow on belly. Local resident (some depart in winter) along Colorado River and desert riparian areas such as at Morongo Valley; also breeds locally on coastal slope at Prado Regional Park, California State University San Bernardino campus and elsewhere, and wanderers found even more widely (mainly fall, winter).

Verdin   (*Auriparus flaviceps*)

4 ½". A small, active light gray bird resident in Joshua tree and creosote desert scrub and wooded washes throughout the Mojave and Colorado Deserts. Adult has yellow head, dark line in front of eye, and small chestnut mark at the bend of the wing. Short bill is sharply pointed. Juvenile lacks yellow and chestnut, has pale base to bill. Usually found in pairs. Call, a sharp *tseep*, a whistled *tee-tew*, and light chipping notes. Now a casual wanderer to coast.

Date & Location Seen:

Black-tailed Gnatcatcher Breeding Male

Sage Thrasher

LeConte's Thrasher

Crissal Thrasher

Black-tailed Gnatcatcher *(Polioptila melanura)*

4″. The resident gnatcatcher of the low deserts and locally in the Mojave Desert (mainly eastern), found in riparian washes and arid scrub of flats, hillsides. Black crown of breeding male and limited white in tail of all birds help distinguish them from Blue-gray (p. 337) with which it overlaps in winter on southern deserts. Range approaches that of California (p. 339) in arid valleys southeast of Riverside; Black-tailed is paler gray below, has more white in tail, and lacks California's "mewing" call.

Sage Thrasher *(Oreoscoptes montanus)*

8 ½″. A small migratory thrasher of open arid country. Grayish above with thin white wing-bars, white tail corners; heavily marked with narrow black streaks below. Compare to Cactus Wren (p. 335). Breeds in high sagebrush valleys just north of us, but here mainly found as a remarkably early spring migrant through the deserts (mainly mid-January through March), with a few reaching the coast and Channel Islands in spring and (mainly) fall.

Le Conte's Thrasher *(Toxostoma lecontei)*

11″. A sandy-gray thrasher with blackish tail, tawny undertail coverts, slim curved black bill. Call a rising *hooweep.* Uncommon and declining resident in sparse creosote and saltbush scrub, especially along washes, in the Carrizo Plain/Maricopa area, Antelope Valley, Borrego Valley, and eastward through the Mojave and Colorado deserts. Shy; runs along ground. Best seen when males sing from open perches in early spring.

Crissal Thrasher *(Toxostoma crissale)*

11 ½″. A localized and very shy thrasher of desert riparian groves and thickets along the Colorado River and now very locally in the Imperial Valley, Borrego Valley, and Coachella Valley; a few also in washes surrounded by pinyon-juniper woodlands in the eastern Mojave Desert mountains. Gray-brown throughout, with rusty undertail coverts, thin black and white lines bordering throat, rapid *chor-lee, chor-lee* or *toit toit toit* call.

Date & Location Seen: _____

_____

Lucy's Warbler
Male

Brewer's Sparrow

Vesper Sparrow

Juvenile

Black-throated Sparrow
Adult

Lucy's Warbler *(Oreothlypis luciae)*

4 ¼". Tiny warbler, pale gray above, creamy white below; rump chestnut (adults) or pale rusty (juveniles); adult male has chestnut crown patch. Dark eye stands out on blank face. Breeds in desert riparian along Colorado River and locally west to Borrego Valley, Big Morongo Canyon and north to a few sites on the Mojave Desert. Rare but regular vagrant to coast in fall, winter.

Brewer's Sparrow *(Spizella breweri)*

5 ½". A slender, pallid gray-brown sparrow with finely streaked crown, thin whitish eye-ring. Note slightly outlined ear patch and pale whisker streak. Local breeder in sagebrush near Cuyama Valley and Mt. Pinos region, Baldwin Lake, eastern Mojave Desert, and a few other sites. Flocks migrate through desert scrublands in spring; smaller numbers also winter there. Rather rare spring and (mainly) fall migrant along in coastal lowlands. Call a thin *tsip*; canary-like song of trills and buzzes heard from spring migrants.

Vesper Sparrow *(Pooecetes gramineus)*

6 ¼". A fairly large, streaky sparrow with white outer tail feathers; shows a white eye-ring, pale crescent behind the brown ear patch, and small chestnut patch at the bend of the wing. Uncommon fall and winter visitor to weedy field borders and desert scrub in the Mojave and Colorado Deserts and more rarely in the drier interior valleys of the coastal slope; rare migrant on the coastal slope, mainly in fall. A few have bred around Baldwin Lake.

Black-throated Sparrow *(Amphispiza bilineata)*

5 ½". An attractively marked sparrow with diamond-shaped black throat, broad white eyebrow and whisker stripes, blue-gray bill; streaked juvenile lacks black throat. Summer visitor (mainly late March to August) in succulent scrub and Joshua tree woodland throughout the deserts (though absent from most of the flatter desert lowlands); a few breeding outposts on the coastal slope. Tinkling calls and a short pleasing trilled song, *tee-tee-trrrr*. Rare on coast and islands, mainly in fall.

Date & Location Seen: _____

_____

Abert's Towhee

Yellow-headed Blackbird
Male

Female

Scott's Oriole
Male

Scott's Oriole
Female

Abert's Towhee *(Melozone aberti)*

9″. Replaces California Towhee (p. 391) in riparian scrub of Coachella, Imperial and lower Colorado River Valleys; more pinkish brown than California, with blackish face. Call a sharp *peek*. Easily found at Salton Sea National Wildlife Refuge Headquarters and along Colorado River.

Yellow-headed Blackbird *(Xanthocephalus xanthocephalus)*

9 ½″ (male); 8 ½″ (female). Unmistakable adult male is as name suggests; also shows a white patch partway out the wing. Female smaller and duller, with yellow limited to the face and breast; immature male intermediate. Call a low, rich *k-ruk*. Raucous song heard on breeding colonies (as at Lake Palmdale, Piute Ponds on Edwards Air Force Base, marshes around Salton Sea and Colorado River), migrants (and a few winter birds) found in irrigated fields Scarce migrant (April, August to early October) in the coastal marshes, parks.

Scott's Oriole *(Icterus parisorum)*

9″. A striking oriole of Joshua trees and other desert woodlands, present mid-March to August. Male is black with lemon yellow underparts, rump, tail base and shoulder patch. Female is olive above with dusky back streaks, yellow-green below, with two white wing-bars. Bill long, straight and sharp (with blue-gray base). Calls include *chuck;* fluty whistled song suggests Western Meadowlark. Very rare migrant and winter visitor on coast; a few winter in wooded desert canyons.

Date & Location Seen:

Black-footed Albatross

Light Morph

Northern Fulmar
Dark Morph

Pink-footed Shearwater

Sooty Shearwater

Black-footed Albatross
(Phoebastria nigripes)

32". Large, very long-winged seabird; regular far offshore, especially May-September. Like a huge dark shearwater, but wingbeats slow, with long glides. Entirely blackish-brown; adults show white on face, uppertail coverts. Heavy black bill, black legs. Our visitors breed mainly in Leeward Hawaiian Islands.

Northern Fulmar
(Fulmarus glacialis)

18". A bull-necked gull-like seabird with a flap-and-glide flight on stiff wings. Evenly gray to gray-brown throughout, with stout yellowish bill with obvious nostril tubes. Less common white morph is mostly white with light gray back, some gray markings on wings and tail. Breeds mainly on islands off Alaska coast; fairly common in our waters some winters, largely absent others. During major flights sometimes found inshore around piers.

Pink-footed Shearwater
(Puffinus creatopus)

19". A large "tubenose" with relative languid flap and glide flight; visits (mainly April-November) from breeding areas on islands off Chile. Gray-brown head and upperparts, mostly white belly and underwings; pinkish bill and feet. Usually well offshore, but can be seen from coastal seawatch points in warmer months.

Sooty Shearwater
(Puffinus griseus)

17". Entirely dark brown shearwater with rapid flap-and-glide flight; underwings flash silvery white. Common well offshore (can be seen from coastal seawatch points), especially April through June. Our birds visit from breeding islands off s. Chile and New Zealand/se. Australia. Short-tailed Shearwater (*P. tenuirostris*, 16"), uncommon to rare offshore November to March, is very similar but with plainer pale gray underwing, shorter bill and tail.

Date & Location Seen:

Black-vented Shearwater

Black Storm-Petrel

Ashy Storm-Petrel

Leach's Storm-Petrel

Black-vented Shearwater   (*Puffinus opisthomelas*)
14". Like a small version of Pink-footed, but with slender dark bill, stronger contrast between dark upperparts and mostly white underparts. Rapid wingbeats alternate with short glides. Visits (mainly September to February) from breeding areas off Baja California. An inshore species, with thousands sometimes visible just off coast, e.g. La Jolla, Newport Beach, Palos Verdes, Malibu, or Pt. Mugu.

Black Storm-Petrel   (*Oceanodroma melania*)
9". Small blackish seabird (but large for a storm-petrel) that flies low over sea surface with deep wingbeats, many course changes. Pale brown bar across upperwing. Visits mainly April to October; sometimes seen from shore (e.g. off La Jolla). Breeds off Baja (and a few on Channel Is.). Tiny, short-tailed Least Storm-Petrel (*O. microsoma*, 5 ¾") visits from Baja erratically in late summer, fall (and accidental after tropical storms at Salton Sea); significantly smaller than Black.

Ashy Storm-Petrel   (*Oceanodroma homochroa*)
8". Nearly endemic California breeder, with colonies on the Channel Islands, where declining. Found in our waters mainly May-October. All ashy brown; smaller, paler-bodied than Black, with some pale gray mottling on the underwings; more fluttering flight.

Leach's Storm-Petrel   (*Oceanodroma leucorhoa*)
8". Dark, medium-large storm-petrel, usually only seen well beyond Channel Islands; year-round, but mainly May to October. Most have white rump, divided by variable dusky line down middle; many Baja breeders have limited or no whitish on rump. Taxonomy complex; slightly smaller, darker visitors from July to September from Guadalupe I. well off Baja (some white-rumped, some dark) may be distinct species. Flight is bounding, erratic.

Date & Location Seen: _____

_____

**Black-legged Kittiwake
Juvenile**

**Arctic Tern
Breeding Adult**

**Sabine's Gull
Breeding Adult**

**Sabine's Gull
Juvenile**

Black-legged Kittiwake (*Rissa tridactyla*)
17″. A northern gull that is occasionally seen – sometimes in numbers – in offshore waters and at coastal piers and promontories from late fall to spring. Adult has plain yellow bill, black legs, solid black tips to pale gray wings; dark gray nape smudge in winter; juvenile has black bill, legs, wing covert bar and tail tip, broad black collar. Casual inland.

Arctic Tern (*Sterna paradisaea*)
14″. Dainty tern, much like Common but with smaller bill, shorter legs, shorter neck, more rounded head. Adult underwings translucent white, with narrow black outer trailing edge. Juvenile much like Common, but inner flight feathers whitish. Fairly common far offshore, mainly fall (mid-August to early October), but a few in late May and early June. Casual inland, mainly June.

Sabine's Gull (*Xema sabini*)
13 ½″. A small gull that migrates (mainly May, August to early October) well offshore (rarely seen from shore). Striking pattern above: dark back and wing coverts, white flight feathers with black triangle forming outer wing. Breeding adults (as seen in May and again in August) have dark gray heads. Bill black with yellow tip. Juvenile has brown back, hindneck. A few sometimes seen over lakes in the deserts, e.g. Antelope Valley, in migration (mainly fall).

Date & Location Seen: _____

**Pomarine Jaeger
Adult**

**Parasitic Jaeger
Adult**

**Long-tailed Jaeger
Adult**

**Common Murre
Non-breeding**

Pomarine Jaeger   *(Stercorarius pomarinus)*
20″. Gull-like seabird with powerful falcon-like flight; steals food from gulls, terns, shearwaters. Long "spoon-tipped" central tail feathers of adult distinctive when present, as is blackish face, heavy chest band (some birds are all dark). Note double white flash on underside of wingtips in flight. Younger birds have heavy barring, lack "spoons." Common offshore, especially April-May, August-November. Heavier South Polar Skua *(Stercorarius maccormicki)*, all-dark with bold white patch on outer wing, uncommon offshore migrant mid-May to early June, mid-August to mid-October.

Parasitic Jaeger   *(Stercorarius parasiticus)*
18″. Lighter in build than Pomarine; adult has pointed central tail feathers. Jaegers breed in Arctic tundra, winter offshore; Parasitic chases terns, and is often seen from shore in late summer, fall around flocks of Elegant Terns. Rare inland migrant, mainly early September at Salton Sea (casual elsewhere inland).

Long-tailed Jaeger   *(Stercorarius longicaudus)*
20″. Smallest, most slender jaeger; adult has longer pointed central tail feathers than Parasitic, limited white in primaries; juvenile much like Parasitic but grayer overall, usually whiter on belly. Migrant far offshore August-September, with a few in late spring; very rare inland migrant, mainly late August to September.

Common Murre   *(Uria aalge)*
17 ½″. Alcids (murres, auklets, murrelets, etc.) are diving seabirds with small wings and rapid whirring flight. This species, our largest, is blackish-brown above, white below; in winter shows black crown, black streak behind eye (breeding birds have all blackish head). Irregular winter visitor offshore, sometimes seen from shore. Breeds on islands along central California coast (a few on n. Channel Islands) north to Alaska.

Date & Location Seen: _____

Pigeon Guillemot
Juvenile

Scripps's Murrelet

Guadalupe
Murrelet

Cassin's Auklet

Rhinoceros Auklet
Non-breeding

Pigeon Guillemot
(Cepphus columba)

13 ½". Distinctive breeding birds are black with large white wing patch, bright red feet; winter adults whitish below, mottled gray above; juveniles similar but smaller white wing patch. Breeds in sea caves on Channel Islands, coast from Pt. Conception north; rare to casual visitor elsewhere on coast, mainly in summer. Winters mostly in Pacific Northwest.

Scripps's Murrelet
(Synthliboramphus scrippsi)

9 ½". Small diving bird, found in pairs offshore (especially around Channel Islands) February to July. Clean separation along neck between slaty upperparts and white underparts; small, thin bill. In flight shows narrow wings that are white underneath. A scarce, threatened breeder on s. California and nw. Baja islands. A few August-September birds, usually seen well offshore, show white over the eye; these are Guadalupe Murrelets (*S. hypoleucus*) which breed mainly on Guadalupe I. off Baja. Scripps's and Guadalupe Murrelets were, until very recently, considered a single species, the Xantus's Murrelet.

Cassin's Auklet
(Ptychoramphus aleuticus)

9". Small chunky dark gray alcid, whitish on belly; at close range note light spot at bill base and white dot over eye. Flight more twisting than murrelet's, wings not as narrow. Found year-round offshore in small groups; some breed on Channel Islands.

Rhinoceros Auklet
(Cerorhinca monocerata)

15". Chunky gray-brown diving bird with stout, yellowish bill; breeding birds have white face stripes, "horn" on bill. Much larger than similarly-plumaged Cassin's. In flight suggests dark football with whirring wings, whitish belly. Uncommon to common winter visitor (mainly November to March) offshore, sometimes seen from coastal points.

Date & Location Seen:

Acknowledgements, Photographer Credits

Over thirty years ago, two of this book's authors (Garrett and Dunn) researched and wrote *Birds of Southern California: Status and Distribution, published in 1981*. Now long out of print and in many ways out of date, that work is still the best single source of information on the birds of this region. Our new book, while intended for a different audience and providing far less detail, owes much to the earlier Southern California book, and we thank all who contributed to that book as well as Los Angeles Audubon for publishing it. We also thank those who have worked tirelessly to learn about and publish on the bird-life of Southern California's varied regions in the years since 1981; these include, but are certainly not limited to: Bob Barnes, Gene Cardiff, Paul Collins, Dave Compton, Brian Daniels, Tom Edell, John Green, Robb Hamilton, Matt Heindel, Oscar Johnson, Sandy Koonce, Paul Lehman, Joan Lentz, Kelli Levinson, Curtis Marantz, Guy McCaskie, Chet McGaugh, Kathy Molina, Michael Patten, Jim Pike, Ken Rosenberg, Jim Royer, Brad Schram, Susan Steele, Richard Webster, Doug Willick, John Wilson, and Phil Unitt.

Brian E. Small has made 453 images from his collection of high quality wildlife photographs available for use in this book. Larry Sansone provided a number of his top photographs for use in the book as well. All of us owe a great debt to all the photographers whose works appear in this book. They consistently met the challenge of capturing a bird's key field marks in photographs of high technical and artistic merit. Their names are listed below.

The letters following the page numbers refer to the position of the photograph on that page (T = top, B = bottom, L = left, R = right, C = center, N = inset).

In addition to Brian E. Small's images, additional book images were provided as follows:

Tom Blackman: 468BL, 488BL. **Jim Burns**: 372B, 484BR. **Olga Clarke**: 28BN, 78TN, 82BR, 224B. **Mike Danzenbaker**: 146B, 488TR. **Jody de Bruyn**: 452B. **Kimball Garrett**: 454T, B. **Julie Gidwitz**: 452TL. **Brendon Grice**: 452TR. **Peter LaTourette/VIREO**: 386B. **Jerry Liguori**: 112TN. **Todd McGrath**: 482TR, BL. **Dick McNeely**: 56BL, 402T. **Dennis Paulson**: 104. **Jim Pruske**: 26TN, 136, 214, 362B. **Jenny E. Ross**: 130CN. **Robert Royse**: 132B, 192B, 276T, 410BR. **Bart Rulon**: 408BL. **Larry Sansone**: 30BL, BR, 38BR, 42TR, 56BR, 94B, 100BN, 108, 112B, 114T, B, BN, 116B, 118BN, 120T, 126TN, 128T, 150B, 152B, 166BL, 178TR, TRC, BR, 184BR, 186TR, B, 190T, 194BR, 198TL, TR, BR, 206BR, 212T, 222BL, 242, 308B, 310TN, BN, 312TN, 318TR, 336B, 370B, 372T, 376BL, 402BR, 448BN, 456TR, BL, 470TR, 480TR, TRN, BL, BR, 482TL, BR, 486TL, TR, BL, 488TN, BR. **Arnold Small**: 198BL, 426B. **Robert Shantz**: 120BN, 122TL. **Bob Steele**: 200CN. **Glen Tepke**: 222BR, 244B, 316, 318TL. **Hank Tseng**: 182BL, 238B, 306, 362T. **George Vlahakis**: 314B. **Brian Wheeler**: 122TR, BR, 126T, B. **Jim Zipp**: 92BL, BR, 124TN.

Index/Checklist of Birds of Southern Claifornia

Use this checklist to keep a record of the birds you have seen. Bold numbers are for the main Species Account page. Common local bird denoted by 'clb'. A complete listing of all the bird species in Southern California is available at **www.rwmorse.com**.

494

Other Species Seen

_____

_____

_____

_____

_____

_____

_____

_____

About The Authors

Kimball L. Garrett

Lifelong resident of Los Angeles, Ornithology Collections Manager at the Natural History Museum of Los Angeles County, past-President of Western Field Ornithologists, member of California Bird Records Committee, and co-editor of the Southern California regional reports for *North American Birds*. With Jon Dunn co-authored *Birds of Southern California, Status and Distribution* and *Peterson Field Guide to Warblers*.

Jon L. Dunn

Grew up in the Los Angeles area, bird tour leader for WINGS, chief consultant to the National Geographic's *Field Guide to the Birds of North America*, host/writer for the *Advanced Birding Video Series*. Serves as a member of the California Bird Records Committee, the American Birding Association Checklist Committee, and the American Ornithologist's Union's Committee on Classification and Nomenclature.

Brian E. Small

Professional wildlife photographer, co-author of two photographic field guides (*Birds of Eastern North America* and *Birds of Western North America*), Photo Editor of *Birding*, co-author of a bird identification column in *BirdWatching*. Thousands of his images are featured in books, magazines, calendars, websites and smartphone apps. Brian and his family reside in Southern California.

Short Index to Species

Use this index to find the main account for every species illustrated in the guide. A complete index is on pages 492 – 496.